Where in the Hell Did You Come From?

Game Warden Ups and Downs & Ins and Outs

Published by The Posey Press

Edited by Jennie R. Posey

Cover by Nicholas Trahan

ISBN-13: 978-0-692-78128-9

Contact:

jennie.posey@gmail.com

Photographs, letters, and newspaper clippings provided by Wayne Fitzwater. Alternate versions of some stories have been previously published.

Where in the Hell Did You Come From?

Game Warden Ups and Downs & Ins and Outs

By Wayne Fitzwater

Dedication

I wish to dedicate this book to the many wildlife law enforcement officers across the nation, who support game management principles, who encourage the "fair chase" of pursuing wildlife in a legal, acceptable and sportsmanlike manner, and who give meaning to the laws and regulations they strive to enforce.

To the crop of young wildlife enthusiasts who may decide to try becoming wildlife law enforcement officers, whose efforts help protect and perpetuate certain wildlife populations for future generations.

To the multitudes of law-abiding, conscientious hunting and fishing sportsmen and women who play an important role in wildlife conservation efforts. In the past, and hopefully in the future, you are an influencing factor in keeping certain wildlife populations within the proper carrying capacities of the lands they inhabit.

Acknowledgements

ALL GAME WARDENS’ LADIES, BLESS THEM!

A tribute is due to those game wardens' ladies who accepted the absences of their men during long duty hours, weekends and holidays; who served as impromptu Fish & Game Department telephone operators for the many inquiries received, particularly immediately prior to the opening of fishing and hunting seasons; who tolerated the intrusions into their homes, which served as a game warden’s headquarters and office; who forfeited household space and arrangement to make room for fishing and game equipment and supplies; who provided space in the freezer and refrigerator for a variety of confiscated items ranging from fish, game meat, furs, fowl, and who knows what else; and who were patient with us when required monthly reports prepared on typewriters that couldn’t seem to spell or print correctly and brought about unpleasant character changes. Special thanks to my dear Alice, who was an invaluable partner and loving wife.

Preface

These stories are the result of my tenure as a Montana Fish & Game Warden working in the mountainous areas of southwest Montana for over twenty-five years, and include the many ups and downs and ins and outs game wardens face on the job. All game wardens have had interesting and unusual experiences, leaving them with many stories to tell. For my fellow wardens who are more reluctant to share their tales, and for those outdoor enthusiasts who may have been on the other end of an interaction with a game warden, I hope the following stories may be of interest.

Game warden duties can range from mundane and routine to challenging, confronting, and hazardous, and sometimes all the way to downright dangerous, especially when working alone, which is common. Many times a warden must make instant decisions with regard to what may or may not appear to be a game law violation. Out in the far reaches of many game warden districts, there aren't any radio or other contacts if assistance is needed. There are no other law enforcement agents that confront as many armed individuals as game wardens. The demands of the job are stressful to game warden families, and it is necessary to have patience, understanding, and tolerance of a game warden's duty demands.

With regard to the numerous women game wardens countrywide—you are to be complimented, so take care, work with pride, and expect the unexpected!

Along with the title of this book, some circumstance within a particular happening frequently resulted in a common remark, "Where in the hell did you come from?" I heard this refrain many, many times over the years, due largely in part to my evasive patrol methods.

Some of the stories shared here were previously published in whole or in part in the Montana Game Warden magazine, which was pioneered by the Montana Game Warden Association and Game Warden Jim Heck. For various reasons of cost, time involved, etc., it ceased being published, but there are still many stories to tell. Here are some of mine.

Introduction

I was born in 1918 on a farm in the Ohio midwest. I first came to Montana in 1936 on a Harley Davidson motorcycle, painting mailboxes along the way to fund my journey. Back in 1939, '40 and '41, I was working for the U.S. Forest Service with District Ranger Vern Edwards in the Gallatin Canyon area, and I also worked at the Squaw Creek game checking station. During winters I was a logger and trapped pine marten, Canada lynx, wolverine, mink, and bobcats on snowshoe traplines.

In 1941, I joined the U.S. Army and served in the North African and European campaigns. Upon discharge, I was awarded the Combat Infantry Badge, Purple Heart, Bronze Star, and Campaign Ribbons. Throughout my more than 25 years as a game warden, my previous WWII military service, several battle wounds, and associated disabilities were at times a hindrance to desired job performance.

Sometime after my military discharge, I returned to Montana and the Gallatin Canyon area, and once again, worked for the U.S.F.S., this time for Ranger "Lew" Peck. Having also met Warden Supervisor Gene Sherman, he inquired if I might be interested in a game warden job. Prior to 1950, game wardens were hired on the basis of job interest and ability, and occasionally through community recommendations or political influence. Having had an extreme lifetime interest in the great outdoors and wildlife, I pondered the offer and wasn't long in accepting.

In November 1950, I was given a Fish & Game law book, a deputy game warden badge, and copies of big game and fishing regulations, and then I accompanied Supervisor Sherman and old-time warden "Len" Clark on a few patrols. I was next told to go to Columbus and get acquainted with the county attorney and the Stillwater Sheriff's Department. After that, I was to review the Stillwater County map and go to work!

At that time, Montana game wardens were not uniformed and they were driving their own private vehicles, with a starting wage of $150.00 monthly. For vehicle use, there was a $30.00 monthly stipend with tires, batteries, gas and a minimal vehicle repair allowance provided. No sidearms were issued then, but some district warden supervisors supported their wardens carrying a gun. I regularly wore my military issue .38 Special revolver with lanyard ring, and always felt as though it should be mandatory while on duty, a necessity based on wardens' power of arrest and the occasional request for assistance from local sheriffs' departments and state highway patrol officers.

Having arrived in the Stillwater County area in November in the midst of ongoing big game hunting and trapping, the Fish & Game activities and inquiries were overwhelming, so working long, long hours seven days a week was essential. After a couple winters and summers, it was the Fish & Game plan to put the Stillwater District in the Billings supervisory region with Jack Kohler as the supervisor. Warden Supervisor Gene Sherman told me he wanted me in Region 3, so I was transferred to the Townsend-Helena District in 1953, and was directed to live in Helena to be in a position to respond to various inquiries received at the state F & G Department headquarters. Old-time warden Frank Marshall at West Yellowstone was retiring, so Warden Ken

Sears was transferred to West Yellowstone from his station at Townsend, and I took his place.

At Helena, being close at hand, I was regularly recruited to assist with chores and projects not particularly associated with game warden duties. Some were aerial censuses of big game and waterfowl, and aerial fish transplants to mountain lakes with pilots Don Brown, Jim Stradley, and Ralph Cooper. I also assisted big game live trapping foreman Jim McLucas with live trapping mountain goat at the trapping site along the south fork of the Flathead River. I helped with trapping and trucking many elk out of several Yellowstone Park elk traps, and aided in taking trout and grayling spawn at Harrison and Agnes Lakes. I lent a hand helping wardens move to newly assigned districts, assisted with fisheries' electro-shocking projects, and aided Bill Bergeson with transplant of Chukar partridge, too.

At Townsend, I had a couple significant court trials, with well-known former Montana Attorney General Wellington D. Rankin defending the culprits.

During that period of time, as before, there were many big game and beaver damage complaints. Being unable to handle all the beaver problems, Chief Deputy Walt Everin called in state trapper Howard Campbell. Campbell, being a one of a kind individual, took immense pride in his beaver trapping skills and his secret potion beaver scent. He openly stated that he would challenge anyone to compete with him skinning a beaver and would do so for fun or money. He could get the job done in less than five minutes! In those days, all beaver trapped by a state employee were pelted by the trapper, then stretched and cured and sold at auction, the same as confiscated game. Wardens had authority to steel trap nuisance beaver on federal and state lands as well. In addition to the steel traps, wardens were provided with Hancock brand live traps, which took considerable time and know-how to use effectively. Quite soon after, the state trapping law was revised to allow licensed trappers to trap beaver on public domain at the direction of the district game warden.

Black bear problems were also frequent, so I asked Fish & Game shop foreman Rex Smart to help me construct a bear live trap. We welded together two 55-gallon drums and fashioned a trigger and trap door. Through the succeeding years, the trap caught numerous black bear. That old retired live trap is on display at the Montana Law Enforcement Museum in Philipsburg, Montana.

When the upper Gallatin and Gardiner areas were opened for post-season elk hunting, additional wardens were assigned duty there, and with the usual severe snow conditions, it took snowshoe patrol to get to the many remote hunting areas. Assisting with the extended hunt for several years, I put in many, many snowshoe hours with the realization that hunter pursuits and activities were different away from the more accessible areas that were regularly patrolled.

I worked the Helena-Townsend districts for a couple years, then as Warden Orville Lewis at Dillon had been promoted to Warden Supervisor at Miles City, I was transferred to the Beaverhead District in 1956 to take his place. Since I arrived during the ongoing big game hunting season, it was evident that the elk hunting activities were probably second to none in the state. At that time, the Region 3 game manager was Joe Gaab, and the two of us patrolled by horseback along the Lima Peaks, Snowcrest and Gravelly areas, and also participated in the calf elk tagging projects during springtime.

It isn't generally known or acknowledged, but for need of a title for newly established game management units to be listed on the next big game hunting maps, I chose the titles of Lima Peaks and Blacktail Ridge. I also submitted the unit boundaries and legal descriptions, which separated these newly established game management areas from adjoining management units.

Through the many years, the Fish & Game Department sponsored various in-service training sessions and game warden seminars. The early training sessions were for the benefit of the newer wardens with warden supervisors conducting the training, namely Ross Wilson, Truce Emmett and Clyde Howard. A couple sessions were held at Fort Missoula, the Blackfoot-Clearwater game range, and in Helena, along with other seminars being held at the University of Montana in Missoula and Montana State University in Bozeman. The intent and hope for these "schooling" sessions was to improve and broaden the wardens' knowledge, but it is questionable if that was always the benefit, especially for some of the older, more experienced wardens who were not altogether receptive to such teachings. The old adage "You can't teach an old dog new tricks" may be an appropriate reference.

I worked from 1950 to my 60th birthday in 1978 at which time, age-wise, I was required to retire. During my hitch with the Fish & Game Department, there were events that were very meaningful for me. One was my award as Wildlife Officer of the Year in 1971, and another was my award of the Otto Fossen Memorial Trophy in 1968. This was given by the Montana Law Enforcement Academy to the top scorer on the pistol range, with a large class of approximately 60 law enforcement officers attending and representing various law enforcement agencies.

It goes without saying that working with many of the state wardens was a pleasure, and very memorable for me.
Through the years there were a number of game wardens that lost their lives while pursuing the job, and some that come to mind are: Marion Ammerman, plane crash; Harold Gartside, drowning; Jack Thompson, heart attack; Gene Sara, death by shooting; and I. L. Todd, heart attack.

There remains many untold and nearly forgotten happenings and events related to my game warden years, but some of the best (and worst!) are included within these pages.

Tools of the Trade for a 1950s Game Warden

Out in the field, and without two-way radio contact until the early 1950s, a warden had to be prepared for anything. The F & G Department didn't provide much in those days, only giving wardens a badge, a book of regulations and laws, a roster of the justices of the peace in their district, and a stipend for the use of the warden's personal vehicle. That's it!

In later years they provided official F & G Department vehicles outfitted with the department's insignia, a flashing red "stop" light for the vehicle roof, cut-off switches for brake and taillights, blackout headlights, red flags, and a flashlight. They didn't start issuing weapons to wardens until 1965.

All the rest of what one might need had to be furnished by the warden, so each kit looked different. Since it was an individual's choice to be armed, I chose to carry my .38 Special. I also regularly used binoculars and a spotting scope, which was not the norm among my colleagues. Two spare tires with a tire pump and valve cores were insurance when out in a huge patrol area, as were screw-and-lever type jacks. I made good use of tire chains, and a log chain paired with a fence anchor that had an auger end and an eye end to get out of sticky predicaments. Carrying a shovel, axe, bucket, and tree saw was handy when I'd come across a fallen tree in a roadway, or for smothering smoldering campfires. For the rest of the miscellany, I always brought a can of gas, a tool kit, a first aid kit, a change of clothing with extra layers, and camp groceries. I also had cans of gas stashed in a couple outer reaches (about 100 miles or so) of my district.

Region 3 Bozeman Fish & Game Personnel

Top row, left to right: Norm Wortman, warden & game range manager, Gallatin Canyon; Joe Gaab, biologist, Livingston (full-time warden later); Len Clark, warden, Bozeman; Clyde Christensen, warden, Columbus; Vern Waples, warden, Red Lodge; Gene Sherman, warden supervisor, Bozeman; John "Red" Burke, warden, Livingston; I. L. Todd, warden, Ennis.

Bottom row, left to right: Phil South, biologist, Dillon; Henry Presinger, warden, Whitehall; K. D. "Pinky" Sears, warden, West Yellowstone; Wayne Fitzwater, warden, Dillon; Bill Sweet, F & G Commissioner, Butte.

Chapter One

“Where in the Hell Did You Come From?!”

Productive Patrol Methods

As I gained experience in the field, I quickly recognized that people who unintentionally violated a fish or game law due to lack of knowledge or unusual circumstance were in a very different category than those persons who intentionally planned, connived and put effort into violating a law or department regulation. Accordingly, I directed considerable effort toward those deliberate lawbreakers.

I delighted in watching the activities of hunters and fishermen from a distance, without revealing my presence or making contact with an individual until I was satisfied that the person was legal or illegal in their activities. I frequently kept notes on my observations too, which proved valuable on more than one occasion when confronted with defiant sportsmen or later in the courtroom. As a result of my many times appearing in a surprising fashion, the response I heard oft repeated was, "Warden, where in the hell did you come from?" On a few occasions, and perhaps influenced by a person's religious affiliation, the reply was, "Warden, where in Heaven's name did you come from?

Patrolling for hunter activities, 1969

Drinking and Poaching Don't Mix

While working the Butte-Silver Bow, Madison and Jefferson County areas, a rancher informed me of some nighttime deer poaching near his ranch. He was concerned due to his cattle being on the ranch's winter pasturage. The rancher stated he had heard single gunshots at night at various times, and in checking on his cattle he had come across deer gut piles, which were revealed by magpies.

I went to the area at nighttime several times for observation, and took up a position on high ground overlooking the ranch meadows. On about the third such stake out, during the wee hours of the early morning, I spotted a vehicle traveling slowly and using a strong spotlight, so I watched for the vehicle's stoplights and listened for a gunshot. Soon after seeing the muzzle flash of a rifle, the vehicle's dome light came on but the driver continued forward.

I kept watching the meadow area through my binoculars, and occasionally would see a flashlight beam. During my watch, I had noticed that the vehicle had one taillight out. I stayed at my vantage point for about an hour, until I saw a vehicle traveling slowly and finally stopping where a flashlight signal was obvious alongside the highway. The vehicle dome light came on, so I assumed a deer carcass was being loaded.

I hurriedly left my viewpoint without turning on my vehicle lights and made the questionable drive out to the highway, racing toward Twin Bridges. I never approached a vehicle with only one taillight, but in my rearview mirror I caught sight of a passing truck missing one. I hastily turned around, with my own vehicle lights still out, and pursued the pickup. At an appropriate highway turn out, I gave a red-light and siren signal to stop. I then called out, "Stay in the vehicle!"

Being in uniform, the driver said to me, "Officer, what's the problem?"

Once I introduced myself as a game warden, I stated that both the driver and his passenger were under arrest for their poaching crime and that the deer would be confiscated as property of Montana. I could smell liquor on the driver's breath, and the two men soon became quite aggressive. I advised them that I could easily radio the Highway Patrol to come and assist, which had the desired effect of settling them down.

The men were issued citations, and as a security measure I radioed the Whitehall night deputy and notified him of the poaching activity with the names, addresses and vehicle license number of the hooligans. Prior to releasing them, I reminded them of the date to appear before the Madison County justice of the peace. Before driving off, the driver asked that familiar question I would hear over and over in my years as a game warden: "Where in the hell did you come from at this hour of night?"

They admitted they had spent time at a Twin Bridges saloon and one fellow jokingly said, "I guess drinking and poaching don't mix!"

The Butte police monitored the radio call to the Whitehall deputy, and the word was spread in Butte about the poachers. I later heard that the fellows experienced some joshing, as they were well known in Butte.

A Surprise Encounter with a Poacher

Within my district, a certain choice elk area had only two primitive access roads. One was in better condition and provided easier access to the hunting areas, while the other was in poor condition and took longer to travel, especially leaving the area. I knew the second road was the more likely one to be used by a poacher, as I had periodically checked hunters on the two roads and had learned that the poorer road was used by those who wanted to bypass the usual check point.

A large nearby ranch that was used mostly for summer grazing covered the lower areas of the mountainous region where hunters went to bag an elk. I had a good relationship with the ranch owner, so I asked the man if he would consider letting me put in a wire gate along his fence line in order to have more immediate access to the lesser used road. The rancher agreed, partly because it would make it easier for him to move his cattle from one

Hidden Fishing Holes with Great Catches

Within the Dillon district, there were a couple ponds in isolated areas that produced big trout, and the nearby ranchers were quite protective of intrusion by fisherman. I finally concluded that it was based mostly on guarding the ponds for their own and friends' and relatives' use, even though the ponds were not on their properties. Keeping this in mind, I would periodically, on the sly, patrol the ponds and had occasion to issue several citations for lack of proper Montana fishing licenses and/or being over catch limits. Naturally, this didn't make for the best public relations with the nearby ranchers, but did convince them that any properly licensed fisherman had a right to access the ponds, which were on public domain lands.

grazing allotment to another. I then spent a day building and installing the wire gate, complete with two fence line brace panels.

Sometime later, I was at a high vantage point where I could see hunters' vehicles leaving that prime elk hunting area. I spotted a vehicle traveling out of the vicinity on the worst of the two roads, so I hurriedly left my position and rushed through the gate to intercept the driver but couldn't keep the vehicle in sight since I was now on lower ground with the terrain obscuring the view. As I approached the access road, I didn't know if the outgoing vehicle was up ahead or still coming toward me.

Spotting the driver's taillights at last, I knew the outbound driver had passed me. Without turning on my headlights, I hastily dropped in behind and put on my flashing red stop lights. The hunter pulled onto the shoulder, and I approached the stopped vehicle. Since this was early in my career and wardens were not then uniformed or armed, except by individual choice, I advised the vehicle driver that I was a game warden and would check the obvious elk for proper tagging along with the appropriate elk license. The elk carcass was properly tagged, but the license did not belong to the hunter. Frustrated, the man said, "Where in the hell did you come from?!"

When I asked him for more details around the suspicious circumstances, the man said his hunting partner had shot the elk, but had to promptly leave the hunting area in time to get to his job in Butte. Suspecting this was not the truth, I radioed the local deputy sheriff and asked if he would phone the alleged hunting partner's number in Butte and ask about his elk hunt. The sheriff's call was answered by a woman, who said, "Heavens no!

He is disabled, and could only do very limited hunting and fishing."

After I hung up with sheriff, I issued a citation with a couple charges and confiscated the elk. During the investigation of the actual license holder, I discovered that the licensee's juvenile son had given the elk license to the poacher friend. Unfortunately, the county attorney would not consider a transfer of license charge due to the circumstances, and a juvenile being involved.

Intrusion into Montana

Within the Beaverhead district there were several places along the Montana-Idaho state line where the only vehicle access was on the Idaho side. One isolated lake was well within Montana and provided reasonably good trout fishing, which was an attraction for Idaho and Utah fishermen who regularly vacationed or spent time in the nearby popular recreational and scenic Henry's Lake area in Idaho. On occasion I would make the drive of 125 miles or so and patrol the area, which also provided some grouse and big game hunting during appropriate seasons.

During one patrol of the lake, I intended to camp out for a few days, and on arrival as I was setting up my camp, a vehicle with three young fellows was just leaving the lake area. I went out from my quite inconspicuous camp to the rough road and stopped their vehicle to check for their licenses and catches. As I was wearing the Fish & Game Department uniform, the one fellow said, "It's a conservation officer," and the other said, "Where in the hell did you come from?"

They were asked for their fishing licenses and I checked the several trout. When they realized I was a Montana warden one fellow said, "You are out of your jurisdiction. We don't have to yield to your request since we are in Idaho!"

They were in Montana by a couple hundred yards of course, and I informed them that the lake was in Montana, which they undoubtedly knew, and that each would be given citations and the fish confiscated. Hearing that the nearest justice of the peace was in Lima, approximately 65 miles away, they showed serious concern.

In looking through their open-top Jeep, one of the "Entering Montana" signs I regularly hung at the border was uncovered. The fellows stated they had found it alongside the roadway, at the base of a tree, but then considering one of the young men was over 6-feet tall, he could have, by standing in the Jeep, removed the sign that I had nailed at about 10-feet high.

I had a bonding schedule from the court with me, and advised the three fellows of the bond amount to be posted along with the citations. All three were dismayed by the bad news I delivered and said they did not have that amount of money, but could provide it at the lodge where they stayed. Having confiscated the illegal fish and issued the citations, I should have taken one person in custody, but instead allowed them all to leave toward the Idaho lodge. They tried to outrun me en route, hoping the rough driving conditions would slow me down, but they did not succeed. Arriving at the lodge, one fellow shook his head and said, "I don't believe it!"

> The Lacey Act is a 1900 United States law that prohibits the trafficking of illegal wildlife, and was expanded in 1980 to include plants and plant products like timber and paper.

Before they went to their quarters, I pointed out that had they crossed into Idaho with their illegal bounty, it would have been a violation of the Lacey Act and they could have been cited with that much more serious infraction. Aghast, one fellow said, "Wow, we're not very bright!"

They then went into the lodge, and after a period of waiting, only two came out with the stipulated bond money. I asked about the third fellow and his companion said, "The last I saw him, he was hurrying out the back door."

I too hurried around back, but it was a futile effort, as there were clusters of cabins and no one in sight. I returned to the remaining members of the fishing party and notified them that a Montana complaint would be held against their friend, and hopefully the fleeing fellow would seriously consider clearing the case with the judge.

Once back at home base in Dillon after a few more days of uneventful patrol of the lake, I contacted the county attorney to apprise him of the details of the situation with the young Utah fishermen. I explained that one had fled, but his name and address was known. I offered to contact the fellow by mail and remind him that there was an outstanding Montana complaint against him, and recommend that he immediately clear it with the Montana justice of the peace. I also sent a copy of the letter to the head of the Brigham Young University, where the young fellow was a student, and within a couple weeks the stipulated bond was received.

Case closed!

One Way to Get the Job Done with the Least Effort

During the years I worked the Beaverhead region, which bordered the Montana-Idaho state line along the Continental Divide, I regularly patrolled those state line areas. It was common for the Idaho big game hunting season to open a couple weeks, more or less, before the Montana hunts. There were several areas along the border where Idaho hunters were likely to intentionally get into Montana, particularly after elk were hunted and pursued in Idaho for a week or more and the animals would cross into Montana where things were quiet.

One preferred hunting spot was near a pass, or mountain saddle, with the only easy vehicle access being an Idaho jeep-type trail. The pass was a natural travel route for game. Wanting to patrol for hunting activities, I drove into Idaho to get to the area on the Montana side. Once there, I pitched my tent in the midst of an alpine fir thicket where I had, years before, cleared a campsite which was very well hidden from view of vehicle and foot traffic. Just as soon as I had unloaded my camp gear, I immediately drove my vehicle to a spot about a quarter-mile mile away, where it was also well concealed behind another island of timber. I returned to the pass and campsite and proceeded to brush out my vehicle tire marks so the area didn't reveal any recent traffic.

Early the second day, a vehicle arrived with three hunters and as they parked not too far away, I could hear them talking and laughing. They soon left, following the state line until they were out of sight. About 10 a.m., I heard shots coming from within Montana, and it was afternoon when I finally heard voices as the three men came up the Montana slope to their vehicle for a bite to eat. As I peered through the timber I could plainly see that one hunter had considerable blood on his pant leg and sleeve. Having finished their meal, they soon started down the slope again with rope and only one gun.

It was late afternoon before I heard their voices again, and after some patient waiting the men were seen struggling up the slope dragging an elk carcass little by little toward their vehicle. Once at their truck with a spike bull elk carcass, they rested and had a bit more to eat.

I hurriedly left my concealed campsite on the blind side of the island of fir trees, and once in heavy timber cover, I went downslope and around the hillside to a place near where the hunters had dragged the elk upslope. I continued out on the open incline and was quite close to the hunters before they saw me approaching.

I heard one of the hunters say, "Uh, oh! That looks like a conservation officer!"

As I drew closer, one of the men said, "You're the first conservation officer I have ever seen along the state line. Where in the hell did you come from?"

I requested their identification and hunting licenses and one man said, "We can show you our Idaho licenses. We got this bull in Idaho, but had to drag it into Montana to get to the truck."

Knowing better, I replied, "The bull looks as much like a Montana elk as an Idaho elk, and considering you did kill it in Montana, you men will be given citations and the elk carcass will be confiscated."

The hunters insisted the elk was legal, but once they were asked to backtrack along the drag trail to the gut pile with the aid of a good flashlight, their claim would be revealed as false. However, it would have taken some time to do. One of the hunters said, “We are bushed, and don’t think we should be required to do that.”

His companion asked me, “Have you already seen the gut pile?”

Without waiting for my answer, the third hunter said, “From the direction you came up here, I suppose you know what you are talking about. So, what’s to be done now?”

I advised them of the procedures necessary to clear up the charges, and one of the hunters said, “If you are as lazy as some C.O.s I have known, the elk will probably spoil right here.”

One of the three inquired whether something couldn’t be worked out so they could keep the elk if the charges were cleared, but I assured them the elk must be confiscated. Resignedly, the leader of the group told his peers, “If this guy hiked all the way up here just to catch us, he’ll get the elk out okay.”

One of the other hunters piped up and rudely asked, “By the way, where in the hell did you come from to have walked your ass off to get here?”

Over the years, I have wondered whether such a patrol with these results would be considered smart and crafty, or lazy and downright dirty?

Speedy Gate Closing

I frequently patrolled the south portion of the Dillon district, near Lima and the Lima Peaks areas, as it was an area with a variety of wildlife. On one such patrol, I went over the Montana-Idaho state line, then back on an access trail across the Continental Divide and into Montana where I could view a large expanse of country and look for hunter and fishermen activities.

From my vantage point, I saw dust from a vehicle traveling the crude mountain road down near the creek bottom, and later I heard a couple gun shots but couldn't zero in on the exact area. Once the vehicle came into better view that long distance away, I recognized it as one driven by a well-known local poacher from Lima, so I maneuvered my truck down the treacherous mountain slope, and finally intersected the road and pulled in behind the driver in question.

I drove rather recklessly to overtake the driver ahead, and was frequently slowed due to a number of wire gates on the road separating livestock pasturages. At one point, with the vehicle ahead in sight, I watched momentarily with binoculars then proceeded on to the next wire gate. With the distance between us being not too great, I saw something white being thrown out of the poacher's vehicle and guessed it was sage grouse, so I noted a couple roadside landmarks in the thick sagebrush growth for when I returned later to investigate and continued my pursuit.

Once I was finally through the many, many wire gates and onto the highway to Lima, I sped to town not far behind the pursued poacher and went straight to the house of the suspect, Hap Hubbard. Knowing one another from past associations and my previously issuing him citations, the fellow said, “Fitz, where in the hell did you come from to get behind me?” I learned later that my vehicle dust had tipped off my presence and influenced him to quickly get out of the area.

The minimum fine for killing a game bird during closed hunting season was $50.00, so I advised him that he could post $50 bond instead of appearing before the local justice of the peace. The fellow went in his house and came out with a sizable roll of paper bills and peeled off the fifty bucks. As he handed them over, he stated, “You know me Wayne, but I’m probably still ahead of the game!”

He then took delight in reminding me that I would be in trouble with the local cowboys by not closing all those wire gates separating the livestock pastures. I had the final word though, as I assured him that every single gate was closed. Of course, I’m sure he thought this was an impossibility, considering I still managed to overtake him despite taking the time to close each and every gate. Later, I returned to the scene of the chase and found two cleanly dressed young sage grouse near one of the landmarks that I had noted during the pursuit.

Everyone Else is Doing It

During the early fall at the start of the grouse, archery, and fishing seasons, I hiked an area of likely sportsman activity. I started at the head of a drainage just below a high, well-known mountain peak that separates the Montana-Idaho state line, and then worked my way down an adjoining drainage toward Deadman Lake, and along the old, old stagecoach and wagon freight road that ran from Virginia City and Bannack, Montana to Corrine, Utah. When I was near Deadman Lake, I watched a fisherman for a few moments before approaching him. When I finally made contact, and he saw my warden's uniform and badge, it was evident he was surprised and a little concerned as he uttered, "Where in the hell did you come from?"

As usual, I asked for a Montana fishing license, and he replied that he did not have one. So, a citation was issued to be officiated by the Lima justice of the peace at a later date. As I handed him the citation, the man stated that a number of Idaho sports enthusiasts in the Idaho Medicine Lodge Creek area had fished the lake for years, hoping his "tip off" might inspire some leniency on my part. Not taking the bait, the citation stayed valid and I informed the man that any Idaho fisherman who transported illegal fish across the state line would be liable for federal prosecution under the federal Lacey Act. That quieted him down right quick, as I guess he felt maybe he "got off the hook" pretty easy.

Paddy G. Rogers
Mutual of Omaha
P.O. Box 2791
Idaho Falls, ID Idaho
September 2, 1970

Montana Fish & Game Dept.
Helena, Montana 59725

Attn: Mr. Wayne Fitzwater

Dear Mr. Fitzwater:

You may not remember my case – fishing in Montana without a valid permit on my person – because it had been lost – but, I just wanted to drop a short note of appreciation for your department's prompt handling of this matter, the refund of my $30 bond, and the courteous manner in which this entire procedure was handled. You and your staff are to be congratulated on your fine work in public relations, something I feel is very lacking between the public and our government at all levels these days. It is a very fine feeling to get the impression you are being taken care of as a person by someone in the state government – and not just taken. Again, my sincere thanks.

Please convey the gist of this letter to both Warden Chet' Duffy and the associate he was with on the day they stopped me, and the two fellows I was with. Their manner was also very courteous and in every way conducive to better public relations.

Also, please convey my thanks to Justice of the Peace Bastien in Dillon for his personal consideration.

In summary, what I have always been told about the hospitality of you Montana folk has been proved true throughout this entire chain of events, and you are to be congratulated.

Sincerely,
Paddy G. Rogers

Cc: Office of the Governor, Montana
Personal file

Unbelievable Recognition

District game wardens issued citations for Fish & Game law violations, and the various local justices of the peace most always officiated the cases. The knowledge, skills and court professionalism varied from one justice to another, and court proceedings were held in a variety of surroundings. The homes and makeshift offices of the justices were frequent locations for hearings, and on rare occasions proceedings were held afield during law enforcement game checking station operations. Hunters and fisherman who had been issued citations sometimes called these "kangaroo courts."

At one location in a small community, the justice of the peace was completely blind. In addition to his civic duties, he was also the owner and operator of a small eatery and bar, where he frequently held court out of convenience. On several occasions, I had to take Fish & Game violation cases to his restaurant. Upon entering the business after taking only a few steps inside, the justice would invariably say, "Fitzwater, I haven't seen you for some time!" It was unbelievable to me that the blind judge had the ability to recognize my presence merely by my footsteps, which only substantiated a blind person's abilities to develop their others senses more fully to compensate for that lost by blindness.

Centennial Valley Isolated Ponds Producing Sizable Trout

Within the huge southwest Centennial Valley, there are about five ponds that produce amply sized trout. Due to the remoteness of the area, it is tempting for some fishermen to get involved with some illegal activity. While patrolling the area of Schulz Pond as usual, I observed two men fishing. After considerable watching with a spotting scope and binoculars, I finally determined that they were setline fishing, which was not permitted. They had their lines attached to low ground stakes, so I proceeded toward them in my vehicle. Unfortunately, the vehicle's road dust was a giveaway to the illegal fishermen that someone was on the way.

Once I contacted the men and checked for licenses and possible fish caught, they stated they were only getting ready to fish and proceeded to get two fishing rods out of their vehicle. When I notified them that both would be cited for illegal fishing regardless, they became quite aggressive and confrontational and said, "Where in the hell do you think you can accuse us out here, forty miles from nowhere?"

Unfazed, I wrote out the citations and handed them over to the men. One of the sportsman said, "You can wipe your ass on mine," as he grabbed it out of my hand.

I warned them not to get overly aggressive, due to the serious repercussions of such actions, and then walked to the pond-side stakes and retrieved the two setlines as evidence. Caught red-handed now, the men's behavior made a quick turnaround, which was a welcome switch as one of the fellows was wearing a holstered revolver—a common show of machismo among the hunting and fishing ranks.

Game Officer Most Likely to Get Shot?

Which law enforcement officer is most likely to be assaulted with a gun? Is it the undercover F.B.I. agent, or perhaps the beleaguered New York City cop patrolling his dangerous beat? Try the nation's 6,000 federal and state game wardens. These unheralded men are actually eight times more likely to be assaulted than other law enforcement agents, according to a nationwide study of game wardens, conducted by the Wyoming Conservation Department.

Most assaults come during deer season when wardens are often alone in the woods and must deal with armed men who are poaching or otherwise breaking the law. Six game wardens have been killed since 1971 and many more shot or threatened with guns. The number of assaults continues to grow each year as wilderness lands shrink.

(Source unknown)

An Attempt to Hide Illegal Fish

Patrolling fishing activities one day, I parked my vehicle at a conducive vantage point above a lake of interest and proceeded to observe the happenings below with my binoculars. I soon concentrated on one fisherman who would occasionally go to a warm spring inlet that was closed to fishing due to the rainbow trout spawning within. I watched as the fisherman illegally caught a couple of sizable rainbows by netting the fish that had gone under an overhanging stream bank, seeking security for their spawning. The fisherman then took those trout and hid them in the nearby tall grass. He was so involved with this illegal activity that he didn't even bother to utilize his fishing rod in the legal fishing waters. In due time, another local warden drove directly to the fisherman and proceeded to check him. Not having discovered the illegal catch, it was a short encounter and the warden departed quickly.

However, the vantage point where I had parked was on high ground with better viewing, and was near the only access road where the fisherman was located. After a while, a couple other fishermen drew near him and he discontinued his wrongful activities. It was then that I left my vantage point to go check the man's fishing license and illegal catch.

After reviewing the fisherman's activities I had documented in my notebook, I notified him that a citation would be issued. Incredulous, the fisherman said, "I was just checked by another warden and everything was on the up-and-up. This double check is very asinine!"

To make my point, I checked the fellow's license one more

time, and again told him he was being cited for illegal activities, retrieving the hidden trout as evidence. Caught red-handed, the man exclaimed, "Where in the hell were you to have seen this?!"

Spawning Trout in a Remote Mountain Lake is Tempting

A remote mountain lake next to a forest trail was seldom fished, but I knew that a few hardy hiking fishermen trudged up that rocky and rough trail to fish. The path normally had a considerable number of wind-fallen trees spanning across it, which created a hindrance for mountain motorbikes to gain access. Knowing that the lake trout were early summer spawners and gathered at the entering stream, I would check the trailhead for human tracks and then decide if the hike was justified. At times, I would stretch a length of dark colored thread across the trail at ankle or knee height as an indicator of trail use, but if a wild animal broke the thread only footprints would be an indicator.

One such trip to the trailhead showed fresh trail use, so I made the trek to the lake. At 100 yards out or so I, as usual, watched as best as possible through the dense undergrowth and trees, and was surprised to see two fellows, with one having a bow and quiver of arrows. I then moved in an inconspicuous manner upslope for a better view, and witnessed the archer attempting to hit a spawner, which he finally did, with a loud shout afterward.

I continued around the hillside and came down the trail well above the two men. When they spotted me, the archer tossed his bow and arrows aside and quickly gave the one trout to the other fellow, who had a fishing rod and creel. The two fellows then hastened up the trail toward me, and when they were close one of them said, "Warden, where in the hell did you come from, miles down the trail?"

The archer received a citation for his unusual and illegal fishing method, and the one fish was confiscated.

High Elevation Viewing for Fisherman Activities

On one planned patrol of Conklin Lake, I had to drive over Lone Tree Pass and Lone Tree Bench to reach a surveillance point high above the lake in order to watch the fishermen activities below. There were four fishermen along the lakeshore, and after watching for a while, three of them appeared to be fishing in a legal manner while one fellow was obviously trying to snag fish from the shoreline. After catching two sizable trout, he stashed them in the grassy, brushy growth at the base of a nearby tree. Waving his arms excitedly, he acknowledged his poaching success to another distant fisherman, who was evidently a fishing partner.

Local cattle stockman had constructed a waterline and gasoline pump from the lakeshore, up the steep, steep slope to a stock water tank up on the bench, and periodically would start the gasoline engine pump to fill the tank. I followed the waterline down to the shoreline, through a lot of growth and rocks, and ultimately to the illegal fisherman. When finally checked, the fellow denied his illegal activity and left his fishing line out in the water, but the line was reeled in at my request and the treble hook was a give-away.

Following my gaze, the fisherman then said, "I know I'm not fishing properly, so I'll reel in and do it right," but once he was confronted with a third trout I had seen him stash, he was somewhat stunned and then said, "What game warden district is yours? I know Warden Todd from Ennis." He then added, "Where in the hell did you come from, anyway?"

As usual, the trout were confiscated and a notice to appear before the Ennis justice of the peace was issued. The fellow indicated he knew the justice quite well and expressed his concern of the Ennis locals learning of his illegal activity, especially my colleague and friend Warden I. L. Todd.

When I told Warden Todd all of this later, he said he knew the guy was a poacher and was pleased he was caught.

That lake is only one of a couple that I know of that had active trout spawning along shoreline areas near the trickling inlet waters.

A Situation Getting the Attention of Local Poachers

At one of the fish hatcheries near my district, the hatchery personnel would cull out some of their large rainbow trout brood stock once in a while. On one occasion, some of those more hefty trout were transplanted into ponds where parents took their children to fish. As the word spread in the small community, neighboring warden Leo Secor and I agreed that soon after the transplant it would be tempting to some local poachers to catch a trout of that size in a local setting. So, we decided we would stake out the pond for a few nights when the moonlight was bright enough that we wouldn't need a flashlight to monitor the locale's activities.

On the second night, a car cruised by the pond and momentarily stopped, but we couldn't tell if anyone got out of the car before it drove off into the darkness. We got out of our truck, which was hidden from view, and tried to get into position to view the pond with binoculars. Since the scanning wasn't good, we quietly crept closer to the pond and heard a voice say, "I've got a big one on," and soon after another voice said, "So have I!"

Cautiously, we approached the poachers and were careful not to make any noise as we stepped on the uneven ground and pond-side growth. We agreed it was best to split up so we could intercept both fishermen at the same time. I reached one of the fishermen first, and when he saw me, he called out in a loud voice, "Warden, where in the hell did you come from?!"

I knew the loud talk was intended to alert his companion that he had been caught red-handed. Shortly after, the second fellow called out, "They've got me, too!"

When the two poachers appeared before a local justice of the peace that happened to know them, he did not hesitate to admonish the transgressors, and said, "You fellows know better. What you've done is like stealing a kid's present from under a Christmas tree!"

Of course, the resulting $27.50 fine assessed wasn't appropriate for the misdemeanor crime.

"We Were Just Sitting There, Whittling!"

Sometimes during late spring, before the regular fishing season opened for stream fishing, the nice sunny weather tended to bring out the urge to go fishing for a few who were impatient. Given that it would still be a couple more weeks before fishing would be legal, I patrolled certain popular creek areas. Depending on the stream conditions, I had a couple places in mind that were quite clear and provided good fishing, whatever the date.

Knowing that most such fishermen are cagey and do not boldly park their vehicle or do their fishing out in plain view, I would quite regularly hike up to a high point adjacent to a promising stretch of waters where I could use binoculars to view much more stream area than I could if I were down in the valley. Once on a vantage point, I would scan the creek area for quite a few hours, or perhaps an entire day. On this particular day, I had sat for a couple hours when I saw two men walking across a ranch meadow and toward a creek. I could see that one was carrying what, at that time, appeared to be a can of beverage. No fishing rods were seen so I surmised that they, along with their dog, were taking a break from their ranch work.

They went out of sight behind a dense stand of willows alongside the creek, and were hidden for some time while their dog ran here and there. After about an hour, both men walked back into view. Once I trained my binoculars on them, it was plain to see that both were carrying whittled out willow fishing poles with the attached fishing lines very obvious in the sunlight. When they stopped they were in clear view, and when the can I had seen them carrying earlier was put on the ground, I could distinguish a picture of a whole red tomato on the label.

Both fishermen proceeded to take a worm from the can and bait their hooks. In a very short time both had caught a couple fish, so I documented the time and my observations, just as I had in many cases before, then I scanned the rocky and sagebrush covered slope for an approach route to their fishing hole. It took me some time to get down to the stream's edge, and the flow was considerably above normal. I looked for a reasonably shallow area to wade across without the benefit of rubber boots. With the thought that the two fellows might quit fishing and head back to the ranch buildings, I ultimately chose instead to wade into the thigh deep water to get across.

I was about an eighth of a mile from where I last saw the fishermen and had gone a couple hundred yards when suddenly their dog started barking very excitedly and aggressively. Annoyed, I felt sure that the dog's barking would alert the two pre-season fishermen. Consequently, I jogged forward to keep the anglers from getting a head start on their story, but the faithful old dog really put up a fuss and made a few challenging charges toward me. When the two men were finally in view, they were squatting down and whittling with pocketknives on pieces of willow.

Getting closer, I realized I knew one of the ranch hands and so I foolishly inquired, "What are you fellows up to?"

The answer was, "We're just sitting here, whittling."

I assured them I had seen them fishing and saw a couple fish caught, but the reply was, "Fitz, you don't see any fishing rods or fish do you? Where in the hell did you come from, anyway?"

Scouring the immediate area, I found no willow poles with fishing lines attached, but in looking across the stream I could see that tomato can so I again crossed in nearly butt-deep water. The worm can was tipped over but there was still considerable dirt with fresh worms inside. As I was about to cross back to where the fishermen were, I saw the tip of a freshly peeled willow with fishing line on it. As it was lodged in some driftwood about midstream, I then proceeded to empty my pockets of their contents and again waded out into about armpit-deep water and retrieved the makeshift rod with the worm still on the hook. When I returned to shore, I issued both fellows citations and clarified procedures for when they were to appear before the justice of the peace.

At appearance time, they were accompanied by a local lawyer and their ranch boss. Their plea was "not guilty" to the charge of fishing during closed season. They had requested a trial by jury, and their scant testimony of, "We were just sitting there whittling," sounded quite innocent. However, after I referred to my notes documenting what I observed and found at the scene, the jury found them both guilty. Because of the time lapse between the day of fishing and the trial date, my documented notes were the winning factor.

Quite some time later the two ranch hands became good friends of mine, and some extra effort in live trapping troublesome beaver from irrigating ditches finally took the edge off of the ranch boss's unfriendly attitude towards me. Afterward, he was a good source for information regarding more than ordinary shooting at deer from the nearby county road.

Closing the Gap on an Illegal Activity

While patrolling a reservoir area and observing the activities of some ice fishermen with a spotting scope, I determined that one of the guys was illegally chumming (baiting a hole) in open waters off the edge of an ice shelf. Watching the fisherman a while longer, I noted that he was regularly scanning the surrounding area and it seemed evident that he realized his methods were illegal. I recognized the fellow as the head of a poaching family and knew he was "coyote smart," which explained his monitoring activities.

I packed up my scope and started my approach across the frozen reservoir, taking a fishing rod with me to appear as another fisherman. When the fellow was occupied with his fishing enterprise, I would jog in his direction, then when he would turn and scan the surrounding area I would quickly stop and pretend to be engaged in my own fishing endeavors. The pursuit worked well and luckily the guy hooked a large fish, keeping him occupied for a longer period of time. I was quite close when he recognized me and said, "Fitzwater, where in the hell did you come from?!"

The fact that he had a local reputation as a fishing and hunting poacher gave me a feeling of great satisfaction at having caught him red-handed. Even though the chumming act with whole kernel corn and salmon eggs was illegal, with reluctance I allowed him to keep the fish caught. It was always a problem to dispose of such a small amount of confiscated items, which by regulation were supposed to be sold at auction. He still was given a citation, though. As I handed it to him, he replied, "Fitz, you know me, and realize I'm still ahead of the game!"

Warden Thought to Have Psychic Powers

Once again, I was on a high vantage point overlooking different river fishing areas while I was on patrol one day, and once more my stealthy tactics resulted in yet another puzzled fisherman who threatened to challenge the citations I issued for the illegal activities that he didn't know I had witnessed. As I sat watching that day, I had taken detailed notes on a group of fisherman in a boat, documenting who was fishing, how many fish each person caught, and how many fish had been secretly hidden away in a cache on the river bank.

When I later checked the fishing party for proper licenses and the number of fish caught, the boat handler and one of the occupants were issued citations for an over limit of fish, and the other sportsman received a citation for lack of valid fishing license. One fellow said to the license-lacking fisherman, "Challenge the warden's claim, because he can't prove you fished!"

The boat handler also piped up, "Where do you get the charge for fish over limit?"

With some satisfaction, I brought out my written notes and reviewed them for the fishermen, telling them that I had observed the unlicensed fisherman and documented the two fish he caught, and also the specific rod and reel he used, which I held as evidence. I also revealed that I would confiscate the several fish that were cached along the riverbank. Once I picked up the rod and reel and told the boat handler about the fish stashed at the riverside location, the boatman said, "Where in the hell were you to have seen this?"

Amazed, one of the fisherman said, "You must have psychic powers!"

Then, the other fellow who encouraged the challenge to my charge said, "I'm going to throw in the towel. The jig is up as far as I'm concerned."

This method of patrol and documentation was highly effective, and I used this same approach when observing the activities of trappers and duck hunters.

An Elk Rack Found During Foot Patrol

I was patrolling the Lima Peaks area on foot one day and had checked numerous elk hunters for proper licenses and elk carcass tagging, and then went on to a creek drainage where there was considerable shooting. After checking numerous hunters, I decided to go to a distant open ridge to survey other open hunting areas. The ridge was a good surveillance location, so after using binoculars to repeatedly 'glass' surrounding areas, I soon realized that it was late afternoon and quite a long hike to my vehicle.

Knowing the upper open ridge and adjacent areas above the dense stands of timber was the best route to hike, I hadn't gone but a couple hundred yards when I came across a bone pile and an exceptionally large set of bull elk antlers southwest of the Deep Creek cow camp. I concluded that it was undoubtedly the remains of a winter kill. The elk rack was of interest to me, so I decided to pack it out with the elk skull still attached. As I had already covered quite a long distance afoot, and the elk antler seemed to get heavier the farther I went, I decided to abandon the giant rack about a quarter-mile into the my trek and planned to return for it later.

Darkness soon made the hiking difficult, so realizing that the cow camp wasn’t too far away, I headed there. When I knocked on the cabin door, the old range-rider cowboy Lynn Nye stared at me in amazement and said, "Fitzwater, where in the hell did you come from?"

After we ate a bite and drank some coffee, I explained how I came to end up at the cabin after nightfall. I told Cowboy Nye about the elk antler too, and the old, bronc-breaking stove-up cowboy offered to take a horse and go pack it to my vehicle the following day. He added, "Fitzwater, you'll owe me a couple drinks when I come to town for the winter!"

As it turned out, in town several weeks later, I treated the old cowboy to a steak dinner, and of course, the couple drinks. That elk antler, at that time, scored in the record class for elk antlers.

Game Warden Wayne Fitzwater with a trophy class elk rack

Chapter Two

Lawbreakers & Troublemakers

State of Montana
Department of Fish and Game
Identification Card

No. 129

Name: Wayne Fitzwater
Division: Enforcement
Classification: State Game Warden
Address: Butte, Montana
is an employee of the Montana Fish and Game Commission

Director: Frank H. Dunkle

Paste Photo here

Description

Date of Birth: Nov. 9, 1918
Height: 5'5" Color of Eyes: Grey
Weight: 130 Color of Hair: Brown
Signature: Wayne Fitzwater

This card is the property of the Montana Fish and Game Dept. and will be returned on severance of service

District Three

Complaining Witness & Assist	Violation	License & Bond Forfeiture
Fitzwater, W. Brann, Ash	Fish w/o rod in immediate control.	$ 25.00 forfeited
Fitzwater, W. Brann, Ash	Possess more than legal limit of game fish.	$ 25.00 forfeited
Fitzwater, W. Brann, Ash	Operate & occupy a boat without a life preserver.	$10.00 forfeited
Fitzwater, W. Brann, Ash	Operate & occupy a boat without a life preserver.	$10.00 forfeited
Fitzwater, W. Brann, Ash	Transport & possess game birds w/o retaining species	$25.00 forfeited
Fitzwater, W. McKiernan, W. Brann, Ashton	Fish for and possess game fish without a license.	$50.00 forfeited
Fitzwater, W. McKiernan, W. Brann, Ashton	Fish with more than a single rod and line.	$50.00 forfeited
Fitzwater, W. McKiernan, W. Brann, Ashton	Shoot a game bird from a public highway, No. 43	$25.00 forfeited
Fitzwater, W. McKiernan, W. Brann, Ashton	Operate a motor vessel after dark without proper lights.	$25.00 forfeited
Fitzwater, W. McKiernan, W. Brann, Ashton	Fail to have a life preserver on a child 11 yr.	$25.00 forfeited
Chesterfield, B. Fitzwater, W.	Purchase improper license.	$25.00
Chesterfield, B. Todd, I. L.	Purchase improper license.	$25.00

District Three

Complaining Witness & Assist	Violation	License & Bond Forfeiture
Chesterfield, B. Fitzwater, W. Logan, Jim Warner, Art	Purchase improper license.	$25.00 forfeited
Fitzwater, W. Foster, R.	Purchase improper license.	$46.50 forfeited
Fitzwater, W. Foster, R.	Purchase improper license.	$46.50 forfeited
Fitzwater, W. Chesterfield, B. Warner, A.	Possess an untagged deer.	$25.00
Fitzwater, W. Chesterfield, B.	Possess two untagged deer.	$35.00
Fitzwater, W. Chesterfield, B.	Possess an untagged deer.	$25.00
Fitzwater, W.	Fish in closed waters.	$25.00
Fitzwater, Wayne	Fish in closed waters.	$25.00
Fitzwater, Wayne Chesterfield, R. [sic] Logan, James	Fail to keep rod and line under immediate control.	(Dismissed by Judge)
Fitzwater, Wayne	Fail to keep rod and line under immediate control.	Write a paper on need enforcement.
Fitzwater, Wayne	Affirm to false statement	$10.00 forfeited
Fitzwater, Wayne	Affirm to false statement	$10.00 forfeited
McKiernan, W. Fitzwater, W.	Purchase improper license.	21.50
McKiernan, W. Fitzwater, W.	Purchase improper license.	21.50

District Three

Complaining Witness & Assist	Violation	License & Bond Forfeiture
McKiernan, W. Fitzwater, W.	Purchase improper license.	21.50
McKiernan, W. Fitzwater, W.	Fish with imvalid [sic] license.	21.50
McKiernan, W. Fitzwater, W.	Fish with imvalid [sic] license.	21.50
McKiernan, W. Todd, I. L. Fitzwater, W.	Fish with improper license.	21.50
Fitzwater, Wayne	Fish in an illegal manner and in closed waters.	$25.00
Fitzwater, Wayne	Fish in an illegal manner and in closed waters.	$25.00
Fitzwater, Wayne	Catch more than legal limit of fish	$25.00 fishing forf. 3 mos.
Sears, K. D. Fitzwater, W.	Fish in illegal manner and in closed waters.	$25.00
Sears, K. D. Fitzwater, W.	Fish in closed waters.	$25.00
Sears, K. D. Fitzwater, W.	Fish in closed waters.	$25.00
Fitzwater, W. Sears, Ken	Hunt and pursue antelope without permit.	$25.00
Fitzwater, W.	Fail to punch date of kill on antelope tag.	$25.00
Fitzwater, Wayne	Attempt to take an antelope from a public road.	$25.00

District Three

Complaining Witness & Assist	Violation	License & Bond Forfeiture
Fitzwater, Wayne	Leave litter on public campground	21.50
Fitzwater, Wayne	Possess and transport an illegal game bird.	$25.00
Fitzwater, W.	Possess and untagged deer.	$25.00
Fitzwater, Wayne	Take a moose during closed season.	71.50 - 30 days suspended
McKiernan, W. Todd, I. L. Fitzwater, W.	Kill a calf moose in the wrong area.	46.50
McKiernan, W. Fitzwater, W.	Kill a cow moose in the wrong area.	$50.00 - 30 days suspended

Lawbreakers & Troublemakers: *Faulty Fishermen*

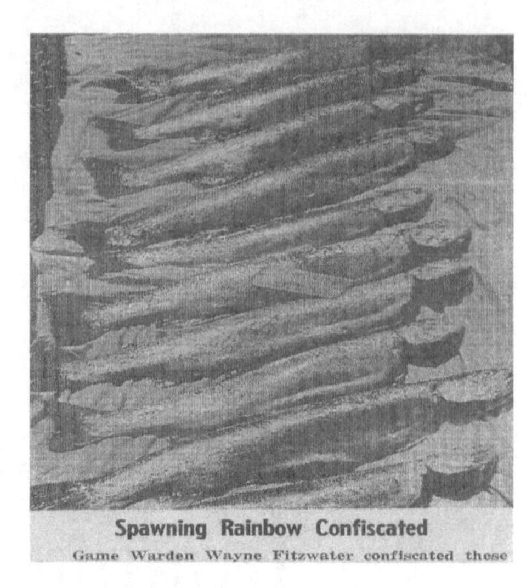

Spawning Rainbow Confiscated

Game Warden Wayne Fitzwater confiscated these

Spawning Rainbow Confiscated

Game Warden Wayne Fitzwater confiscated these Rainbow trout Thursday that were illegally taken at the inlet waters of Clark Canyon Reservoir. The 10 trout averaged some four pounds each and were spawning when caught. Fitzwater said the persons charged will face two violations: using illegal equipment and taking fish in closed waters. The fish were caught bare-handed, he said, in the shallow inlet waters. The Rainbow were given to Parkview Acres.

(Source: *The Dillon Daily Tribune-Examiner*, Dillon, MT, May 2, 1969)

Pegged as a Poacher

During winter months when sportsmen activities in the field were somewhat slack, I would go to one of my chosen vantage points where the fairly dull activities of reservoir fishermen could be monitored, often for many hours. For this kind of long-range observation I used a spotting scope, because there was no cover in the area that would allow me to observe without being detected as a "sneaky game warden." After a couple hours of such scoping, my eyes would sometimes fail to immediately focus once taken away from the one-eyed viewing. Sometimes a headache developed, which could be conducive to a nasty disposition.

On this particular late winter date, there were only a few bank fishermen with their backs turned against a cold, chilly wind, and they were fishing open water near a spring flow inlet. The surveillance seemed to indicate that one lone fisherman, off on his own and bordering the closed to fishing inlet flows, had taken one fish illegally, and from his suspicious actions appeared about to try again. I watched as he made a hurried short walk to his vehicle and stashed a good sized trout. He sauntered back to the stream bank and soon, very slowly, went down on hands and knees and reached under an overhanging clump of sod. With one hand, he tossed a sizable trout from its hiding spot onto the bank of fall grass. That settled it—the guy was due for a ticket.

I eased away from my surveillance spot and slowly drove in the direction of the illegal fisherman. About halfway there, I stopped and used my binoculars to look the fisherman's vehicle over and get the license plate numbers in the event that he would leave hurriedly and perhaps try to outrun me, which could sometimes happen. I chose that moment to quickly radio the base station for a 10-28, vehicle registration information, and when received, I wrote the registration name, address and other details on a Notice to Appear citation, then proceeded to the area to contact the fisherman.

When I reached him, the fellow was very friendly and showed a valid fishing license but stated fishing had been "lousy." Then telling him that I had witnessed his illegal activities, I advised the fisherman that I was issuing a citation for the violation. While I added a physical description and other details to the N.T.A., the poacher was looking over my shoulder and noticed his name and address already entered on the ticket along with his vehicle license number. He stated, "That's my dad's name and address and he is Senior," so I added Junior to his name on the form. The fellow was quite puzzled and surprised at his name and vehicle description already being on the citation for acknowledgement of taking fish in an illegal manner.

In the meantime, a couple other fisherman who had been some distance away came upon the scene and openly showed their amusement and pleasure that the culprit was getting his "just dues." One of the spectator fishermen had tried to motion me aside a couple times, but I completed the N.T.A., then went directly to the poacher's vehicle and retrieved the two well hidden illegal trout.

One of the onlookers blurted out, "Fellow, they sure have your number!" He proceeded to laugh and laugh until it was a source of irritation to the poacher. Realizing he had somewhat antagonized the guy, the heckler moved away, all the while chuckling with his friend.

Annoyed, the culprit fisherman said to me, "With those big fish in there, I'll bet they have done the same thing, but never got caught."

Vantage Point Viewing

There were times along the Beaverhead and Big Hole Rivers that I scanned stretches of the river from a high vantage point above, instead of just going on foot along the riverbank to check fishermen. On several occasions, I observed boat fishermen stashing caught trout at some point along the riverbank, so I would pinpoint that exact place by some obvious landmark along the shoreline so that I could go and retrieve the fish later. While doing this long-distance observing with binoculars or a spotting scope, I would also make notes as to the color and type of clothing worn by anyone fishing and also the type and color of individual rods and reels being used, and by whom.

Once the boat fishermen were checked at the end of their river run, there were many occasions that the fishermen would claim a legal limit of trout or a person in the boat would claim they didn't fish and were along just for the enjoyment of the float trip. Thanks to my notes and careful observation, I knew these claims were false, so when I advised certain boat occupants they were getting citations, I would point to specific individuals and state the citation charge and then go to the particular place along the riverbank that the trout were stashed. Often, one of the fishermen would blurt out something along the lines of, "Game Warden, I am puzzled how you succeeded in selecting certain individuals for citations, and finding fish we had hidden along the riverbank."

I'd just smile and reply, "It's all part of the job!" and leave them puzzled. It paid to be thorough!

A Learning Lesson

Before construction of the Clark Canyon Dam that formed the Clark Canyon Reservoir, there was considerable fishing activity on the Lower Red Rock River and Horse Prairie Creek. Quite a lot of the fishermen were from Utah and Idaho, and I had received several reports of anglers catching over the limit. Word was that some stored their excess fish in a freezer at the Buffalo Lodge Café, and others boxed the fish up and sent them by Union Pacific Railroad back to Utah. Unloaded of their extras, the visitors usually continued fishing before leaving for home.

Accordingly, I concentrated on checking visiting fishermen's activities. I knew that a couple Utah fishermen had purchased some older pickup trucks and licensed them with Montana R.P.O. (registration purposes only) license plates. The Montana plates, being more acceptable to landowners with prime fishing streams, helped them gain access to those otherwise restricted waters. I focused my efforts on these particular out-of-state fishermen's activities for a time, and when they finally arrived in the small Armstead community and were preparing to leave for Utah with over-limits of trout, I intended to check them and their catch of fish.

Waiting for them to embark on their journey home, I was parked on the east side of the river in Armstead. As I proceeded to go to their lodgings across the railroad track and river, a train pulled in and blocked the railroad crossing for quite some time. I sat there, impatiently waiting in my vehicle until I couldn't take it anymore, and looked up at the locomotive engineer and foolishly said, "Why don't you move that damn engine?!"

The engineer replied, “Why don’t you?”

Stuck on the other side of the train, I missed checking the fishermen and their haul. Instead, they left southbound in two separate vehicles with Utah license plates. Thankfully, I had taken down their plate numbers earlier, so I too headed southbound on the main highway and radioed the deputy sheriff stationed at Lima and asked him to stop and detain the men until I arrived.

Once I caught up with the fellows, they were obviously puzzled by the stop by the deputy sheriff, the arrival of the game warden, and just how the trout over-limit was known. They did indeed have possession of too many trout, so I confiscated the contraband fish and strongly advised them of the seriousness of transporting illegal game across state lines, which was in violation of the Lacey Act.

One of the fisherman with an attitude problem said, “Warden, you just screwed up a good thing!”

Fortunately, they had adequate money to pay the fine assessed by the local justice of the peace. Unfortunately, it turned out that was most of the money they had on hand, so there was much grumbling when they told me they would need to wire for money at Idaho Falls so they could get home to Utah.

Improvising Fishermen

At one of my usual vantage points, where I had a clear view of fisherman activities through a spotting scope, I concentrated on two men who were walking along the bank of a spring flow into a reservoir. By the men's actions and arm pointing, it was certain that they were excited to see the large trout in the narrow spring flow.

Finally, after some hesitation and looking around the surrounding area for other people, the one fellow removed his jacket and waded in the flow of water and stood on each side of the jacket collar so the water would flow through the two sleeves. The other fellow went upstream quite a distance and waded downstream toward the man with the jacket. As soon as the other fellow was near, the man with the jacket threw it on the stream bank. The two soon held up two large trout and then hastened toward their parked vehicle quite some distance away.

I then left my vantage point to go have a chat with the two men. As I approached them at their vehicle, the two retrieved fishing rods from the pickup bed and were standing alongside it when I arrived.

Offering a greeting, I said, "How are you fellows doing today?"

This was a poor approach because it encouraged a lie from a fisherman, when I already knew of their illegal pursuit. The fishermen said, "We really hit the jackpot today!"

After checking their fishing licenses and revealing I had been watching their unlawful activities, they were advised that they both would receive citations and the beautiful trout would be confiscated. What an unusual and crafty way to capture two spawning trout!

Regulations Outlined for Brook Trout

State Game Warden Wayne Fitzwater, Monday, clarified brook trout fishing, under the new Montana regulations for 1968-69.

The entire Big Hole drainage, with the exception of the main Big Hole River channels from the Divide dam, upstream to the River Bridge at Wisdom, is open to fishing for "brookes" the entire year.

Daily possession limit on brook trout is 10 pounds, with no number or size limit.

(Source: *The Dillon Daily Tribune-Examiner*, Dillon, MT, date unknown)

Fishing from a Raft on a Mountain Lake

While approaching a mountain lake one day, I stopped short to watch two fishermen on a raft, which repeatedly drifted back to shore due to a brisk wind. The two men would then paddle to the upwind side of the lake and again drift downwind, repeating the cycle over and over as they fished from the raft.

Strangely, I didn't see any obvious fishing rods and after the first drift across the lake, each of them retrieved two setlines before paddling to the upwind side of the lake. When I approached them as they were retrieving their setlines on the next downwind float, I watched as both inconspicuously dropped their lines in the quite shallow waters at the end of the float. I waded out to the raft, and on the far end spied a fish-stringer with four hefty trout in the water.

I checked their licenses as was my routine duty, and then the men were notified they would be cited for the four setlines. In rebuttal to the charge, one of them said, "This is the way we always fish a lake. One line each is legal, and the fish are, too!"

I went to my vehicle and took my fishing rod with a treble hook and unbelievably retrieved all four setlines that were still baited! When I told the men that all four trout would be confiscated, they were quite angry, and both exclaimed, "One line should be legal, so how can you confiscate all four fish?!"

Fishing Too Good to Stop

One lake in the Dillon warden district is accessible by a fairly steep trail from a parking lot at a nearby picnic area, and pan-sized grayling are the only fish in the lake. The lake shore is beach-like granite sand, and evidently due to lack of an adequate food source, the fish are stunted at eight to ten inches maximum. It is quite common to catch two or three at about every cast, which is unusual when compared to other fishing holes. Quite a few fishermen are familiar with the productive lake and if they are oriented toward catching and eating scaled grayling, they will regularly fish there.

Overstepping Authority

While working the Helena district, I had numerous Fish & Game violation cases before a justice of the peace, A. J. White, who was very professional in his court proceedings. George Spomer, the warden from an adjoining district, had a case involving fishing closed waters before Justice White, and after the complaint was read to the defendant, the justice levied a fine. Immediately afterward, Warden Spomer openly said, "Judge, my minimum fine for those fishing in closed waters is $50.00!" Justice White quickly replied, "Warden, I'll have you know that I am the judge and I am to say the amount of the fine, and not you as the officer!"

On one trip hiking along the trail while on patrol, I met a fisherman coming down from the lake. Since he was wearing a rubber-coated army-style backpack, I requested the fellow's fishing license and to see the backpack contents. I was more than a little surprised to count over 30 grayling! I issued a citation and then relieved the guy of his packsack. I carried it down to the parking lot and confiscated all the fish that were in excess of the legal limit, leaving him with only what he could have rightfully caught. The guy admitted he got carried away and didn't stop.

A Question of Jurisdiction

On patrol along the Jefferson River, I contacted a fisherman and found the fellow did not have a valid Montana fishing license. I issued a citation and directed the man to appear before a justice of the peace in Butte. Once before the justice, the man was asked for a plea to the charge, so he pleaded not guilty and reiterated that the court had no jurisdiction since the violation wasn't in Silver Bow County.

I reminded the fellow that, unbeknownst to many, the Silver Bow county line came to an unusual wedge-shaped point at that location and joined with the Madison and Jefferson county lines, so the Butte justice had jurisdiction. Later, it was learned that a law violation in such close proximity to other county lines and within a certain distance factor meant that the jurisdiction could be in either county. However, I produced two maps which clearly showed these unusual county line boundaries, so the Silver Bow County judge officiated the proceedings and rightfully assessed a $27.50 fine for failure to have a valid fishing license.

A Challenging Couple

The Big Hole River headquarters are in the well-known Big Hole Basin and provide stream, river, and high mountain lake fishing below the Continental Divide, which is the Montana-Idaho state line. The upper basin streams are predominately brook trout waters that attract many fishermen interested in pan-sized fish. Over the years, from 1950 to present, numerous game wardens were assigned duty there and were based out of Butte, During the 1960s, a sheriff and old-timer who later became a game warden, by the name of Howard Larsen, worked that warden district.

Larsen was a "raw boned" six-footer and was a fair man, but one not to be challenged by hunters and fishermen who may have violated a Fish & Game law. At the time, I was working the west Dillon district, and was living in Dillon. My district adjoined Larsen's Big Hole district at Big Hole-Grasshopper Pass, and when either one of us was in the area, we would invariably attempt radio contact in order to exchange information of interest to both of us. On one occasion, we made radio contact and agreed to meet in nearby Jackson for lunch.

Following our meal, Larsen asked me to accompany him on an afternoon patrol of the upper basin. We checked the activities of several fishermen, and at one location we observed a woman fishing with a man standing alongside her. After some time, we went to check them for proper licenses. The man wasn't very friendly, and abruptly took the fishing rod from the woman. When asked for their fishing licenses and a creel check, the man said he was the fisherman and was only coaching the woman. The man produced a valid license, but the lady did not have one, so she was informed by Warden Larsen that he would have to issue her a citation.

Immediately, and in an aggressive and confrontational manner, the man said he was the fisherman and he was only showing the woman how to fish and that a citation was not justified. However, during our prior observation of the two, we could see that the woman was very adept at casting and changing her artificial fly. We also observed that she removed fish she had caught several times when the man was not standing nearby. Warden Larsen felt quite confident that a citation was valid.

While checking the sack of fish they had caught, there were a good number of fish, and the woman told us the fishing had been good and followed up with, "Now I suppose I'll get a ticket for over the legal limit?"

After dumping the sack of fish on the stream bank, and with both of them exchanging worried glances, we told them that the limit for Eastern brook trout was ten pounds with no size or number limit. They both said they weren't aware of that, but the man persisted that the citation was unjustified and said, "Both you wardens are assholes, and you can go to Hell!"

Warden Larsen reminded the man that there was a time and place for the woman to appear before a Dillon justice of the peace, where she could answer to the charge of fishing without a license. The man then said, "We won't be there!"

As he headed to his car, he gave Warden Larsen a shove sideways. I knew this would not go over well with Larsen, and he sternly told the man that his attitude and aggressive act just resulted in reason for his arrest. Consequently, both the man and woman would be immediately taken before the justice of the peace in Dillon. The man was then escorted to Larsen's vehicle door and ordered to get inside. The man put both hands above the vehicle door and braced his body outward. Larsen then quickly grabbed one of the man's arms by the wrist and then downward between his knees and shoved him head-first into the vehicle. The man was caught off-guard and so shocked, he was speechless. This ended the confrontation.

The woman was asked if she could drive their car to Jackson for safe keeping and then ride with Larsen to Dillon. She indicated she would, and that the car belonged to her. My vehicle as also in Jackson, so I followed them to Dillon. The man was released from his arrest, and the two had adequate money between them to pay the assessed fine. Warden Larsen then took them back to Jackson, and along the way the woman apologized for all the problems they had caused.

Incriminating Beer Can Evidence

During winters that lakes and reservoirs were adequately frozen to a safe depth, numerous ice fishermen would try their luck catching trout and ling in certain waters. I spent hours and hours checking their activities and fishing successes. As usual, I would observe their activities from a distance before making contact with the fishermen.

On one patrol, I watched as a fisherman was fishing out in the open without any shelter and had augured holes through the ice to open water. Hoping to maximize his efforts, he was using two fishing rods, which was illegal at the time on that reservoir. The fisherman also had a six-pack of beer, and once a can was empty he would go off a ways to a third hole in the ice and submerge it.

I could plainly read the beer can labels and made notes of how many cans had been disposed of in the littering manner, along with how many fish he caught on his extra rod. Once I approached the fellow, he quickly reeled in the very short second rod and attempted to conceal it under an extra jacket on a makeshift sled used to get his fishing gear out to his preferred spot. The fellow was from Idaho but had a proper Montana fishing license. When I issued the citation for the extra rod and beer can littering, I confiscated the number of fish he had caught with the second rod. The fisherman was quite upset about being issued a citation, particularly with reference to littering, as he said, "Warden, you don't see any evidence of littering, do you?"

When I told him that I had seen him sinking empty beer cans, he replied, "You would have a difficult time proving it. Where in the hell were you, anyway?"

When the man finally appeared before the justice of the peace, he pleaded guilty to the use of the second fishing rod but then pleaded not guilty to the littering charge. He posted cash bond, and the justice advised him that he would go to court trial for the beer can charge. Later that same day I returned to the fishing site, and with a stiff piece of number 9 wire I patiently hooked and retrieved three of the submerged beer cans. I then took photographs of them on the ice surface alongside the augured hole.

The next day, I notified the justice about my success retrieving the submerged beer cans, and submitted them to be held as evidence. When the county attorney issued the complaint, he suggested that the fellow be advised by mail of the incriminating evidence, so I sent the man a formal letter. About a week or so later, the justice told me that the culprit had paid the bond designated for the littering charge, and the case was considered closed before it ever made it to trial.

Hiding One's Guilt

One of my warden districts in the 1950s had several ponds that were spring-fed and grew pan-sized trout, which were the size many fishermen desired. There were times when fishermen could catch a legal limit in just a short amount of time, which meant a very short period of enjoyment. Often, I parked in a grove of trees some distance away and watched fishermen's activities before checking their licenses and catches.

It so happened that a few fishermen were tempted to use more than one fishing rod, which of course was illegal, and as access to a couple ponds was open and a clear view was possible, I could observe some of the fishermen reel in a second rod and then quickly put in in their vehicle when I arrived. Surveying their activities through binoculars and documenting how many fish had been caught on each of the rods was the determining factor as to how many fish would be confiscated when a citation was issued.

This particular day, I observed a solitary fellow who was catching fish regularly, and so when I was sure he had caught the legal limit, I assumed he would leave as a happy fisherman. Instead, he left his obviously baited line and rod out in the pond and caught a couple more trout. I noticed what appeared to be some type of paper wrappings blowing on the ground and guessed he was probably having lunch, so I proceeded to go in to check his license and catch.

When I approached him and asked to see his license and the fish he had caught, I was surprised to see there were only two fish in his creel. The fellow said, “That's all I've caught so far!”

I then decided to let him know I had been observing him and was quite sure he had already caught his legal limit, plus two more. Hearing this, he became quite mouth, and his body language was aggressive. Footprints and disturbed dirt around the left rear wheel of his vehicle caught my eye, along with a screwdriver laying on the ground nearby. I guessed he had pried the vehicle's hubcap off and out the missing fish inside.

He noticed me looking at the wheel, and he suddenly changed his attitude. He finally admitted what he had done, and that his sneaky method wasn't very good. He blamed it on a neighbor of his who had told him it was a good way to conceal small fish and grouse.

A Rare Opportunity for a Bonus in Gratitude

When I was patrolling the Boulder River area near town, I was notified that the fish hatchery truck would be in the vicinity and would like to have some help releasing a load of catchable size trout, so I asked the Jefferson County Sheriff Office to give me a radio call when the truck came through town. Some time later I received the call, met the truck, and assisted with fish releases at various locations along the river.

After the hatchery truck left the area, I had lunch in Boulder and planned to patrol river spots where we had just released the trout. I knew from previous experience that eager fishermen enjoyed fishing release areas with exceptional luck, due to the hatchery trout being docile and tank fed, so not as wary as wild trout.

During late evening, I observed several fishermen at one of the release sites and proceeded to check their catches and licenses. Just before sunset I checked one last fisherman. I discovered the fellow did not have a valid license with him, but instead he claimed he had left his license at his place in Butte. I had encountered such claims in the past, and some were honest but not usually. Since I was going to my headquarters in Butte later that evening, and I felt assured that fellow was truthful, I issued a courtesy citation and advised the fisherman that I would see him within a couple hours.

Once arriving in Butte, I went to the house number given, and upon knocking on the front door I was greeted by a petite and attractive lady. I explained I was looking for the man I had cited earlier, and she invited me in to wait for the fellow. Walking through the door, I immediately noticed a pleasant feminine scent. The man appeared and produced his valid fishing license, which was dated weeks before, so I returned the previously confiscated fish.

The man expressed his gratitude for my visit, and was quite elated that the fish he had caught were finally returned to him. The conversation was quite short, but then the man said, "Game warden, I have a couple souvenirs to give to you." He left the room, and came back with two metal tokens that he pressed into my palm. Examining the tokens, I realized the building was a "house of ill repute" and that the fellow was the brothel's pimp! With a sly smile on his face, he said to me, "You can, if you are so inclined, redeem the tokens!"

Lawbreakers & Troublemakers:

Tricky Trappers

"Warden, You are Everywhere!"

As the fur trapping season was approaching, it was a common practice for serious trappers to contact ranchers who had a stream with a good beaver population and encourage them to request a landowner beaver permit from the local game warden. It was beneficial to the ranchers for beaver to be trapped in order to alleviate the serious problem of damming up irrigation ditches and flooding areas, particularly hay fields, that would be too wet to harvest with machinery, and so convincing them wasn't too difficult. As a result I issued many, many such permits. With considerable reluctance, I would also provide a listing of good beaver trappers, knowing very well that a few trappers were eager to start trapping beaver in late October and early November when pelts were reasonably prime. They were also anxious to get a head start trapping mink before the season opened November 10th, which increased their take of money-making furs.

Knowing these illegal mink trappers from past experiences, I would concentrate on patrolling those ranch areas. In one instance, I went to a crude cabin at a cow camp that two rugged old-timers were using as their trapping headquarters. Even though the ranch owner had previously given me permission to use the cabin anytime, the trappers were not present when I arrived, so the I awaited their eventual return.

Once hardy old mountain man and long-time trapper Lew Weidner arrived, he was quite surprised to see me, but offered a greeting and said, "Glad to see you're on the job. Would you like to come in for a cup of coffee?"

As the rugged old fellow stoked up the wood stove fire and prepared to brew the coffee, I was seated at the makeshift table. As I leaned back against the cloth-enclosed storage space below the support for the chimney, I detected the obvious odor of mink. The farther I leaned back, the stronger the odor. As the old trapper was occupied brewing the coffee, I quietly parted the cloth and saw quite a collection of mink pelts strung on a wire, so I removed one pelt and was blowing through the fur as the trapper turned around to face me. Calmly, I said, "It is a fairly prime pelt."

The trapper responded, "Darn it, we were about to bring the mink hides to you. You just cannot keep them out of beaver traps!"

I responded by saying, "I realize the effort to trap, skin, and stretch so many mink, but I'll ask how many times through these many trapping years have you turned in any mink pelts to a warden?"

The trapper then said, "You've got me there."

Having been a trapper for many years myself, I was a poor farm kid that bought his first Harley Davidson motorcycle with the proceeds from trapping money, so it was with great remorse that I confiscated all the illegal mink pelts. When the other trapper, his brother Rance Weidner, arrived at the cabin and learned what had taken place he finally said, "Warden, I believe I remember you from somewhere," and then added, "Hell, I remember you from up north at the Brady ranch, back in the early 1950s, where we were trapping!" Exasperated, he then added, "You're like cow shit in the pasture—you're everywhere!"

Dyed in the Fur Trapper

Trapping activity seemed to have been at a peak during the 1950s, and there were some very good dyed in the wool trappers covering considerable distance on foot, in vehicles, and in boats to better take mink and beavers. The competition was keen, so some ordinarily conscientious trappers drifted out of the legal ranks and boat-trapped river areas for the more valuable mink, prior to that November 10th opening date.

I had several vantage points adjacent to the Beaverhead, Red Rock, Ruby and Big Hole Rivers where I could, from a concealed place, scan certain sections of river channels to identify boat-trapping activity. Once it was evident that a trapper was boat-trapping, I would then decide at what place I might make contact with the trapper to check his catch, license, and equipment.

Due to any number of circumstances, but especially in accessing the river from my vantage point, there were many, many times that it wasn't an easy matter for me to properly check a trapper and make a determination whether he was completely legal with his activities. Some of the more sly, crafty, and conniving trappers would put out considerable effort to keep from being caught trapping illegally. For instance, I knew of one particular fellow who was boating a section of river, and I noted that at the end of the river run he would not have any fur beavers, except perhaps what might be legal on a landowner permit. As a result, I later canoed that same section of river and checked for traps. Luckily, my investigative efforts satisfied my suspicion that many of the sets were meant for mink, which were not yet open for legal trapping. Once I found a mink in a trap, I proceeded to place a colored dye in the fur and left it to be collected by whichever trapper claimed the catch.

Not much later, on a day when I observed the particular trapper in question at the end of his river run, I made it a point to check him. As usual, he had only a couple beaver, which was legal on a landowner permit, but I happily noticed that the trapper's rubber gauntlet gloves showed evidence of the colored dye that I had previously placed in the fur of two trapped mink. When the fellow removed his gloves, his left hand was also stained with the dye. After checking the trapper's license, I called the fellow out about his illegal mink trapping activities. This, of course, was at first denied. After some down-to-earth talk and mention of the unusual color on his gloves and hand, the trapper stated it must have been from some trap dye he had used, and he stuck to this made up story until I advised him of the dye that I had placed on the two trapped mink.

After some pondering while pulling his boat out of the water, the fellow joked about the procedure and agreed to go with me to where the mink carcasses were cached. He must have realized that in order to continue trapping the surrounding area, and being confronted by a game warden, it would be best to be somewhat cooperative and legal.

I had known this trapper's father quite well and made a casual remark to the fellow that his dad was recognized as a "dyed in the wool" trapper. The fellow laughed and said, "And he has a dyed in the fur son!" which brought forth a chuckle from both of us.

Contact in a Remote Area with a Possible Confrontation

For a time, I was working the Butte Basin lowland areas. While traveling above the stream in Bison Canyon, I saw a wisp of smoke coming from down in the brush-covered creek bottom. I found a place to park my vehicle off the traveled road and hiked down the slope to the creek, then toward the source of the smoke. Due to the dense brush, I left the creek bottom and went up on the slope to get a look at a crude campsite, and watched a fellow moving around a small tent and meager campfire.

At that distance, I couldn't determine what the fellow's activities were, so I approached the camp in a cautious manner. The camper was completely surprised and shaken by my seemingly sudden presence. With some steel traps hanging nearby, I realized the old fellow was a trapper. After I offered a greeting, which wasn't well received, and an acknowledgement that the fellow was an animal trapper, the man was very nervous and slowly went toward a gun leaning against his tent. Concerned, I advised him not to move any closer to the gun. I next asked the fellow if he had caught any animals, which he denied. After looking around the area for possible animal pelts and finding none, I asked if he had a trapper's license. He shook his head no, so I informed him his activities were illegal, and with the steel traps as evidence he would be issued a Fish & Game Department citation.

While writing up the citation, I learned that a friend had dropped him off the day before, and then after a few days planned to check on the fellow's welfare and trapping success. I reluctantly took the old trapper into custody and to my vehicle so he could appear before the local justice of the peace. Before leaving the camp, I told the fellow that later, at an appropriate time, I would help him dismantle his camp if needed. The old trapper flatly stated he didn't want any help from a warden. With that, we headed into town to rectify matters with the justice of the peace. On the way there, the grizzled old-timer said to me, "Warden, you took a hell of a chance coming into my camp, as I don't take kindly to game wardens."

After presenting my case, I recommended that any fine be suspended and only court costs be assessed, which was ultimately agreed to by the justice. Once the case was closed, the steel traps and gun which were held as evidence were returned to the trapper, but I didn't bother to offer help tearing down his camp.

November 3, 1975

Honorable Thomas L. Judge
Governor, State of Montana
Capitol Building
Helena, Montana 59601

Dear Governor Judge:

Recent news articles have discussed, pro and con, the carrying of sidearms by Wardens of the Montana Department of Fish and Game. Some such items indicate that the carrying of weapons by these officers is unnecessary.

As Peace Officers Wardens may be called upon at any time to handle difficult and dangerous law enforcement matters of all types. Most certainly they cannot ignore violations of any Montana law, or any emergency requests for assistance from other Peace Officers or private citizens. Further, nearly all persons Fish and Game Wardens come into contact with in the field are armed. Undoubtedly the overwhelming majority of hunters are law abiding citizens. However, a few are unpredictable and experience proves that some are extremely dangerous. It would be an injustice to the Wardens and their families to require them to face armed, potentially dangerous individuals, without adequate protection. Being unarmed would undoubtedly encourage some persons to refuse to comply with their legitimate requests, or take offensive action, especially during the current rise in violent crime throughout Montana.

During some 35 years in law enforcement I am aware of many instances in which Fish and Game Wardens, particularly those working in the sparsely settled areas of Montana, have been called upon in emergencies to assist other Peace Officers or private citizens. About 10 years ago, at the request of the Montana Department of Fish and Game, I assisted in instituting a Firearms Training Program for Wardens. I had an opportunity to train most of the Wardens throughout the state and at the Montana Law Enforcement Academy in Bozeman. Based on my observation and close association with these men I

Honorable Thomas L. Judge
November 3, 1975

sincerely feel that they are the most carefully selected, best educated, and best trained Peace Officers of any law enforcement agency in the entire state of Montana. As Governor of Montana I am convinced that you can be extremely proud of the outstanding leadership and dedicated wardens comprising the Montana Department of Fish and Game.

The fact that the Wardens are visibly armed and that most people are aware of their extensive training in the use of the firearms they carry, would normally be a deterrent to anyone considering offensive action against them. Such knowledge should logically also encourage potential violators to comply with the Montana laws the Wardens are charged with enforcing. As Sheriff of the largest Sheriff's Department in the state of Montana, I respectfully urge you to insist that all Montana Fish and Game Wardens be authorized to carry firearms while in the field. I am confident that with their intelligence, training, experience, and the outstanding supervision afforded them, they will carry such firearms with the utmost discretion.

May I also humbly state that based on my extensive experience in the training and use of firearms by law enforcement officers throughout the United States as a Firearms Instructor for the U.S. Border Patrol and for some 18 years in the F.B.I., the Model 66, Smith and Wesson, .357 revolver is probably the sidearm best adapted for the work of the Montana Department of Fish and Game for a number of important reasons, which space does not permit me to elaborate on.

If you so desire you may disseminate all or any part of this letter to the news media.

Sincerely,
/s/
JOHN C. MOE
Sheriff

JCM:cb
cc: Wesley Woodgerd, Director
Montana Department of Fish and Game
Orville W. Lewis, Administrator Law Enforcement Division, Montana Department of Fish and Game

Lawbreakers & Troublemakers:

Hooligan Hunters

Conniving Hunters

At one time in the 1950s, the wardens in one Fish & Game Department region were issued individually numbered paper punches for use in areas of concentrated hunter activity, like the upper Gallatin River Canyon and Gardiner extended elk hunts. The thinking behind the use of the individually numbered paper punches was to avoid the double-checking of successful elk hunters by the several game wardens in those fairly confined hunting areas. I followed the guidelines for use of the punches, then added my own extra policy of inconspicuously cutting a slit in one ear of a tagged elk. To avoid confusion, I also informed the other wardens patrolling the area about my extra procedure.

On one stop during that era, I checked a successful hunter and punched his elk tag and big game license. I noted that there was another man in the pickup truck, but had no reason to contact him. That was not the duo's last encounter with a game warden, though. Over the next couple days, the two men in the pickup were seen by several wardens parked in plowed out snow turnouts, using binoculars to scan surrounding areas for elk.

One of my colleagues checked a hunter with an elk, not knowing he was one half of the pair of hunters, and saw that the elk tag was punched with my numbered punch but there was no slit in the ear. Suspicious of wrongdoing, and quietly noting the hunter's extreme nervousness, he questioned the hunter. During the ensuing conversation the hunter stated that his hunting partner had gotten an elk earlier, which was back at their temporary quarters, so the warden and hunter went to the temporary set-up so he could further investigate. The warden checked the second hunter and his claimed elk, which was properly tagged but had no corresponding punch mark on his license. It did have a slit in an ear, though.

The two elk were confiscated and probed for bullets, which were substantiated as two 30-06 caliber shots that were fired from the same rifle that belonged to the more hardy hunter. The other fellow finally admitted that he had not shot an elk and had given his hunting license to his hunting partner—so, citations were issued for shooting over the legal limit. However, the justice of the peace who heard their case deemed the one elk to be legal and to be returned to the hunter who had shot both elk.

What a roundabout way of claiming an elk!

A Method of Marking

As the big game hunting season neared, quite a few hunters set up temporary hunting camps in advance of the opening day. During one pre-season patrol, I was making my rounds in an area with a couple camps and learned that one camp had been occupied for several days prior to the opening day. So, just on a hunch, I skirted around the timber area surrounding the camp, and quite some distance above the site there was a gathering of magpies. I approached the birds and was not surprised to find a deer gut pile.

I hiked back down the slope toward the hunters' camp. In a thick stand of jack pine along the way, I found a nice buck deer carcass, field dressed and covered with a tarp to ward off birds from feeding on the deer meat. I cut a slit in the hide, placed a metal tag in the slit, and continued on my way.

After the big game hunt had been in progress for a few days, I finally managed to get back to the camp and found three deer hanging nearby. In checking the three hunters present, I informed the hunter who claimed the tagged buck that he was being cited for killing the deer during closed season. Denying my allegation, the accused hunter demanded to know the basis for the charge on the citation. So, I asked him to accompany me to the deer carcass where I removed the metal tag as evidence that the animal was taken during closed hunting. Frustrated and embarrassed, he exclaimed, "There are days when you just can't win!"

A Case of Broken Honor, Dedication, and Trust

During my assignment to the Helena warden district, I was summoned to the headquarters by the chief deputy for an assignment. I was informed that a rancher in an area north of Helena and south of Great Falls had information about elk being killed illegally and transported through the ranch by three men. He thought the culprits may have possibly been Fish & Game Department employees.

I was directed to investigate and report back to the chief deputy. So, I contacted the rancher personally and, surprisingly, learned that the rancher recognized two of the men transporting the elk from the Region 4 Fish & Game Headquarters. Having learned this, I reported back to the headquarters' chief deputy, and asked that I be relieved of continuing the investigation due to the extenuating circumstances.

The chief deputy excused me from further involvement, and recruited investigative assistance from the Lewis & Clark and Cascade counties sheriffs' departments. To his shocking surprise, it was found that the men involved were a game warden supervisor, a regularly assigned game warden, and a probationary game warden! All answered to a court decision, paid the price of their unbelievable acts, and were relieved of their Fish & Game Department duties. Naturally, the shock of this happening went through the Fish & Game law enforcement ranks, and caused a degree of concern and mistrust with the sporting public.

Sheriff's Officers Find Elk Meat on Sun River Bottom

Great Falls--(AP)--Sheriffs from two counties hauled a quarter of an elk from the debris-littered bottom of the Sun river Friday afternoon and said they were "fully satisfied" the meat from two elk illegally slaughtered by three deputy game wardens had been thrown into the river.

The officers, who unsuccessfully dragged the river for 1-1/2 hours Thursday, caught the meat on a grappling hook about 3 p. m. Friday. They called off the search then.

The elk quarter was fished from the water about 200 yards below the Sun river bridge, from which the former state fish and game department employees said they had thrown it when it spoiled.

Convicted on illegal elk killing charges in a Helena justice court Tuesday were District Supervisor Truce Emett of Great Falls and Deputy Wardens George S. Spomer of Great Falls and Ernest T. Toth of Havre.

The three were fired from their jobs after they pleaded guilty.

Emett is serving 75 days in the county jail at Helena and Spomer 60 days. Toth was fined $300.

Officers dragged the river to confirm the trio's story that the meat had been thrown into the river.

Taking part in the boat search over an area of river filled with old automobile frames about four miles west of Great Falls were Lewis and Clark County Sheriff Dave Middlemas and Deputy John Bakker, Cascade County Sheriff D. J. Leeper and Deputy John Krsul.

After the former warden's story was substantiated Middlemas said, "I had made up my mind to find that meat if at all possible."

The Montana fish and game department Friday announced the temporary assignment of two deputy game wardens to fill vacancies created by the discharge of the three employees.

They are Keith Burke of Conrad, a department employee since 1941, who was transferred to Great Falls, and Otto Kebschull a department employee since June, 1941, who was moved to Havre.

Burke will be replaced in the Pondera-Teton area by Howard Larson, former Sanders county sheriff. Kebschull has been one of three wardens working out of Missoula.

Name of the third deputy was not announced. But the department said Thursday night, "Three game wardens have already been transferred to the Great Falls-Havre area for patrol duty."

Friday's announcement said, "Final assignments for these posts will not be made at this time."

The discharged deputies said they shot an elk on a ranch near Wolf Creek, Sept 25-27, "on the spur of the moment."

(Source: *The Independent Record*, Helena, MT, October 11, 1952)

Two Fawn Deer and Only One Valid Deer Tag

As I was driving to an elk hunting area one winter day, I saw a vehicle parked along the remote county road, and as there was snow on the ground, the occupant's footprints showed that the one person had gone up a slope east of the road. The wind had partially covered the footprints, and I was about to follow the human tracks to determine the person's activities when I observed a hunter, identified by a bright orange vest, quite a distance up the slope. Changing tactics, I instead drove out of sight of the hunter and awaited his arrival at the road.

It was obvious that the hunter was dragging an animal in the snow, and when the fellow came to a fence above the road I was surprised to see that he, quite easily, literally threw two fawn deer over the fence. I hastened out of my truck and approached the hunter, asking for his hunting license, which was minus the deer tag that was attached to one deer carcass. When I informed the fellow that the one untagged fawn was illegal, the fellow said, "Warden, I am a meat hunter for my family. I would think that the two small deer would be equal to one adult deer."

This, of course, was not how the Fish & Game regulation was written. He was again advised that the untagged fawn would unfortunately be confiscated, to which he replied, "Damn it, you ruined my day, taking my deer and giving me a citation!"

A Race for the Truth

Many times, a game warden will be confronted with circumstances that don't jibe, and then he must put his inquisitive and suspicious instincts into play until he can determine if things are as they seem. Such was the circumstance when my colleague Warden Secor and I were paired up to patrol a heavily hunted elk area in southwest Montana. We came into a hunter's camp with three elk hanging, so we proceeded to check the hunter's license and required tags on the animal carcasses. One elk carcass had the required tag, which seemed to be okay. The hunter-rancher explained that an elderly hunter friend of his had gotten the elk late the previous day. Unfortunately, the friend had become somewhat ill and was exhausted, so he had gone back to the ranch and by now may be on his way home to Iowa. The guy produced the non-resident license to match the animal tag and said, "I thought it was best for him to leave his license to correspond with his tag."

Being of suspicious nature and with considerable doubt, which is a common game warden trait, neither of us readily accepted the statement, but then again it could have been the truth. Once out of camp we both said, almost simultaneously, "We'd best check this further!"

Knowing where the guy lived, we decided to quickly travel the 18 miles to his ranch to determine circumstances there. As we left the mountain area and drove speedily across the remote valley with its unimproved dusty roads, we were leaving a sizable trail of dust behind us that was visible for quite a few miles. Once at the ranch, we asked the rancher's wife about the old fellow to whom the license was issued. The lady replied, "Good heavens, no! He went back to Iowa several days ago for business reasons."

With that valuable piece of information under our belts, we left without any undue visiting or pursuing the matter further. About the time we arrived at the end of the long ranch lane, an obvious dust cloud on the county road from a fast traveling vehicle could be seen heading our way. Warden Secor and I looked at one another and smiled, knowing it was undoubtedly the hunter trying to get to the ranch to attempt to get a story concocted with his wife that would coincide on both ends.

When the rancher arrived where we had temporarily parked, he had a grin on his face and said, "I knew the jig was up the minute I saw that cloud of dust out across the valley ahead of me." He added, "I guess that is one elk we'll lose. I'll admit, I tried to pull a fast one and will shoulder the blame. We just hated to have that license go to waste for the cost involved."

Getting the Job Done with Repercussions

During the Montana big game hunting seasons, the Bull Mountain area of Jefferson County was a popular area for many hunters, and especially those from Butte. I had numerous confrontations with hunters that were not particularly cooperative while being field checked for proper hunting licenses and tags, and whether a big game animal claimed was legal and properly tagged.

A new game warden was hired and stationed at Whitehall. Being not too far away in Dillon, I coached and encouraged the new warden, and advised him that he would undoubtedly be challenged in some respect by various hunters that were not particularly fond of game wardens or their duties. At my suggestion, the newly hired game warden established a one-man checking station along one of the few roads exiting Bull Mountain, and he proceeded to check numerous hunters late in the day.

His checking station activities went well until a vehicle with two hunters was stopped, with the warden requesting their big game licenses. The driver rolled the window down a few inches and quickly flashed his and his partner's licenses in the warden's direction, but the warden stated that he must have their licenses to document certain information. He had noted that there was animal hair and blood on the vehicle trunk and bumper areas, so he again requested their licenses and stated it appeared that they had an animal in the vehicle's trunk.

The men didn't cooperate and rolled up the car window. Feeling very frustrated, the warden put his hand on the butt of his revolver as a show of seriousness, but only got a “go to hell” expression from the driver. As the hunters pulled away, the warden shot the left rear tire and the driver stopped and got out yelling, “What in the hell is going on here?!”

The warden was still holding the gun pointed toward the ground and replied, “The darn gun went off accidentally.”

Not surprisingly, a harsh exchange of words followed.

Needless to say, for the hunters to continue on, the spare tire in the trunk was required. When getting it out, a deer carcass lacking the proper tag was revealed, and a citation was issued. When the case was presented before a justice of the peace, the hunters indicated they were threatened, but the justice, after listening to the testimony, did not include that in his final judgment.

The new warden was still serving his one-year probationary period when the checking station fracas unfolded. Once the regional warden supervisor learned of the details, along with a couple other questionable activities on the warden's behalf, he was not recommended for permanent job status.

Hunters Have Great Day; Wardens, Too

Hunters from the Butte area had a big day Sunday.

But so did the game wardens.

Six hundred and forty-five cars passed through a checking station manned by members of the Montana Fish and Game Dept. near Buxton on the opening day of the big game season.

Game Warden Louis Kis of Butte said he and four associates counted the following:

5 elk,
137 deer,
5 antelope,
1 moose,
1 goose,
200 ducks.

But Kis and game wardens Wayne Fitzwater, Dillon; Leonard Secor, Sheridan; Howard Larsen, Butte; and Federal Game Management Agent Ashton Brann, Helena, detected 24 violations. Kis said these included:

2 men with over-the-limit fish catches,
1 grouse out of season,
20 deer untagged or improperly tagged,
1 elk with no tag.

Kis said he would not be working at any checking station Monday, "I'm going to be busy in court."

(Source: *The Montana Standard*, Butte, MT, October 19, 1959)

Confiscated big game carcasses outside a checking station

Fish & Game Enforcement Checking Stations of Great Benefit

During the last half of my tour of duty in southwest Montana, I initiated and conducted numerous warden enforcement checking stations at multiple appropriate locations, including Blacktail Creek, Four Corners, Big Sheep Creek, Lima Port station, Horse Prairie Creek, Wise River, Dillon Highway south, Cactus Junction, Bull Mountain, South Boulder River, Reynolds Pass, and Wibaux. The two checking stations at Lima and Wibaux were set up at Montana Highway Department truck weighing stations on Interstate Highways 15 South and 14 East. Both were intercepting fishermen and hunters leaving the state. Those two stations checked out-going sportsmen from mostly the eastern half of Montana, rather than the smaller stations in the southwestern parts of Montana that were oriented toward sportsmen's activities in more localized areas.

The checking results from all the stations revealed the true number of violations that the field wardens missed due to the huge areas they had to patrol in their assigned districts. Despite this, the need for keeping individual wardens in assigned patrol districts could not be over-emphasized in order to keep pace with district activities. It should not come as a surprise that I had a couple game warden friends who did not want any game checking stations in their respective districts, because they believed that the station results might have a reflection on their job efficacy.

Having considerable knowledge of checking station operations, I established some guidelines and operating procedures. First, each station needed a competent and ambitious warden crew. Second, the checking station location and adjacent area were of great importance to make the operation run in an orderly and effective manner. Consideration needed to be given to handling incoming sportsmen vehicle traffic, which ranged from light to heavy. Balancing the safety of the warden crew with the needed element of surprise presented a challenge when setting out roadside signs indicating a station ahead. Not giving much advance notice discouraged turn-arounds and vehicles stopping short in efforts to remedy potentially illegal situations. This was a common occurrence necessitating a quick pursuit and vehicle response from the checking station, and so two Fish & Game vehicles were positioned for such situations, and also for pursuing sportsmen who drove through the station without stopping to be checked.

Many wily and shrewd characters in the fishing and hunting ranks tried to outwit and out game law enforcement. Even though we tried to minimize the declaration of an upcoming station, adequate and very obvious signs alongside the highway for warning of a sportsmen stop were mandatory for safe and effective station operation. The flagman had to actively alert travelers of the operation, and also be aware that some drivers are a danger to themselves and others. They were frequently the first to recognize that certain vehicle occupants, as indicated by their dress and/or vehicle contents, should have stopped.

Immediately surrounding the station, there had to be adequate vehicle turn-out space so no roadway was blocked. Station crew had to agree where the necessary questioning and interrogation would take place, preferably out of the weather and removed from hearing distance of others. At one law enforcement session at the University of Montana law school, it was stated that to question a suspected game law violator in a closed office environment may require reviewing the Miranda warning, so we had to account for that as well.

Even the greeting offered by the flagman of the station had to be considered. At one vehicle stop, the flagman asked, "How are things going for you?"

The reply was, "Good up until now, as you will find!" This was a reminder that on stopping a vehicle, the warden's greeting and opening statement was important and the usual, "How are you doing?" or "Any luck today?" was inappropriate, as it tended to lead to a falsehood if the vehicle occupants were found to be in an illegal category. Driving this point home, during the course of a station’s collaboration with a federal wildlife officer, the federal officer was adamant about the opening statement, which he repeated as, "We are State and Federal Wildlife Officers here to check any fish or wildlife you may have, the appropriate licenses, and also your vehicle contents."

Other logistical matters that needed to be addressed included the need for facilities to hold confiscated game, which required cooler surroundings or an ice chest. The station crew also required access to proper clothing for weather changes from cold to warm, and dry to wet. A coffee maker was a wonderful morale booster and could often go a long way in easing relations when questioning stopped sportsmen. Arrangements for necessary food and lodging had to be resolved for the station crews, too. It goes without saying that adequate first aid kits were a must.

It was of benefit, and also a courteous gesture, to notify the area highway patrolman, sheriff, and community police department of checking station activities, as a warden may have had to request a vehicle stop. A police channel radio and telephone was also quite useful. All officers in the checking station crew had to be cognizant of unexpected confrontations, from mild to serious, involving the unpredictable persons contacted or "cornered," so to speak.

All of these recommendations combined yielded productive and effective game checks that were otherwise impossible to replicate with the vast territory that Montana Fish & Game wardens had, and still have, to patrol.

A Fellow's Status Should Make Him Immune

During a patrol of an antelope hunting area, I was at a high location where I could view the activities of several hunters in the large basin below, which was covered with sagebrush and grass. Through my binoculars, I could see a couple groups of antelope. One of the groups had two hunters approaching, and I expected the animals to run off and out of rifle range. Noticing that the distance between the two hunters and the antelope wasn't too great, I then realized the two hunters were in a ground swale and still out of sight of the antelope. As the two men went up the gentle slope of the swale and nearly reached the top, they suddenly squatted down when they saw the antelope. After what was undoubtedly a shooting plan huddle, the larger of the two hunters passed the rifle to the smaller man, who then cautiously rose up and fired a first, then a second shot.

I had counted how many antelope were in the group, and as the same number ran off a short distance, I saw the larger hunter literally snatch the rifle from the other hunter. As the antelope had only gone a short distance, the buck antelope was off to one side and broadside to the hunter with the gun, and the fellow downed the buck with a single shot.

While I was watching their activities, I observed a puzzling act between the two hunters as they hugged one another in a manner not typical for two men. Then again, after the buck was shot, I observed them hugging again in that affectionate manner.

Since they had shot an antelope, I hastened to the area. After covering the distance as quickly as possible, I approached the two men field dressing the buck. When I asked for an antelope permit, only the smaller fellow produced a valid permit. Upholding the law, I stated I was issuing a citation to the larger man, and before clarifying why, he said, "Warden, do you know who this man is?" and then added, "He is Father and obeys God's Laws and the laws of the land."

Perplexed, I continued to notify the larger fellow that the citation was for him killing a game animal without a permit. After some thought, I then told the man with the permit that under the circumstances the buck antelope should be confiscated as property of the state - but, he would be allowed to keep the buck due to a severe shortage of cold storage space in Dillon.

As word was passed around, as it so often is, I learned that the relationship between the two men was known by many to be in a romantic category.

Scanning for antelope and hunters in the Frying Pan Basin area, northwest of Dillon

Hunters' Acts a Giveaway

Soon after transferring from the Helena to the Dillon warden district, I planned to patrol the Snowline (Lima Peaks) areas accompanied by the Region 3 Big Game Manager, Joe Gaab. We patrolled the popular Lima Peaks elk hunting areas on horseback, and at one site we observed two hunters far upslope. In viewing them with binoculars, it was evident the wardens' presence was of concern to them, as they continued to peek at us from mountainside cover.

Now quite interested in them, we worked our way up slope until we made contact with the two horseback hunters. As suspected, the two men were in possession of two illegal elk, so I issued the necessary citations and confiscated their elk.

As an aside, the circumstance of Joe Gaab working efficiently and conscientiously as the region game manager was later deemed by the Helena Fish & Game Headquarters supervisory personnel to be inappropriate. Their opinion was that due to his college degree being something other than a wildlife degree, he was not qualified to be a game manager. So, having an interest in game warden duties and the desire to stay with the department, plus the ability to do the job, he transferred to the warden force. The Fish & Game Department could have lost a good employee!

Novice Duck Hunter's Dilemma

When I worked the Helena areas, I was assisted quite often by Federal Wildlife Agent Jim Birch, who lived in Helena and was often eager to get afield away from administrative duties. I had re-posted the boundaries of the Helena Game Preserve (now known as Gates of the Mountains Game Preserve), which had been indistinct and not commonly known to many waterfowl hunters. Reports had been received that some hunters were hunting within the game preserve boundary, so the two of us made it a point to patrol the area as often as possible.

On one such patrol, we used a haystack on the O'Connell ranch as a vantage point to be able to see any hunter activities adjacent to and within the game preserve. During late afternoon we observed a vehicle slowly traveling a back road, then park alongside a fence which was part of the preserve boundary. There was a very obvious game preserve sign on a nearby post, and we watched as a man got out of the car and hastily grabbed a coat and gun. He brazenly climbed over the fence and followed a ditch waterway, and soon jumped some Mallard ducks and proceeded to shoot at a couple, only to miss. Very soon more ducks took to the air, and the hunter shot four times in succession. He downed two ducks, with one dropping across the fairly deep water-filled ditch. The one duck was easily retrieved, but with the depth of the water the hunter, not wearing boots, couldn't seem to find a suitable crossing to fetch the other. Instead he proceeded on with hunting many ducks within the game preserve, and shot considerably more than the legal daily bag limit.

After considerably more watching from our elevated place of observation, Federal Warden Birch indicated the hunter was quite gutsy with his activities, which already included hunting within a game preserve, using an unplugged shotgun, and undoubtedly shooting an over limit of ducks. We decided it was time to make our approach, and proceeded on foot in the direction of the hunter, but had to detour around brushy willow, swampy cattails, and a deep water ditch, which put us right up to the end of legal daily waterfowl hunting time.

Once the hunter was in sight, some more ducks took to flight and "bang, bang!" The hunter fired twice, so Warden Birch said, "This guy is really pushing his luck with those last two shots, which were well after legal hours."

It was nearing darkness when we finally made contact with the hunter. It was very obvious, as he was carrying several ducks by the neck with more in his hunting coat pockets, that he was heavily laden with birds. The three of us walked out to where the hunter's car was parked and we asked for his hunting license, which had a new crease from that day's purchase.

Warden Birch checked the hunter's gun, and advised him that it was not properly plugged as required. He also did not have the necessary duck stamp, and he was in possession of an over limit of ducks. The bewildered hunter exclaimed, "And I went to all that trouble gathering all those birds, and had to get my butt wet in that cold water, just for this!"

About that time, I said to the hunter, "I wish to inform you that isn't all," and showed him the very obvious game preserve sign where he had entered the area.

The fellow pondered for a few moments then said, "I'm new at this duck hunting, and it looks like I've gotten a bad start, so maybe you officers will excuse me this time and I'll make it all right next time out?" He did maintain he had not seen the game preserve sign, had borrowed the unplugged shotgun, did not know a federal duck stamp was required in addition to the state bird license, was told the duck possession limit was the same as what he had—not knowing the daily limit was one-half the allowable possession limit—and he had forgotten to borrow hip boots, which should have been part of his duck hunting clothing.

The novice hunter was issued a total of five citations, and when I appeared in court to clarify the hunter's predicament, the judge simply stated, "Ignorance of the law is no excuse." However, he was quite lenient with his decision.

For months afterward, Warden Birch would burst out with his hearty laugh when the subject of this novice duck hunter came to mind or was mentioned.

Ignorance May Be Bliss, but It's No Excuse

During one waterfowl hunting period, I had received a couple calls from a rancher about "more than normal" shooting along a ranch slough. The rancher voiced concern about his cattle that were scattered throughout the pasture and the dense willows along the slough's edge, and indicated that some of the shooting was just before dark.

Following up on his complaint, I went to the area and climbed up on top of a stack of baled hay for a better view of the flat valley. A few shots were fired here and there, and from my viewing spot I could pretty well surmise what was being shot at, simply by seeing ducks take to wing. Legal shooting hours soon ended for the day and the area was quiet for some time. I could see hunters trudging through the rough frost-heaved pastures to their vehicles along the county road.

After a while, no more vehicles or hunters could be seen, so I guessed that the area would remain quiet. Then just about dusk, and about too dark for a hunter to identify a bird, I heard a flurry of three shots coming from an area of cottonwood trees and heavy willow brush. I hadn't seen any remaining vehicles along the road, and wondered where the hunter would go to leave the area, so I hurriedly left my comfortable vantage point and jogged in the direction of the shooting.

I finally saw one hunter walking toward a ranch bridge across the slough and guessed that he was headed for the ranch. Once close enough, I stopped to view the guy through binoculars and could see that he was carrying a sizable bird. Occasionally along that slough, a hunter would luck out and get a shot at a

Canada goose. There had been a couple instances where one rancher's domestic, heavy-bodied, and off-colored geese had been shot by an over-eager, inexperienced nimrod.

As I approached, I could see that the hunter had stopped for a breather from walking over those rough mounds of sod and was sitting on a clump of dry ryegrass instead of the moist ground. Where I was standing I was about two and a half miles from my vehicle, I hadn't brought my flashlight, and daylight was fading fast.

When I came into contact with the hunter, I asked to see his hunting license and checked the pump shotgun for proper plug, but did not, at that time, mention that the hunter undoubtedly shot after legal hours. I then asked, "Did you do any good?"

The hunter replied, "Yeah, I got one. My old lady will not be quite as mad that I wasted gas and time by going hunting." Then he said, "I threw the bird across that fence in the tall grass if you want to see it."

When I saw the "bird" I was somewhat surprised and asked the hunter, "Do you know what it is?"

He replied, "Yeah, a goose of sorts. I don't know one from another because I'm new at this hunting. I borrowed my boy's gun and came out because of an invitation from my rancher friend where my wife buys our beef. He told me he had lots of wild ducks and geese along his slough."

I then picked up the "goose," an ugly, off-colored, long-necked and long-legged blue heron and again asked him, "Do you know exactly what it is?"

And again, his reply was, "No, not exactly, except a goose of sorts. Is it a good one?"

In the partial darkness, I advised the hunter about what he had shot, that it was unlawful to kill a blue heron, and that he would receive a citation for possession of the illegal bird.

The tired and inexperienced hunter slowly got to his feet, using the shotgun as an aid with the gun barrel pointing directly under his chin, and I thought to myself, *I'm sure glad I unloaded the gun!*

He came over and nudged the dead bird with his foot and said, "It does look different!" Then he added, "Now my old lady will really be mad, because she handles the purse strings, so I guess I'll just stop at Grogan's Bar and make a night of it, and make the catchin' hell worthwhile."

During that era, the unlawful shooting of "shite-poke" (blue heron) was common practice for a number of shotgun shooting enthusiasts along the ranch sloughs and ponds, and also around rookeries. The shooters felt those birds and "fish-ducks" seriously damaged fish populations.

For this accidental shite-poke hunter, perhaps a hunter safety course and a swift reminder to "learn to recognize your target" may have been appropriate punishment, but undoubtedly the most dread and maybe most effective punishment was going home to face his irate, penny pinching wife.

Conflict Between a Waterfowl Hunter and an Officer

I periodically patrolled Elk Lake, which was popular for fishing and was near Faye Selby's Elk Lake Lodge, which was popular with fishermen. Selby was quite possessive of the area, and had a cinch on access to a "secret" lake not far from his lodge, appropriately called Hidden Lake. To gain access to Hidden Lake and its prime fishing, Selby took fisherman by boat from the lodge across Elk Lake, leaving them at the head of a foot trail leading to Hidden Lake, and then he would pick them up at day's end.

I had been notified that a U.S. federal game agent from the Billings office would be at the federal Red Rock Lakes Refuge, and I planned to contact the agent regarding refuge patrol matters. I arrived at the refuge headquarters to meet with the visiting officer, and learned that the game agent had gone to Selby's lodge. Not wanting to miss my opportunity to discuss my patrol concerns, I too headed to the lodge to see if I could catch up with the agent there. I arrived at Elk Lake Lodge just as Selby was returning with a couple fishermen. Since the waterfowl hunting season was open, Selby was carrying a couple ducks he had bagged.

The visiting game agent, Ken Rohen, being a stern and aggressive officer, approached Selby and checked the ducks while asking for his bird hunting license. Selby handed his license to the agent, but it was only a Montana license, minus the required federal duck stamp. In a harsh manner, the agent advised him of the violation, and then added, "Your shotgun isn't properly plugged, as required. And, you shot the ducks while the boat was in motion."

The agent went on to further inform Selby that he would be taken to a justice of the peace at the county seat in Dillon, and it was evident that this severely upset him. The exchange of words between Selby and the game agent was fast developing into a heated confrontation, and was soon followed by a tussle between the two. Up to then, I had not intervened, but I could see it was a serious quarrel, so I stepped between the two brawlers and attempted to convince them it was only a misdemeanor violation, and didn't warrant building the case into a more serious charge.

Luckily, that calmed things down. I convinced the agent that Selby was a respected, good citizen and suggested to him that a notification for Selby to appear before a justice at an agreed date and time would be honored and the case would be settled. An agreement was made to the satisfaction of both men, and the case was later resolved. To gratify the federal game agent, I later sent a report of the proceedings for his and his supervisor's records.

"Game Warden, Someone is Using My Private Road!"

After some years of providing the shuttle service to fishermen from the lodge to the head of Elk Lake, where there was a trailhead for hiking to Hidden Lake, Selby spent some time and labor establishing a road between the two lakes. He drove his vehicle across the frozen-over lake one winter, and left it on the opposite side of the lake from the lodge to be used as a shuttle the following summer. Selby considered the short road his, and resented use by anyone else. "His" road, however, was actually on U.S. Forest Service land.

I was at the lodge checking license sales books one day, and since I was there anyway, I also checked any fishermen in the area. It wasn't long before a very upset Selby exclaimed, "Someone is using my road, and I want you to find out who it is and stop it!"

After discussing the matter with the district Forest Ranger, we agreed that Selby actually had no claim on the road between Elk Lake and Hidden Lake, which was established without authorization from the Forest Service and was actually in violation of certain USFS policies. When Selby learned that neither the Forest Service or the Fish & Game Department would intervene and that he was in violation of certain federal guidelines, he softened his complaining but vowed to learn who had intruded in his area and confront them.

Selby didn't know it at the time, but this particular situation influenced the Forest Service to bypass his lodge with a roadway to Hidden Lake, making it accessible to many more fishermen. As a result of this drastic change in his "private" access, Selby finally sold the lodge facility, which actually was on Forest Service lands on a lease basis anyway.

Poor Response to Coaching

A shallow mud-bottom lake in my district was a popular duck hunting area. Since the lake was within the Red Rock Lakes National Wildlife Refuge, I accompanied Federal Game Warden Ash Brann and we positioned ourselves at daybreak to observe waterfowl hunters' activities. There were quite a number of duck hunters in the area that had positioned themselves in the early morning hours, and were awaiting the legal shooting hour when ducks were flying.

Evidently, one hunter had arrived somewhat late and had launched his small boat with only his oars. Not being familiar with the muddy lake bottom, he was having difficulty getting his boat in a shooting position. The fellow was very noisy, with the oarlocks rattling against the aluminum boat hull. Consequently, a number of well positioned, and now irritated, hunters were calling to him to stay put and quiet down. The fellow ignored the coaching and complaining, but as it continued, he finally stood up in his boat and said, "To hell with all of you. I'm outta here." So, that morning's hunt didn't go well.

Our patrol wasn't a waste of time, though. Before the day was over, we did write citations for hunters killing over limits of ducks and for not retrieving all ducks shot, due to some being considered not as desirable for eating.

Some of the hunters were affiliated with an area duck hunting club, and one provision of membership was that any member given a citation for any violation of a Fish & Game law or regulation would automatically lose his membership. Despite the several citations we issued over time, no one had to forfeit their membership. I eventually surmised that the need for club support, particularly financially, was the main consideration in allowing them to retain their memberships.

An Overinflated Spare Tire

During the sage grouse hunts, I set up a temporary game check point on the only exit road out of sizable sage brush and grassy basin. During late afternoon and evening, I checked several hunters and everyone checked out okay and all appeared to be legal. I asked the exiting hunters if they had observed other hunters that were successful, and one fellow said they had passed a small stream where four hunters were parked and appeared as though they were repairing a flat tire. He also stated that his hunting party had stopped momentarily to offer assistance, and noticed there were lots of sage grouse heads, legs, and wings laying around and blowing in the wind. I kept this in mind as I continued to check hunters as they exited the area with no problems, except to caution a few about their failure to retain the appropriate grouse body parts for identification of the game bird.

Later that evening, a group of four hunters drove up to the checkpoint. All four had the legal limit of grouse, and all had proper licenses. Just in passing, I mentioned that another hunter had told me about some tire trouble they had encountered. As soon as I mentioned it, I noticed two of the hunters exchanged a quick glance at each other. As I checked their field dressed birds, all had proper body parts attached for identification. When I walked around the vehicle, I noticed the spare tire was mounted on an outside bracket, and also observed the "flat" tire was mounted back on the rim. However, I also noticed the tire's tube was inside the vehicle. When I mentioned this to them, they said there wasn't enough room inside the vehicle for the tire with the four of them and their guns.

Even though they provided a reasonable explanation, I had a gut feeling that things were not as they should be. I approached the mounted spare tire and lingered there long enough to observe and exchange of glances among the four men. I wanted to remove the tire from the rim, but I was concerned that being alone with four men could encourage confrontation, so I told them I would radio the Lima deputy sheriff and give him their names, addresses, and vehicle license number and description. One of the men was wearing a holstered revolver, so I asked him for it and placed it on the hood of my vehicle. One of the men said, “What's the matter, warden? You afraid?”

“Not at all, not at all,” I replied with a smile.

I then asked them to get inside their vehicle and remain there. My radio call wasn't answered by the sheriff's office, and I learned later that the Dillon and Idaho Falls radio stations hadn't monitored my call. Fortunately, a Montana Highway Patrolman, Frank Brown, had received the call but couldn't reach me by radio. When he finally came in radio range, he offered his assistance if needed. I advised him that he was approximately 20 miles or 15 backroad miles away from my position, and told him if I needed assistance I would let him know.

When I removed the tire from the rim, it was packed with sixteen bare sage grouse carcasses wrapped in a moistened cloth and the tire was lined with plastic, which to me indicated premeditation. One fellow tried to assume all the blame, but all four were cited and fined, and they lost their hunting privileges for two years.

Lawbreakers & Troublemakers: *Plundering Poachers*

Who Said, "A Friend in Need is a Friend Indeed?"

While out on patrol one day, I saw a man shoot from his car, which was parked alongside a public road. Shooting from public roadways was illegal, so I proceeded to stop and check what the guy might be shooting. As we were talking, I saw a couple ducks fly from a nearby spring creek close to a ranch house. I took temporary leave of the shooter, whom I instructed to wait, and checked the area but failed to find a dead duck. I returned to the fellow's car and looked through its contents, finding an illegal antelope and a couple cottontail rabbits, plus considerable amounts of dried blood, animal hair, and feathers, which indicated the guy, at some time, had transported other creatures in the trunk of his car.

The shooter was cited for the possession of an illegal antelope and shooting from a public road. When he appeared before the judge he didn't seem at all overly concerned about his situation, and pleaded guilty to the charge. The man stated he did not have any money to pay the required fine, so the judge indicated he would be committed to jail. Hearing this, the shooter said he was sure he could get the fine money from a friend, so it was agreed that I would accompany the fellow to get the required $200 for the fine assessed.

As the poacher and I left the courthouse, the man stated he wanted to go to a particular saloon in town to find his friend. On our arrival there, I informed him that I would not accompany him into the bar as I was on duty, and cautioned him not to go out the back door or do anything foolish that would worsen his predicament. Within a short time the man came out with the fine money, which was taken directly to the judge.

A couple days later, I decided to go to that particular saloon since I wasn't working and, out of curiosity, see if there were any familiar poacher faces present. The opportunity was right to visit with the owner-bartender, so I struck up a conversation. Being in plain clothes and off duty, I told the bartender that word was going around town that a certain friend of his was caught poaching and was fined a hefty $200.

The bartender stated that he thought the guy got too careless. He also thought that the fine was too much because it was in fact $300 instead of $200, as he had provided the fine money! I didn't give too much thought to the $100 difference between the actual fine and what the bartender said he provided, but it was soon evident to me that the poacher had gotten an extra $100 and undoubtedly must have pocketed the surplus cash.

I didn't reveal my identity or mention the discrepancy, because it may have been reason for a serious conflict or area shoot-out between the poacher and his bartender friend. However, while at the saloon, there were a couple of incoming customers who bought a drink and the bartender sliced off a small chunk of seasoned sausage as a bonus. The sausage was probably made with a variety of meats, such as a poacher could provide. A friend in need is a friend, indeed!

A Poacher's Timely Rescue

During patrol duty out of the old Eagle Creek cabin near Gardiner in the early 1950s, Game Warden John "Red" Burke mentioned to the crew of wardens that a particular old poacher was undoubtedly in the area and would be shooting and tagging elk for licensed hunters, who usually stayed around Gardiner playing cards and partying. The warden crew all kept this in mind, and during one particular day after the usual early morning surge of hunters into the vicinity, I was in the Travertine area. From a vantage point where I could monitor quite a large expanse through my binoculars, I observed one lone hunter high up on the snowy slope. It was evident he was, little by little, dragging an elk carcass a short distance to where it would freely slide down a steep incline and be much nearer to a vehicle loading point. Once the elk had slid to the bottom of the slope, the lone hunter was quite some time carefully working his way down to the carcass.

Wanting to check his permit and tags, I snowshoed over to make contact with him. I first checked the elk carcass for proper tagging, but found no tag. The hunter said he didn't want to lose a tag while dragging the carcass, which wasn't an unreasonable claim. At that time it was a common practice to temporarily remove a tag under such circumstances, as long as it was properly validated. The hunter reached in his pocket and removed not one but three elk tags, and was trying to put two back, but I insisted the hunter surrender all three. I asked the old fellow about the tags but only got vague replies to my inquiries. Because of the severe cold and chilling wind, I directed the fellow to go with me to my vehicle about a half-mile away so I could continue asking questions.

Once there and warmed some, I informed the hunter he was being charged with the possession of an untagged elk and possession of another person's tag. Identification was requested from the hunter and finally he produced a well-worn and barely legible driver's license. The name was the same as that provided by Warden Burke during his briefing on the known poacher.

The old fellow told me that someone had dropped him off earlier that day, so I took him into Gardiner, where the man asked to stop and make a quick phone call. After he finished his call, we went directly to the justice of the peace. Once certain required procedures were completed, the judge read the filed complaint and asked for a plea to the charge. The poacher never seemed to acknowledge the request for a plea, and instead of answering, he talked randomly and insensibly. The judge repeated that he must have a plea, but the fellow only seemed to ignore the request.

I could see that the judge was becoming impatient, and I was about to assist with explaining the proceedings when there was a knock on the judge's door and two fellows stepped inside out of the cold. The justice of the peace advised the two men that he was officiating, and that they must wait there. One of the men that had just entered interrupted him and explained that they were friends of the guilty old fellow, and if he was in any kind of trouble they were there to try to help. Before the judge or I could clarify the need for a plea, the old poacher said very distinctly, "Guilty!"

One of the newcomers came forward as the judge levied a fine of $200 and promptly peeled off four $50 bills, saying to the judge, "Here is payment for the fine, Judge. Is that adequate to settle this for our old friend?"

Case closed!

Foiled Escape Route for an Elk Poacher

On occasion, game wardens in adjoining districts would patrol an area together, but usually each district warden would patrol alone in many outlying and very remote areas, with only on and off two-way contact with sheriffs' offices and Fish & Game base stations. Radio contact was many times affected by mountain terrain and adverse weather conditions.

Collaborating with Warden Leo Secor from the Sheridan district, he and I would sometimes patrol areas where working jointly was more effective. On one such patrol, we were checking for elk hunter activity in an area that was quite remote and not readily known to many hunters. One of us would stay at the junction of a jeep trail and a foot trail that led to a hunting area we wished to patrol, and the other one would hike up the foot trail. This particular day I did the hiking while Warden Secor did the waiting.

On the foot trail, and a couple miles into the area, I encountered a hunter who reported considerable shooting in an area higher up the mountain. Thanking him for the information, I continued up the trail to investigate, but I came across another hunter who also reported the shooting activities. He said he thought it was some horseback hunters who had shot elk, and would undoubtedly go out on a trail on the east slope of the mountain. Hearing this report, I hurried back and met Warden Secor at our vehicle.

We drove approximately 45 miles around the north side of the mountain, then headed south to where the horseback trail ended at a vehicle and horse trailer parking lot. We waited there for several hours, and finally during the late evening two hunters and one pack horse appeared.

I checked the half elk carcass they had brought out with them, and found there was no tag. Asking the hunters to explain the situation, they claimed the tag was with the other half of the elk left on the mountain. But, when their hunting licenses were checked their elk tags were intact. A citation was issued and the one half of the carcass was confiscated.

Due to the hunters' actions, and one of them being a known poacher, both of us wardens had doubts about what had actually happened on top of the mountain. Before daybreak the next morning, we went to the two trailheads on the west and east sides of the mountain. I hiked up the west side trail following the horse tracks, and arrived at a sizable meadow area. With considerable tracking difficulty, I sat observing ravens in an area a quarter of a mile or so at the edge of the surrounding timber. Following the ravens' activities, I found the other half of the untagged elk, and a hundred yards away I found a whole and untagged elk carcass. Both were confiscated and, with a lot of effort, taken out of the hunting area over a period of a couple days.

Upon questioning the horseback hunters later, the two men first denied their connection with the whole elk carcass but finally stated that it was to be claimed by a hunter friend who was injured and couldn't hunt. The untagged elk was confiscated and a citation was issued to the hunter who who killed the elk for his injured friend. The other hunter who claimed the two elk halves admitted that they were to be given to what he called a "needy family," so his intended generosity cost him a fine and no more hunting that season.

Game Warden Wayne Fitzwater issuing a game violation citation

Premeditated Poaching Plans

During the 1950s, I regularly assisted with patrol of the Gardiner re-opened elk hunt, which had become known as the "Firing Line." With a significant migration of northern Yellowstone Park elk to the re-opened hunting area in Montana, it was really a hunt of last resort but did attract many hunters, with some being somewhat desperate to go home with an elk. While there are many, many stories about happenings during the Gardiner extended elk hunt, I especially remember one which involved a hunter from eastern Montana.

I snowshoed the Decker Flat, Eagle, Pole and Phelps Creek areas quite regularly, and during one such patrol I made contact with a hunter trying to drag an elk carcass down from a steep slope near Eagle Creek, where it could then be more easily dragged out by horse to be loaded onto a vehicle. I checked the hunter's license and documented the necessary information in my hunter field check logbook, then proceeded to check the elk carcass for proper tagging. On one leg of the animal was a securely tied string with only a metal eyelet, which was part of the elk and deer carcass tags at that time. I pointed out that there was no tag there, and the hunter replied, "It must have come off while dragging the elk down the steep slope." I knew this could be a possibility because it had happened on past occasions.

Wanting to give him the benefit of the doubt, I suggested that the hunter backtrack the skid trail and look for the tag, and I would stay in the nearby area and keep watch on the elk carcass, which might be claimed by another desperate hunter. The fellow agreed and set off along the skid trail.

Meanwhile, I snowshoed up on another slope and stopped to view the surrounding areas with binoculars. While looking in the direction the hunter, who was supposed to be looking for the lost elk tag, I noticed the fellow had merely backtracked on the skid trail just far enough to be out of sight. Instead, he was sitting on a rock outcropping and not looking for the game tag he claimed to have lost. As stealthily as I could, I worked my way around the side of the hill and was quite close to the hunter before he saw me, at which time the man was surprised and quickly started kicking around in the snow as if he might find the tag at that particular place.

As many game wardens might react, I immediately surmised that something was amiss regarding the claim of a lost tag by the hunter. I advised the fellow that we would go back down to the elk carcass, where it would be tagged with a confiscation tag. Then we would hike out and resolve the seemingly illegal situation in some manner. While hiking out, I finally told the hunter that I was convinced that things were not as described, and it would be advisable for him to relate the true facts.

After showing considerable nervousness, and doing some pondering, the fellow admitted he didn't bring a valid elk tag to the Gardiner area, and had rode along with friends. He only brought the tag eyelet on a piece of string, with the idea of using it as a guise for a lost tag if he was lucky enough to get an elk. At that time, game wardens could issue a replacement tag while in the field if circumstances justified doing so, but in this case the hunter was charged with taking and possessing an elk without a valid license.

That was my first experience of intentional deceit by a hunter. It was certainly a learning experience for me, and probably also for the hunter, who was assessed a hefty fine by the Gardiner justice of the peace.

A Vigilant and Capable Game Warden

While patrolling the upper Gallatin extended elk hunt, I heard many repeated stories from old "retired" big game poachers, which I considered on the job training to be kept in mind for future reference. With their recollected stories fresh in my memory, along with using my assigned numbered paper punch on successful elk hunters' licenses and game tags, I also slit one ear of any claimed elk. The ear slitting was an extra step on my part, but the other wardens working the area knew this was my normal procedure.

During the extended elk hunt, fellow warden Art Warner saw an elk carcass in a pickup truck outside a hunter's cabin, so he approached one of the members of the two-man hunting party and asked to check his license and game tag. The license and tag had been punched sometime earlier by me, but there was no slit in the elk's ear, so Warden Warner initially thought that perhaps I had forgotten to complete the additional step. Warner sensed that the hunter was somewhat nervous, so he did some questioning and carefully watched the fellow's reactions. During the conversation, Warner noted a gathering of Canadian Jays, known as "camp robbers," flying from behind a woodpile behind the cabin. He asked the hunter to accompany him to the woodpile, where he discovered an elk carcass with no game tag on it, but it did have a slit in its ear. Warner immediately issued a citation and confiscated both elk, which severely upset the hunters.

Not long after, Warden Warner and I learned that the two men had killed both elk, but had only one license and tag. They were hoping to leave the hunting area undetected and head southbound towards their Madison County homes. Colleague warden I. L. Todd, from the Ennis district, later reported that the two men were know to be poachers and he was delighted that they were caught.

A "Well Done" Escape

One afternoon, I met a neighboring warden that was in town on business. During our conversation I mentioned that I had been informed that a certain restaurant owner was mixing considerable deer and elk meat with beef to be served in burgers, meatloaf, and chili. The visiting warden immediately became excited about the prospect of catching the owner and was insistent that we go to the restaurant to eat. I assured my warden friend that this restauranteur was quite a sly fellow and was no careless, darned fool.

At the restaurant, the owner-chef acknowledged our arrival with his normal, "Hello Fitz," and then went about his duties in the kitchen. The waitress was a friendly and accommodating person, and when ordering, the visiting warden said, "I'll tell you what I'm really hungry for, and that is a very, very rare burger with a big slice of raw onion."

I ordered a bowl of chili, as the old chef had a reputation for making the best around. When the food was served, the chili, as usual, was delicious. The burger, however, was very, very well-done, which didn't really surprise me, but my warden friend called it to the attention of the waitress. Before she could get to the kitchen, the old chef called out, "Sorry about that overdone burger, but I just forgot and left it on the grill too long," and then added, "I'll gladly make you a good Denver omelet or ham sandwich at no charge, as I am out of hamburger for today."

Of course, the visiting warden had planned to keep a portion of the rare meat in the burger he had ordered so he could take it to the lab to have it analyzed and possibly identified as wild game meat. Even though we didn't succeed in catching the restauranteur that time, I did issue a couple Fish & Game citations to him over the years because he was also an avid hunter, fisherman, and trapper. During one such encounter, as the fellow became older and fond memories surfaced, he told me, "I know I have it coming, especially after that burger deal with that warden friend of yours."

Old Hap' was a sly poacher and a good cook, but still a fine fellow and friend.

Pheasant Nest Egg Robbers

While working the Townsend, Toston and Radersburg areas in valleys with good pheasant populations, I observed two young looking fellows who were toting a small bucket with a carrying bail. Somewhat puzzled as to their activities, I observed them with my binoculars as they zig-zagged around ground areas of considerable growth, and I continued to be perplexed. When they flushed a couple hen pheasants, it dawned on me they were looking for pheasant nests and were robbing them of eggs.

When I later caught up with them in the field, the pheasant eggs in their containers were evidence of their poaching. Realizing they were undoubtedly gathering the eggs for an adult, I asked who that person might be, but the fellows wouldn't give me a name. I issued them citations, and they were required to appear before the county juvenile officer and answer to the poaching charges. I was not present at their hearing, but the juvenile officer later informed me the two delinquents still refused to divulge the name of the person who had asked them to poach the eggs.

Considering the two juveniles didn't have any record of misconduct or problems locally, the juvenile officer assigned them several work details around town for community betterment.

A Case of Accumulated Evidence

A report to the county sheriff's department from three hunters revealed that they had come across two elk carcasses that had seemingly been poached illegally and the carcasses abandoned. The hunters noted the elk carcasses were salvageable, so they had reluctantly and crudely gutted them and then placed some brush over the exposed meat to protect it from scavenging ravens. Once their task was complete, they went to a ranch house and phoned the county sheriff's department to give their report. The sheriff's department radioed me, and in a couple hours I arrived at the ranch and was directed to the scene of the elk kill.

The three conscientious hunters' efforts to crudely field dress the carcasses certainly saved the meat from spoiling, but could have put them in bad light if a warden had arrived at that time! So, I completed field dressing the elk and put confiscation tags on them. I next scouted the surrounding area and found a third elk that had been killed and dragged about a mile to where it was loaded on a vehicle. Following the drag trail required some concentrated tracking, as only some minute traces of elk hair revealed the route on the bare and uneven ground.

At the loading site, another vehicle was parked with hunters still afield, so I waited a couple hours for them to return. When they appeared, I questioned the two hunters to determine if, by chance, they had seen the other vehicle or knew the occupants. The hunters said the other vehicle was parked there before their arrival, and that they had recognized the license plate county prefix number. Helpfully, they also remembered the pickup vehicle color and noted significant body damage. I thanked them for their time and hastened back to the scene of the elk kill.

Examining the carcass bullet entry holes, I was able to determine the direction of the shooters. I also recovered a bullet in one of the carcasses, which had expanded but still had the bullet base intact. I spent the remainder of the day scouting and luckily determined where the poacher was when he fired his shot and found one empty 30-06 shell case!

Once back home, I phoned the county sheriff and gave the vehicle license prefix and a description of the poacher's vehicle in the hopes that they may eventually identify the owner. Considering the matter somewhat settled for the time being, I went about my business of patrolling for several weeks. Then, surprisingly, I received a report from the county sheriff which provided the name and address of the owner of the suspected poacher's vehicle. An accompanying warden, Warden Chesterfield, and I drove to the distant county to question the vehicle's owner. When all the accumulated evidence was reviewed with him, the fellow finally admitted guilt.

He later appeared before a justice of the peace, but never revealed his hunting partners' names, so he was charged with killing all three elk and abandoning the two not field dressed. While he was allowed to keep the one elk he had properly tagged, he was still fined $200 and lost his hunting privileges for two years. So, his stance to not reveal his hunting partners' names cost him two ways!

K. D. "Pinky" Sears' Philosophy

Now that I am retired, I have been asked numerous times if certain comments about Warden Ken Sears (also retired and now deceased) were true.

One story about Warden Sears comes from when I was assigned to the Townsend-Broadwater district and Sears was transferring to the West Yellowstone district. As the incoming warden, I had asked Sears if he would provide some names of area poachers, so he handed me the local telephone directory and said, "There you are." His philosophy must have been, "Most everyone is guilty until proven innocent."

To put all kidding aside, I worked many, many hours with Sears and put him in a special game warden category. He was very conscientious, capable, and efficient. He had a memory "like an elephant," and little patience with those who outright lied when caught red-handed. During his tenure as a Montana game warden, Sears was a credit to the warden force and I am extremely proud to have worked with him for many years.

Region 3 Fish & Game Wardens

Front row, left to right: Joe Gaab, Wayne Fitzwater, Chet' Anderson, William Smith

Back row, left to right: William (Bill) McKiernan, I. L. Todd, K. D. (Pinky) Sears, Gene Clark, Don Wright, Art Warner

A Nonchalant Interview of a Suspected Elk Poacher

The Ennis district game warden, I. L. Todd, reported that a squatter at one of the U.S. Forest Service patrol cabins was thought to have poached a cow elk, and Warden Todd asked to be accompanied to question the suspected poacher. So, Warden Sears from West Yellowstone and I met Warden Todd at the isolated cabin site with the understanding the he, as the district warden, would lead with the questioning.

Warden Sears, a very impatient person, assumed that Warden Todd would immediately get down to business with the inquiries. Instead, Warden Todd took out his pocket knife and deliberately whittled on a piece of wood, all the while talking about the weather and elk being seen in the area, and other seemingly insignificant subjects. Finally, Warden Todd told the suspected elk poacher that he had heard from a reliable hunter in that same area that he had seen him with one-half of a cow elk on his pack horse. Of course, the guy denied poaching an elk and said he had packed an elk out for another hunter who was on foot.

The questioning was progressing as Warden Todd desired, but Warden Sears was obviously very upset by the proceedings. Sensing Warden Sears' restlessness, I decided to scout out some of the surrounding heavily timbered and highly brushy areas in the meantime. Luckily some Canadian Jays led me to a timbered area where I found what appeared to be two halves of an untagged cow elk, which I marked with a metal ID tag that I tucked under both halves of the elk's hide.

When I returned to the cabin area, I took Warden Todd aside and told him about finding the hidden elk in the timber. While I was gone investigating, Warden Todd had checked the poacher's pack saddle and found elk hair and blood. He told the poacher the Bozeman lab could match the hair and blood with the elk carcass I had found, which was an untruth during that 1950s era. Warden Todd then said, "Fellow, the jig is up," as the cow elk carcass had been found and would be confiscated since it was untagged, and a citation would be issued for him to appear before the Madison County justice of the peace.

The fellow then said, "I have an elk license with a tag I should have used. You will never know the hard work and sweat to get the elk out of that hellhole!"

Hungry Sheepherder

Many people will remember the government trapper Morgan Hall, who worked the southwest Montana area during a time when there were several large sheep outfits plagued by severe depredations from coyotes and black bears. I accompanied trapper Hall when he was putting out "coyote getters" and 10/80 baits. While he made his rounds, he would stop at the different sheep camps to learn of depredation problems. He mentioned to me that some sheep herders fished nearby streams and probably without a fishing license. I told him, for the sake of good relations with the sheep herders, I wouldn't press the issue unless it was an unusual circumstance.

On one such trip with Hall, we visited one of "Pink" Mayberry's sheep camps. As we entered the camp site to talk with the herder, there were three cleanly dressed mountain grouse hanging from a rope line between two trees. Hall shook his head in disbelief, and, after some casual visiting, he introduced me to the herder as the local game warden. The herder grimaced and said, "Damn it, I've had it."

I told him with the grouse right in front of me, I was obligated to acknowledge the violation and review the necessary procedures associated with the citation. After I fulfilled my duties and Hall and I were preparing to leave, the herder said he had been out of grub for a couple days and asked Hall to stop at the Mayberry place and let them know his severe camp needs. Hearing this, I interjected and suggested that when the herder saw Mayberry he should ask the rancher to post bond or pay any fine the justice of the peace would levy. Luckily, I had taken a sizable lunch and Hall had a box of some basic camp groceries he always carried in case of a breakdown out in the boondocks, so we gave them to the herder. I later learned Mayberry did indeed take care of matters with the justice of the peace, and all was resolved.

Duty During Record Cold

It was January 19, 1954, and the second day of my temporary duty assignment in Helena, when the call came to the local sheriff. The caller reported an illegally taken deer in the town of Lincoln. Interested by the caller's account, when the sheriff called to notify me of the report he indicated he might join me in the investigation the following morning.

Early the next morning, I arose to discover that it had gotten very cold during the night, and I had considerable difficulty getting my panel truck started. I had to remove the battery and bring it indoors to warm up, and had to place some kerosene highway flares under the oil pan so the engine would crank over sufficiently to start. Once the vehicle was running, I checked in with the sheriff and was told the temperature was way below zero and, that, due to office work, he had decided not to go.

I proceeded on to Lincoln anyway and contacted a couple of people who were supposed to know where the illegal deer carcass was hanging, along with the name of the logger who had shot it. I soon located the carcass, marked it, and left it where I had found it. Then I took off in search of the culprit, who was rumored to be at a friend's cabin.

When I arrived at the cabin, I discovered the suspect and three other loggers were playing poker and drinking booze. Not surprisingly, things did not go well. There was an exchange of harsh words and a few threats were made. The situation was getting worse, so I explained, as I had done before in similar situations, that violations of Fish & Game laws were only misdemeanors and it would be rather foolhardy for them to provoke the situation into something a lot more serious.

Evidently they had retained some of their good judgment, because that pretty much quieted them down. However, they still made excuses, claiming the deer was just for food, and that it didn't seem right to arrest a man for merely shooting a deer for needed food. Encouraged by his friends' statements, the poacher then piped up and added, "There is a provision in Fish and Game law that in case someone needs food, they can violate the law."

I foolishly replied,"You don't look to be hungry!"

Paying no mind to the excuses offered, I advised the logger he had best wear some extra warm clothes to go to pick up the deer, which was behind his cabin. The man hastily replied that he didn't need any damn game warden telling him how to dress. The mood of his friends had changed by now to one of kidding the poacher and general merry-making. They all downed a toast to the poacher as we left to retrieve the deer.

Once the carcass was collected, I headed for Helena with the poacher in custody. The route took us over the Continental Divide at Flesher Pass. A few miles down the road, the man began to get belligerent and unruly, so possibly his "one for the road" drink was kicking in. After a few more miles of increasingly boisterous talk, the man grabbed the steering wheel, which nearly put the vehicle into the roadside snow bank. He followed this by kicking violently at the two-way radio control box below the dash, and after a few kicks he managed to knock the control from its mounts so it was just dangling by some wiring. Meanwhile, I was trying to keep control of the vehicle while my passenger's rampage continued. Again, the man grabbed for the steering wheel, so I cracked him sharply on the arm with a small blackjack that I carried. This must have smarted a good bit because he temporarily sat back up and held his arm in his lap.

This lull in the action gave me an opportunity to aim the truck into a turnout and come to a stop. The abruptness of the stop slid the drunken man up against the dashboard, giving me a chance to reach across behind him, open the offside door, and push him out into the snow with my right foot. Although the vehicle was all but stopped, I heard a thump against the side of the truck and my first thought was that I might have run the ornery guy over, but in a second he was lurching drunkenly to his feet and seemed more confused than hurt. I quickly locked the truck door and informed the bugger he would now be walking to Helena, so he'd better get going, thinking the cold and fresh air might sober him somewhat.

To all appearances, the smack on the arm and the tumble out of the vehicle had a certain calming effect on the man, and he began trudging unsteadily down the road ahead of me. At this point, I called to him that he had better put something on his head to protect his ears from the cold, but the advice went unheeded, and in a short distance the logger just stopped and sat down on a snow bank and mumbled something about the walk being "for the birds." I decided to let him sit there for a while and sober up a little, as it was obvious that he wasn't going to do much more walking. Then I began to notice the man's ears and the sides of his nostrils showing the first signs of frostbite, so I told him he could get back in the truck and ride into town on the condition that he keep his mouth shut and not act up. Feeling this was the best deal he could likely get, he got up and staggered back to the truck. I wondered if the truck would start after being stopped, but it slowly turned over and we were off again for Helena. In the minimal heat and protection of the truck, the troublesome passenger was soon sound asleep, which made the remainder of the trip quiet, but cold.

In Helena, the poacher was jailed and later appeared before the justice of the peace. His poker playing and boozing buddies paid the substantial fine for his killing a deer during closed hunting season.

It was announced later that the coldest temperature ever recorded in the lower 48 states had been recorded that night on Roger's Pass: 70 degrees below zero. I had driven on Flesher Pass, which is about 7 or 8 miles south of Roger's Pass and has an elevation of 6100 feet while Roger's Pass is 5100 feet. I am fairly certain that it was at least that cold on Flesher Pass, if not colder. Years later, a roadside monument acknowledged the record temperature at Roger's Pass.

Jittery Poacher

While I was the Helena district game warden, the Fish & Game headquarters office advised me that they had received a phone call that a fellow in a vehicle on the road had just shot a swan on a pond near the complainant's house, and a vehicle license number was given. With this helpful information, I ran a vehicle registration check through the sheriff's office. I then called the suspected person's residence and was informed that the man was a postal employee and was at work. Next I went to the post office and asked the desk clerk if the man was there, and learned that he was on duty.

As I was talking to the clerk, I noticed that a fellow in the back part of the room quickly dropped a box and very obviously left in a hurry. The postmaster came on to the scene and asked a couple of employees where in the building the fellow was, and one employee said, "He just went racing out the back door."

The postmaster replied, "Did he say where he was going?"

No one responded, so I went to the back parking lot and saw the fellow sitting in a vehicle. Given his strange actions in the post office, I immediately presumed that he was the swan shooting culprit. I motioned for him to get out of the vehicle, and the jittery fellow complied. After a brief questioning that revealed my suspicions to be correct, I advised the man that he must appear before a local justice of the peace to answer the complaint of illegally shooting waterfowl and doing so from a roadway.

The justice assessed a fine and suspended the man's hunting rights for a period of time. The people who had witnessed the shooting and notified the Fish & Game Department inquired about the resolution of the case and stated they were having the dead domesticated pet swan mounted by a taxidermist for family memories.

Questionable Sleeping Quarters

Before the construction of Canyon Ferry Dam and the resulting large reservoir, there were ranches in the Canton Valley. As you might expect, there were also the accompanying rancher complaints of nuisance beaver periodically. Most commonly, the ranchers complained of beaver diverting irrigation ditch waters to areas where it wasn't intended or needed. Many times the beaver had diverted irrigating waters onto hayfields that were ready for cutting but too wet for haying machinery. To alleviate these problems, I live trapped a number of beaver through several years.

I once received such a complaint from a well-known lawyer and rancher, and I proceeded to live trap beaver in several of his ranch irrigation ditches. Because I needed to remain close by for live trapping the beaver before traveling to other, distant areas to release them, I stayed in the ranch bunkhouse along with several ranch hands and cowboys.

As usual, I would check in with the county sheriff office at Townsend, and when I mentioned to Sheriff Thompson that I was staying at the ranch bunkhouse for convenience, he told me it wasn't a good move, and suggested I stay in an unoccupied jail cell. When I asked why, he said most of the ranch hands were state prison parolees, which could possibly be risky for me, and particularly so, considering I regularly carried a revolver and occasionally some money.

I spent the greater part of four days resolving the serious beaver problem, and had no conflicts at the ranch. While I was there, I noticed some deer legs and a couple deer heads and hides that were quite old, so I kept those in mind for future reference, and in the meantime I went about my beaver eradicating business. However, during future patrols in the Canton valley, I would check various ranch dumps, and during one visit, I found the legs and head of a fawn deer that were quite fresh. Checking around the various ranch outbuildings where I was trapping beaver revealed a skinned deer carcass.

I informed the sheriff of my findings, and he told me that he would come and standby when the contact with the ranch crew was made. That evening, after the crew had gathered at the cookhouse, I advised them of the fawn deer carcass and told them if any one fellow would admit to the poaching, he wouldn't involve any others. There were glances around from one another and a period of hesitation when finally one fellow said, "I'm your man." The sheriff later told me that if one of the parolees was the poacher, it would have been very bad for his legal status. Luckily, the fellow who claimed guilt wasn't a parolee.

Football Playing Cowboys

I received word that a couple cowboys had tried to sell a few quarters of elk while a crowd of people were attending a yearly gathering in a small ranch community. The information wasn't in detail and it only mentioned a ranch where two out of state college football players were cowboying for the season.

I drove the distance to a cow camp cabin where I assumed the two fellows were staying. I waited there for some time, and then noticed several magpies gathered out along a fence row. Being curious, I went to check on things and discovered an area of fresh dirt and some elk hair exposed on the surface of the ground. Now really suspicious, I got my shovel out of my truck and dug down only a couple inches, then a little deeper, and uncovered four legs, head, and most of the neck of a cow elk. I put the tainted and very smelly elk remains in the bed of my pickup truck, and drove around the ranch a bit to see if I could find the culprits. With no one around, I left.

Out on the county road, I met a local rancher and asked if he knew the two cowboys. The rancher said they were trailing cattle from another ranch that was several miles away, and should arrive in the cow camp's adjacent pasture by the afternoon. With that information, I drove to a high point where I could view quite a lot of the fairly open country toward the ranch where the cattle drive was to end. After being there for a couple hours, I finally saw the lead cows and one rider coming my way. After more waiting and watching, and with the lead cattle going through an open gate and into the cow camp pasture, I opened a roadside gate and drove slowly over to a couple of cowboys on the flanks of the drive. I asked them about the two cowboys at the cow camp cabin, and was told they were at the rear of the drive.

I waited an hour or so, and once the two suspected riders were near the final gate, I approached them and advised that they were being cited for killing an elk during closed hunting and were under arrest. As the last of the cattle went through the gate, I told them to unsaddle their horses and turn them loose in the pasture, and then put their saddles in my pickup bed. When the two saw the rancid elk head, legs, and hide, they exchanged worried glances but made no comment.

During the drive to the justice of the peace court in town, the two men were very quiet. To break the silence, I reviewed the court procedures and explained that the justice would ask for a plea of guilty or not guilty, and their response would then dictate further procedures. I had radioed ahead to the sheriff's office to assure that the justice would be available.

Once the men pleaded guilty to the charge and were fined, they stated they did not have the funds to pay the penalty but had some money due from the ranch owner for their cowboy services. Since they couldn't immediately pay what they owed, they were notified it would be jail time until their bond was posted. This was clearly an unappealing idea for them, and the two cowboys said they could likely draw the money from their ranch boss. Given the late hour, I offered to drive them the numerous miles back to the ranch headquarters. They managed to be paid for their cowboy duties, and were also promptly fired from their jobs.

That ended the poaching case, and the two were very distressed at the financial loss from their summer efforts as cowboys. Their money situation put them in a critical category to get back to Alabama for their continuing college pursuits. Having learned that they were good at livestock roping, I suggested that they might consider participating in some ranch jackpot roping events or small rodeos in hopes of winning some cash prizes to improve their financial circumstances.

The following Christmas, I received a card and short letter from one of the cowboys, Clea, stating that their roping efforts had paid off and had somewhat rescued them from financial dire straits.

A Surprising Show of Appreciation

For a while, I worked the district near the Jefferson county copper mines. Many of the miners had immigrated from countries overseas, bringing with them substantial mining experience and a good work ethic. While reviewing license agents' books of sales for fishing and hunting licenses, I observed that some of the information required to establish Montana residency was questionable at best, so I requested a listing of persons living in the mining area who were legal immigrants but not U.S. citizens. As time permitted, aside from my other demanding game warden duties, I then reviewed the license agent application forms against the listing of immigrants, which revealed several questionable license purchases.

I issued many citations for the illegal purchases to the guilty miners. When they appeared before the justice of the peace court, their illegal licenses were revoked and they were cautioned about further purchases due to their failure to apply as U.S. citizens, and because they did not always meet Montana residency requirements.

My strict adherence to the law raised considerable concern locally and I was summoned to the county attorney's office, where I was questioned about the proceedings. After stating my case, I was admonished for having downtrodden the local hard-working miners who added so much to the community well-being.

Some time afterward, I was contacted by some family members of several of those who were cited and, surprisingly, was thanked. They told me that the citations influenced their kin to start striving to gain U.S. citizenship. It was a gratifying feeling for me to have influenced their decisions to gain citizenship and then comply with Montana license purchase requirements.

A Nighttime Gunshot

A couple reports of nighttime deer poaching created the need for a night patrol in a river valley area. A colleague of mine accompanied me to a vantage point to listen for gunshots and to scan the valley areas for spotlights. There were so many ranch security and dwelling lights and no particularly suspicious happenings that when a single gunshot was heard, we had difficulty in determining its source. We decided to sit tight and hope some light movement or unusual activity might reveal the exact area.

After a considerable length of time waiting in the penetrating wind on that chilly night, we finally spied some moving vehicle lights, but the type of light was unusual and puzzling. Finally, a ranch security light revealed a ranch tractor and a deer carcass in the hydraulic front lift bucket. From our viewing location, it was a problem determining the exact ranch location. Luckily an open barn door and surrounding objects made identifying the location achievable, so we closed in on the suspect. With the tractor engine still hot from use and access to the barn gained, we easily found a whitetail deer carcass. The rancher was issued a citation and we confiscated the illegally obtained deer.

Feeling somewhat put out, the rancher flatly stated, "I feed the damn deer all year on my hay and grain fields, so I ought to be entitled to one."

I told him I was very familiar with wildlife thriving on private lands, many times year-round, but in our position as game wardens we were obligated to acknowledge the killing of a game animal during stated closed hunting season and/or without a proper hunting license. I did assure the rancher I would appear before the justice of the peace with him to help explain and clarify the rancher's point of view.

A Nose for Crime

I received word from a log pole cutter that he had heard a couple rifle shots near where he had been working in an isolated mountain area. I knew that a logging crew was operating in the nearby area, so after some contacts with a couple cowboys at a remote cow camp, and a couple sheep herders at their camp, I decided to go to the logging area for some surveillance. When I arrived at my desired location, I went up on a vantage point where I could scan a lot of the surrounding vicinity and listen for gunshots. After quite a while of watching, a couple pickup trucks came down from the logging area, then stopped at a tool shed and took some tools inside. The one pickup soon left, but the three guys in the other lingered awhile before they finally turned the vehicle around and went back up the mountain toward the logging site. I surmised they may have left tools at their worksite.

I stayed at my vantage point, and then sometime later the vehicle came back to the tool storage shed where one of the loggers threw a tarp back and exposed a buck deer carcass. I watched as they took the deer in the shed and were inside for quite some time. When the one fellow came to the shed door with the deer head, legs, and hide, he took a quick look around and then he walked to a pile of sawdust and dirt and proceeded to dig out a sizable hole and put the animal parts in, and then he covered them back up, and pushed a tree stump and tree limbs on top.

When he returned to the tool shed, the three men soon came out with four quarters of deer and put them in a large wooden tool box in back of the truck cab. They soon left and went a couple miles to the country road, then out on the paved highway toward Lima. After going several miles, I drove quite close behind the pickup to get the license number, then soon stopped the pickup and informed the men that they were getting a citation. The driver said, "For what? Are you a highway officer?"

Evidently he had not looked at the warden badge or my jacket shoulder patch. I replied, "I'm the local game warden, and the citation is for transportation and possession of an illegal deer." I advised the driver to go on to Lima to appear before the justice of the peace, and I'd follow behind and meet them there.

Before I could finish my instructions, the driver piped up and said, "You don't see any deer, do you? And say, where in the hell did you come from to be accusing us?"

Smiling, I answered, "When I drove up close behind you, I smelled deer," which brought on some laughs and head shaking.

When the men appeared before the justice and the complaint was read, one of the guys said, "The warden accuses us of having an illegal deer, but he hasn't seen any such deer for such a charge."

"I know Warden Fitzwater, and I am sure he has a basis for the complaint," the justice responded, and then added, "He has a nose for such things." This elicited more head shakes and nervous laughter.

After the court proceedings, the justice went to the pickup with the poachers and watched as the deer quarters were removed from the tool box and marked as confiscated. I then explained to him all the proceedings from the logging area through to Lima, and all he said was, "Well, I guess my comment was appropriate!"

Duck Club Poacher

One of the districts I was assigned to over the years happened to be inside the borders of the federal Red Rock Lakes National Wildlife Refuge. Within the refuge, there was an area open to waterfowl hunting. As a result, several hunting clubs had facilities for their club members' relaxation and comfort, often serving chef-prepared food.

Within one "duck club," it was supposed to be the policy that any club member cited for violating waterfowl hunting regulations would lose his membership. The regional United States game agent, also known as a federal warden, advised me that he intended to patrol the hunting area and inquired if I would accompany him and assist with the patrol, and I agreed to do so. The federal game agent, having worked California's extensive waterfowl areas, took the lead in suggesting the best methods of patrol.

Before daybreak, the two of us, sitting in an extremely shallow draft boat, got into position for observing the hunters' activities. I was coached to concentrate on a particular shooter, who was regularly downing birds. During my observation, I was to start documenting how many birds were shot, and to identify the shooter by clothing worn, a description of the boat, and the area of shooting.

I soon observed the hunter having a heyday downing ducks. Once the early morning waterfowl flights tapered off, we pushed and paddled in the very shallow water with untold mud depths to the site of the shooter, who was then retrieving a legal limit of desirable ducks and preparing to leave for the club house. We intercepted and stopped the hunter, and checked him for required licenses, plugged shotgun, and legal bird limit. When this was complete, I advised the hunter that he was being cited for shooting more than the legal limit, and that we would meet him at the clubhouse to verify the extent of his poaching. Meanwhile, us wardens retrieved the pathetic over-limit of ducks of different species. It was obvious that the hunter was very selective in the ducks he possessed in his boat, which were all Mallards and the best choice for eating.

Odd Duck Disposal

At a later waterfowl hunting season, I climbed to a vantage point to observe duck hunting activities, and after the morning hunt, I observed a couple duck club hunters leaving the facility. They had quite a large gathering of ducks held by their necks, which they took to a frost-heaved meadow and buried the birds with a shovel. From that distant vantage point, it appeared that it could be a waste of birds violation. Later, when inspecting the birds' burial site, I discovered that the buried ducks had only their breast meat removed. The federal warden later told me it was a common practice in California and considered legal.

Later, at the clubhouse, the poacher was cited in the presence of the club members. The man stated his shame and admitted to the unsportsmanlike act, which I'm sure must have been terribly embarrassing for him. In the justice of the peace court, he paid the fine assessed and lost his bird hunting privileges for two seasons, which was more effective than the monetary fine.

Interestingly, the incident involving the duck club member poaching more than the legal limit of ducks resulted in no loss of club membership. He was one of the greatest financial supporters, and so did not lose his club membership despite his shameful act. So, money and loss of hunting privileges speaks louder than words!

Revelation While Patrolling the Outer Fringe of a Bird Refuge

Duck hunters weren't the only troublemakers at the Red Rock Lakes National Wildlife Refuge. The north side of the refuge is quite remote, and the headquarters are on the south side. Patrolling on the north end one day, I stopped my vehicle to scan the lake waters with my binoculars, looking for the presence of trumpeter swans. While scanning the vast region from my car parked on the north Centennial Road, I spotted two men covering quite a large area. After a couple hen ducks were flushed, it was obvious they were stealing duck eggs.

I watched for some time, and then put on my often-worn hip boots and planned a foot route to the men. There was no high cover for my approach, so I realized I would undoubtedly be spotted before reaching them. As I drew closer, I tried to pinpoint the scarce vegetation growth that would make a good hiding spot for contraband if the men ditched their take of eggs so I could go back and check later. It was fortunate that I did so, because the men did indeed leave their duck egg container as they hastened off in another direction without any indication they had spotted me.

> Formerly known as the Red Rock Lakes Migratory Waterfowl Refuge, it was established by the federal government in 1935 at a time when the trumpeter swan population was at a critically low level. Through the years of protection the refuge has afforded, the resultant swan population increase is proof it has served a good purpose.

For fear I would not recover the egg container due to the sea of marsh grass and other growth, I found their bounty and then hustled at a good pace in the thick grass until I was finally within shouting distance. After a couple loud calls, I managed to get them stopped.

They looked at the pail of eggs, and the glance between them was an indication they knew they were caught. They were advised they would be taken the long distance around the lake area to the refuge headquarters, where those in charge would then officiate the egg poaching case. When I handed the culprits off, I turned the container of eggs over to the refuge official as evidence of their illegal activity.

Thinking back, I am quite certain the fellows, had they been successful in their escape, could never have found that container abandoned in that vast area with few obvious landmarks. Since I didn't have a chance to positively identify the hen ducks the poachers had flushed, I have wondered if it was puzzling as to which family the ducklings belonged when the eggs were hatched.

Bargain Shopping

On one trip to the Red Rock Lakes Refuge, with snow on the ground, I accompanied the federal game warden on patrol. En route near the 7L Ranch, I observed a couple guys up on a mountain slope, and asked the federal warden to stop so I could take a better look. Being an impatient individual, he asked, "What in the hell do you see now?"

I saw that the two men were dragging something, and guessed it to be a game animal carcass. We pulled up the road a bit, and when the two men were close to the roadside we backtracked to meet them. As we drew near, I recognized one of the men as Andy Forsyth, with his hat and usual cigar. Andy said, "Fitzwater, I've fed them for years, so I guess I'm entitled to one deer on the house. Plus, my hired hand likes venison."

Naturally, a citation was issued to Andy by the federal warden to help bolster his standing with the state Fish & Game Department. When Andy appeared before the relatively new Lima justice of the peace, I had to remind him to remove his hat and cigar. The justice read the complaint and asked for a plea, so Andy said, "Not guilty."

The new justice, who had not yet heard a case like this, was quite nervous. Not realizing the procedure following the not guilty plea, he hesitated and replied, "That will cost you $27.50," when in reality the case should have gone to trial.

Andy shrugged in response, and said, "If that's all it will cost, I'll plead guilty!"

A Poacher Caught in Due Time

After my retirement, I have made many visits to see my daughter Lorri, who lives in Tucson, Arizona. On one trip, we paid a visit to the Arizona-Sonora Desert Museum, where there is a large open area for the desert bighorn sheep exhibit, and one ram was very outstanding and of particular interest to many visitors. Quite some time later, I heard that an exceptional ram had been shot and taken from the museum by a guilty poacher. However, the culprit had yet to be found.

On my next couple of visits to Tucson, I contacted the Arizona Game & Fish Department and inquired whether the poaching case had been settled. The answer was always "No!" During one such inquiring phone call, an employee indicated the case wasn't of great interest to the department since it involved private property considerations. My ears perked up and I asked if there was any outstanding evidence, such as an empty cartridge case or obvious vehicle tire marks, or if vehicle paint was found on the many spiny desert plants in the area. The answer again was "No."

However, the poaching case remained of interest to me, and regularly came to mind. Then, I happened to read in a newspaper that the large desert bighorn ram head-mount had been found. Evidently, a California highway patrolman stopped a motorhome for a highway violation. The ensuing conversation between the officer and motorhome driver revealed that both were interested in wildlife matters. After their exchange of interests, the motorhome driver said "Officer, I have something to show you" and then proudly showed the officer a head-mount of a large desert bighorn ram.

The officer marveled at the beautiful mount. Fortunately, the observant and knowledgeable officer also noticed that the ram head had no marking to indicate it was taken legally, which is a requirement. Further investigation led to the determination that the mounted ram was that of the desert bighorn poached at an earlier time at the Arizona-Sonora Desert Museum!

I ultimately heard the final outcome of the poaching case from a relative of mine, who was a colleague of the California Highway Patrolman, and it shows how some events come to pass.

'87 Ram Slaughter Nets Ex-Firefighter 5 Years

By Dee Ralles

TUCSON—A former California firefighter received a five-year prison term Monday for a December 1987 mutilation-slaying of a prized bighorn ram at the Arizona-Sonora Desert Museum.

Stephen Richard Doyle, 38, also was ordered to pay $8,015.10 in restitution to the museum by Judge Pro Tem Howard Hantman of Pima County Superior Court.

Doyle had pleaded guilty to all of the charges that he faced in the slaughter of the ram—first-degree burglary, theft by control, criminal damage and using a gun silencer.

The ram's killing, which outraged Tucson residents, took place early on Dec. 7, 1987. Doyle cut locks to fences leading into the museum, 12 miles west of downtown Tucson, and then cut locks to an enclosure occupied by the bighorn sheep and its mate, which was pregnant at the time.

The ram was shot and its carcass dragged into a cage, where the horns were sawed from the head.

"I had this cockeyed notion that it would make a good trophy," Doyle said.

Doyle, a former captain in the San Ramon Valley, Calif., Fire Department, was arrested in June 1988 as he was driving a stolen motor home near Susanville, Calif. Horns found in the motor home turned out to be form the ram.

Doyle was extradited to Arizona in 1990. Doyle, who had been sentenced I California to a four-year jail term for the motor-home theft, had just been released on parole after serving one year in jail.

Doyle must serve half of the five-year term before being eligible for parole. However, because he is being given credit for the 479 days he has already served in Arizona while awaiting trial, Doyle will be eligible for parole in about 14 months.

(Source: *The Arizona Republic,* Tuesday, August 20, 1991)

Chapter Three

The Ones That Got Away

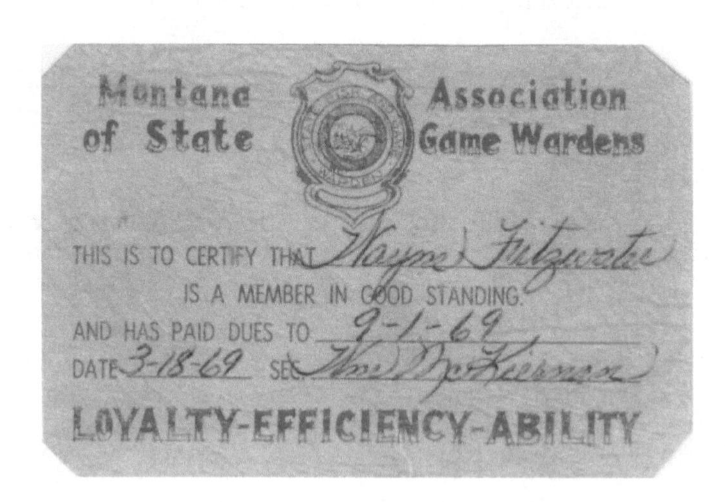

Montana Association of State Game Wardens

THIS IS TO CERTIFY THAT Wayne Fitzwater

IS A MEMBER IN GOOD STANDING.

AND HAS PAID DUES TO 9-1-69

DATE 3-18-69 SEC [illegible]

LOYALTY-EFFICIENCY-ABILITY

Coyote Bill and His Shenanigans

When I arrived at Dillon as the district warden, I soon learned that a local character known as "Coyote Bill" was one to be watched, as he had a reputation as a rugged, true mountain man who hunted and trapped. My first encounter with him certainly confirmed his suspicious status in my book.

Shortly before my arrival in Dillon, the state gave approval for Montana sportsmen to initiate a program to live trap and transplant Yellowstone National Park elk in order to bolster elk populations in certain other areas. The elk that had been live trapped in Yellowstone were trucked by Fish & Game personnel and private individuals who volunteered their services and trucks.

A Dillon group participated in the project and Coyote Bill was one of the volunteers, using his own livestock hauling truck. Once the elk were loaded, the group agreed to assist one another at the various release sites. Things went well until Coyote Bill didn't show up as planned. Once the last of the trucks was unloaded, the others waited and waited for Coyote Bill but he was not to be found, even after a couple fellows backtracked to see if he had had any mechanical troubles. When one of the transporters finally caught up with Coyote Bill in town and questioned him about his failed arrival with the load of elk, he said he got lost and ended up having to release the elk somewhere else. That "somewhere else" happened to his favorite hunting area at Snowline and Lima Peaks.

Meanwhile, Regional Game Manager Joe Gaab and I had been making plans to patrol the Lima Peak area, knowing there was a substantial elk population. During one patrol, several hunters complained to me that a certain access road was blocked by a broken-down truck. I went to investigate, and lo and behold, there was old Bill's truck with a wheel off and a crude note stating, "Broke down and will move as soon as possible," with the trees on both sides preventing driving around the blockage.

I noted that the loading ramp was in an up position, but the disturbed ground revealed that Bill had unloaded his horse. I stayed and waited there until well after dark, but Bill and his horse never arrived.

The next day I went back and waited several more hours for Coyote Bill to show. Once he did, he was minus his horse and sporting blood-stained clothes. Finding this suspicious, I had a few questions for Bill—what exactly had he been up to?!

Bill stated he killed an elk and said, "Fitzwater, I tagged it too, because you are like cow shit on the ranch—you're everywhere!"

He then told me that after killing the elk late the previous day, he had staked his horse at a grassy meadow and camped out for the night. Early the next day, he hiked back to the truck, remounted the wheel, and drove to his horse and the tagged elk carcass.

It wasn't long before I learned from people in town that several local widows were regularly provided venison by no other than Coyote Bill. Not surprisingly, many people thought it was a commendable act, and not a serious violation of Fish and Game law.

I never did manage to cite Coyote Bill in my years working the Beaverhead district, and this was not the only time old Bill outsmarted me, but that's another story. This was just one of the many shenanigans he pulled over the years!

An Unproductive Effort to Reveal Possible Poaching

A local legend by the name of Steve Logan had a couple of knowledgeable old-time stone masons build a very decorative stone fence on his property, and for quite a period of time Logan was hauling in various kinds of stones from outlying areas. During that time, a rancher in an area where Logan was seen loading rock told me that on a couple of occasions, he had heard gunshots. This was unusual, considering there were no open big game hunts. The rancher also said that while cowboying for cattle, he found ravens were congregating in an area and his curiosity revealed an elk gut pile.

One late afternoon a few days later, I observed Logan coming to town with a load of rock, so I followed him to his somewhat remote home site. Once there, I asked Logan, "When do you intend to unload the rocks?"

Then, with a sly grin, Logan said, "Well Fitz, if you are up to it, I'll unload it this evening." He added, "Fitz, I know what you have in mind, so thanks for the help."

Once the trailer was unloaded, I checked it for animal blood and hair only to find very, very little, which was quite old. Over a period of time, I became good friends with Logan, and much, much later he said to me, "I'm sure you realized that you were a day late and a dollar short when you helped unload the rocks!"

Dastardly Animal Control

One year, I was patrolling a large grass and sagebrush area during the annual sage grouse hunt. During my patrol, I had a chat with a cattle rancher where numerous bird hunters were afield, and the evening conversation revealed that the rancher didn't particularly like the grouse hunters milling about near his buildings. He also complained that too many antelope stayed on his pasturelands.

I was familiar with the antelope population in that sizable basin. The group was not in excess numbers, but due to the lusher and greener pasture, as one might expect, many antelope congregated on his ranch. I told the rancher that the hunter and his gun was the most acceptable manner for controlling the antelope population, and added that I would direct antelope hunters to his area as a means to try to reduce antelope numbers.

I never heard another complaint from the man, and within a couple years the rancher sold his property and moved to Dillon to serve as an elected county employee. In town, I would occasionally have coffee and a visit with him. After quite a few of these meetings, he stated, "Fitzwater, your method of antelope control didn't help my situation, but I had my own way to do it." Then he said, "I used my .22 caliber rifle and belly shot quite a few of the pasture invaders."

I was taken aback! It was a shock to learn this, and I soon took the rancher's revelation to the county attorney. However, the lawyer did not wish to file a complaint, saying, "It's water under the bridge."

Soon after making his confession, the rancher died. I have wondered if perhaps the fellow I considered a friend may have confessed his actions to me merely to clear his conscience, knowing he would soon be passing on to due to his severe health issues.

Thinking back on it, I remembered finding several decomposed antelope carcasses in the general area near the man's ranch, and often did so when gatherings of ravens and magpies flew away. Many hunters would report similar findings when I contacted them in the field. After discovering the antelope remains, I always contacted the local game manager, a biologist, to report my findings, but nothing was ever found to have caused the deaths except .22 caliber gun shots.

After quite some time, I got to thinking. Had I had access to a metal detector at the time, it may have revealed a lead bullet in the antelope remains. Years later during the annual big game archery hunts, several archery hunters were cited when a rifle or revolver bullet in a claimed archery kill was revealed by a metal detector.

Questionable Testimony and Extenuating Circumstances

Extended mule deer hunts were quite common in the 1950s and early 1960s in southwestern Montana. One such hunt was declared in a portion of Madison County's Sweetwater area. The Sheridan warden, Leo Secor, and I were assigned to patrol the region.

On one such patrol, I contacted a couple hunters with bagged deer well into the Beaverhead County Carter Creek drainage. When the two hunters were contacted and questioned about the area of the kill, they stated the kill site was a considerable distance to the east, along one of the numerous off-road trails south of the county road. Knowing the area well, I doubted their story and asked them to accompany me back to the claimed kill site, which they agreed to do. Disappointingly, after spending considerable time looking for deer gut piles and a boarding point, none were found and the hunters stated that the large expanse of sagebrush and numerous jeep trails made it impossible to re-visit the kill site. Despite this, I issued citations for killing deer in a closed hunting area anyway, knowing they would be disputed.

Later, when appearing before the justice of the peace in town, the two hunters pleaded not guilty and a trial date was set. During the trial, the men still testified that the deer were killed in the open hunting area. Without any substantial evidence, I knew it was a questionable case that would undoubtedly be lost. But, to clear my doubt and support my suspicion, I later went back to the area searching for any telltale signs. After a couple visits to different spots in the vicinity of the suspected kill site, I finally found rifle cartridge brass in the tall grass along the roadside, and noticed magpies flying up around an area 100 yards or so beyond the presumed Madison-Beaverhead County boundary. I made my way over, and found the weathered and deteriorated remains of two deer gut piles, which were well within the closed hunting area. There were no obvious deer carcass drag marks, but I did find one tuft of deer hair on a lower roadside strand of barbed wire in the closed area.

I made inquiries to Beaverhead and Madison County road maintenance personnel as well, but they could not pinpoint the county line. Some time later, I studied a county map and learned that that particular stretch of county line ran directly north-south, and was north of the illegal kill site. Providing further satisfaction for my insatiable curiosity, I did eventually find an old, solid, squared post on a roadside fence line, which was a county line marker. Even though the tardy discovery of evidence may not have been of much judicial value at that late date, and with a lot of water under the bridge so to speak, I still found it educational.

Another Poaching Case Lost

On occasion, game wardens in adjoining patrol regions would work together. In one instance I asked my neighboring colleague, Warden Chesterfield, to assist in a nighttime patrol of a deer poaching hot spot. This area had a significant river-bottom deer population, and at nighttime several deer moved to the open hay meadows on a nearby ranch. This soon became known to quite a number of dedicated deer poachers, and was of considerable concern to the rancher as he had many cattle on the ranch's winter pastures.

The two of us went to the area and positioned ourselves on two nearby high vantage points nearby where we could view quite a substantial area of the hay meadows. During the early nighttime hours, there were a number of vehicle travelers. Several of them slowed down and used spotlights to see the congregation of deer, with some deer quite close to the highway.

Before midnight, the vehicle traffic tapered off, and after a couple more hours of watching with no highway activity, Warden Chesterfield indicated that our patrol efforts may be futile. I disagreed, and radioed over that it would be wise to stay put until after saloon closing time. Then sure enough at about 2:30 a.m., Chesterfield radioed that he was watching a slow-moving vehicle using a spotlight and that the driver had stopped momentarily to watch deer, and I suggested that he roll down his vehicle window to better hear a gunshot. Not long after, the suspected deer poacher continued on toward my scanning area, and then turned around and hurriedly went back, then again turned around just beyond Chesterfield's scanning range.

Traveling slowly, the vehicle occupants continued spotlighting deer. When the vehicle brake lights came on, we heard a single gunshot, and the vehicle's dome lights illuminated. I advised my patrolling partner to sit tight and try to identify some vehicle markings. From experience, I informed Chesterfield that undoubtedly the vehicle would continue on while someone would go across the hay meadow and field dress the deer. I predicted that after an hour or so, the driver would come back and turn around, and then stop and load the deer carcass.

Sure enough, after a while, Chesterfield could see a flashlight signal for the vehicle to stop. We both quickly left our vantage points and hazardously headed to the highway. Then, by chance and rather unfortunately, several other vehicles were traveling both directions on the road, so pinpointing the poacher's vehicle quickly became an impossible task. What a frustrating and trying time!

After Chesterfield and I passed one another, we decided to speedily continue on in hopes of overtaking the poachers' vehicle —but with no success! Being familiar with the sly and wily ways of experienced poachers, I surmised that the poachers may have driven into a rancher's lane or off a couple little-used side roads and sat tight until they were sure the coast was clear to leave.

On two other occasions, I repeated nighttime patrolling at that same poaching hot spot and succeeded in nabbing deer poachers by following the same stake-out methods. One encounter was very threatening. In such instances, I would often emphasize the seriousness of making a Fish & Game misdemeanor crime into a much more serious criminal charge. Luckily, this often changed the poacher's attitude.

Warden Fitzwater, about 1962

An Investigation of an Elk Overkill with No Results

While I was snowshoe patrolling one early morning I heard many rifle shots, but due to a strong wind blowing I couldn't pinpoint the exact area of the shooting. As I continued my patrol and covered quite a lot of area, I eventually contacted a couple hunters who had also heard the shooting. They told me they had seen a small herd of elk in the distance through their binoculars, which during the shooting bunched up, then milled around and scattered.

Even though it was late in the day by that point, I snowshoed to the area they described and was surprised to find several dead untagged, unclaimed elk. There were no hunters around, and in snowshoeing between the several unclaimed elk, I was again bewildered to find that all had the belly cut open and entrails only partially removed. I surmised that the shooters were conscientious enough to do so, and undoubtedly had a certain peace of mind in keeping the elk carcasses from bloating, and possibly preventing spoilage.

Unable to leave the somewhat cooled elk carcasses in good conscience, I finished a more complete field dressing of the four unclaimed elk as the daylight was dwindling. I then followed the footprints back to the place the shooters stood while taking their shots, and one footprint revealed an unusual boot sole imprint, which I sketched on a notepad. I scoured the immediate area for ejected cartridge brass and only found two empty 30-06 and .308 cases, which I kept as evidence.

As it was dark by then, I covered the elk carcasses as best as possible to prevent the many ravens congregated in the area from damaging the exposed elk meat before I began my trek back to my truck. It was quite a long distance, probably three miles out to the Gallatin Canyon highway, so I followed the drag trails downslope to where the terrain leveled off, where it was evident that the two poachers had help in dragging two elk out to a loading area alongside the highway.

Once at the highway, I awaited a ride back to the Almart Lodge, but no warden arrived to pick me up, so a hunter gave me a lift after a very tiring and frustrating day. Once at the lodge, I found the couple other wardens assigned to patrol the area with me comfortably sacked out in their bunking quarters. When I complained about not having either one there to pick me up at the highway, they said that every hour they had made a pass along the roadway looking for me. Still annoyed by my supposed abandonment, I quizzed them about who they may have checked with elk alongside the highway, but they had no checking record and didn't share any information of value.

Early the next day I went to the parking area where the two elk were loaded and checked for any sign of the unusual boot sole imprint but found nothing. While I was there, I interviewed a couple hunters for possible leads in the poaching case. Thinking the two poachers may have lingered at one of the several bars and restaurants in the canyon, I checked those haunts next, but there were no unusual boot prints alongside the parked vehicles, and only two trucks with two elk atop, which were properly tagged.

Outside, the gusty winds may have obliterated any such foot prints, so out of desperation at one of the bars, I went inside and openly asked the customers which of them claimed the elk loaded in the pickup trucks. A couple men raised their hands. As I had already checked their elk tags and found them to correspond with their licenses, I then asked the hunters to expose their boot soles, which didn't meet with much approval. One somewhat liquored fellow said, "What in the hell is this all about?"

Once I explained the elk overkill circumstances, the mood of the hunters changed for the better and one approached me and complimented me with a handshake, which left me with a feeling of gratitude.

Disappointed but not deterred, I left the bar and went to review the records at the North Canyon checking station, but none indicated the two poachers had gone through the station. As had happened in the past, some sly and conniving poachers had gone south out of the canyon and were free of being checked, getting by with their overkill of four elk. However, I did later learn that the four elk carcasses were permissible, based on the poachers opening the elks' paunches.

Confiscated big game carcasses outside a checking station

A Night Patrol Dry Run

The region's game warden supervisor received a report from Yellowstone Park Ranger Chapman in Gardiner that a couple elk had been poached at night, both inside and outside of the park's boundary. I was chosen to go and accompany a recently hired park ranger to stake out the area. We got into our surveillance position after nightfall and watched for any vehicle traffic with our vehicle windows down in the very cold night air to better listen for gun shots.

For most of the long wait, we saw nothing. Finally, a couple of hours after midnight we heard a single gunshot, but couldn't zero in on the exact direction it came from. The two of us stayed put watching for any vehicle or light, but saw none so we remained at our vantage point until daybreak. After the sun came up, we drove the back roads several times before heading back to our respective stations, but still found no evidence of an elk kill. We repeated our nocturnal patrol for three more nights, but never had any success in apprehending the poacher.

Reflecting on our fruitless patrol, we both decided that with a very bright moon, some poacher had risked shooting an elk without a spotlight amongst the several animals near the road and might have wounded one, but there was no blood or drag trail in the roadside snow.

One Move Ahead of the Game Warden

I once had an old codger tell me about an incident when he had outwitted me and had the "horse-laugh." I well remembered the incident, but never knew the details until the wily culprit, Coyote Bill, relayed them to me a number of years later.

He was known to be quite a deer poacher during those years when deer populations were at an all-time high, and he took an active part in the deer population reduction. I was going to the well-known Scudder Creek deer wintering area when I noticed a fresh vehicle track leaving the traveled road. I proceeded to investigate, and hidden from view in a sagebrush pocket, I came upon and recognized an old pickup truck with stock racks. I noted that Coyote Bill had unloaded his unusually well-trained black horse, and the horse tracks leading up the mountainside were headed toward a ridge that harbored wintering deer.

I had already checked Coyote Bill with his legal bag of deer earlier in the week, and knew the venison was being given to several aged widows that were recognized locally as needing some help. Now it was evident that he was out for more venison, so I surveyed the slope and saw Bill's horse go out of sight over the ridge. Snowshoeing at a hastened pace, I was hopeful of overtaking the old fellow and catching him red-handed.

By the time I reached the ridge top, unbeknownst to me, Coyote Bill had already spotted me. With a deer carcass laying across the riding saddle, he then had the horse lay down in a slight ground depression amid waist-high sagebrush, which would be out of my view. Once I had followed the tracks over the ridge and out of sight, the old fellow had his horse get up in a sitting position and then he reloaded the deer and proceeded to his truck.

After I had snowshoed some distance on the opposite back slope, I thought it would be best to go back to the ridge top so I could scan more of the area. Once there, I glassed the area toward his truck and saw the vehicle just leaving, and realized that Bill had luckily and intentionally out-maneuvered me. But, not knowing for sure the old fellow knew of my presence, I decided to make tracks down to my also hidden vehicle and head for town to check some of the old codger's various haunts, perhaps catching up with him while the trail was hot.

Once in town, I checked every known place where I thought Coyote Bill might be or where he might stash a deer carcass. Unfortunately, the old fellow, deer carcass, truck, and horse were nowhere to be found for a week or more, and then I knew for sure I had been outsmarted.

In contacting the assistant county attorney with the details of the proposed case, I was denied a complaint against old Bill for lack of evidence, except what I had seen. With the community knowing of Coyote Bill's generosity in providing several needy widows with good, clean venison, which with their garden produce they canned and stored to get by, I wasn't inclined to feel I was seriously shirking my warden duties, but in fact I was!

As a last resort, I planned to go back to the hunting area and determine if, and where, a deer might have been killed and dressed. I knew Bill normally removed the head and legs from an animal carcass to lighten the load, so I felt sure there would be adequate evidence of an illegal kill. Alas, it so happened that I was assigned patrol duty in the Gallatin Canyon and could not pursue it further. What terrible luck! Undoubtedly, the ravens, golden eagles, and coyotes had eliminated the gut pile and carried off the deer head and legs.

Several years later Coyote Bill just had to rub this old game warden, and told me about the details of his deception and his black horse laughing for outwitting the law. I assured the old fellow that I was familiar with his deer poaching activities, and his questionable generosity toward the impoverished widows in town.

Outside an old cabin used by big hame hunters

Scot-Free Poachers

An old-timer residing in the small community of Monida, where an access road entered the isolated Centennial Valley in my district, advised me of some questionable hunter activity in a remote area of the snow covered, blizzard-prone area. He said the suspicious activity was several days old, during blizzard conditions in the valley. I asked for investigative assistance from neighboring Warden Chesterfield, who came from Butte with a snowmobile.

We unloaded our snowmobiles at Monida, and traveled the many miles to the area of the suspected illegal elk kill on the side of the valley. Once there, a gathering of ravens led us to some gut piles. We scoured the area foot-by-foot but found only a piece of hard plastic, which we assumed came from some part of a snowmobile. Lacking any more evidence, we left the area and contacted the Monida fellow for any more possible information. He could only tell us that he saw one pickup vehicle with a license plate with the state number 3 prefix. At the poaching site there was snow drifted in ruts, which indicated at least one vehicle had made it there through the deep snow.

I knew a local ranch family who originally came from Yellowstone County, and I knew the make of snowmobiles they owned. So, over the next few days Warden Chesterfield and I checked many snowmobiles in the field and at dealers' to try to fit the plastic piece found at the poaching site with many models and makes of snowmobiles, but had no success.

Meanwhile, I was advised that I was scheduled to attend a warden training session in Great Falls, temporarily interrupting my efforts. During a break in the training, I walked around town and stopped at a used car lot where a fellow had the engine hood up on an International pickup. As I stood by the fellow looking at the vehicle engine, I saw the cooling fan shroud and immediately realized that the piece of plastic we thought was from a snowmobile would actually match the International fan shroud. When I returned to Dillon, I contacted Warden Chesterfield and the Beaverhead county attorney for his comment related to the case, which wasn't at all encouraging.

Warden Chesterfield and I ultimately decided to go to the ranch of the suspected poachers to look at their pickup truck and two snowmobiles. We didn't find any elk hair, blood, or other evidence that might be incriminating, but we did learn that a family member east of Billings owned an International pickup, so we got clearance to travel there to continue the investigation.

Once there, we brought along the Yellowstone County district warden, Gene Sara, who knew the rancher well from regularly buying fresh eggs from him. While we were inspecting the International pickup engine compartment, Warden Sara unwittingly pointed to the fan shroud and said, "Your piece matches."

We then contacted the Yellowstone county attorney and were reluctantly given a complaint and warrant, which we served, and then took the suspect to the local justice of the peace, where he pleaded guilty and paid a fine. The other two family members, for lack of evidence, were not given citations by decision of the county attorney.

About a month or so later, Warden Sara advised me and Chesterfield that another Yellowstone rancher had told him that a gathering of magpies and ravens at a remote illegal dump site was being attracted there by some food source. Warden Sara checked and determined it was small packages of elk meat that someone had discarded, but there was no indication of who put it there. There was no specific evidence related to the family from Beaverhead or their relative in Yellowstone County that could be presented to the county attorney for a complaint, so they got off scot-free!

Unpredictable Justice of the Peace Decisions

With the many Fish & Game citations I issued that went to the justice of the peace courts, the determinations and penalties assessed were quite variable. Over the years, I sensed a difference in judgment from a justice of the peace that was appointed to office as compared to a justice of the peace voted into office by local voters. However, in almost all instances, I made an effort to appear in court at the same time as the cited violator. This was of benefit for the judge to make a case determination, and also for me as a warden when asked about the specifics and details of the violations being reconciled.

Even with the often differing testimonies of the warden and the defendant, the justice also considered various other factors. Sometimes the defendant appeared to be outright lying; other times they claimed hardship on having to pay necessary fines, which may or may not have been true. Whether or not the defendant showed regret or remorse was another aspect in the judgments handed down from the court.

Unfortunately, lying in court by those cited for Fish & Game law or regulation offenses was a common occurrence and difficult to prove as perjury! I was often quite distressed and upset at the seemingly, in my mind anyway, lenient or inappropriate judgements issued in numerous court cases over the years, and especially if a particular case involved a great amount of time and physical effort to develop adequate evidence for issuance of the citation. But, even though it was quite troublesome, I accepted the gamble and the fact that "it all paid the same!"

Case Dismissed

While working the Townsend and Helena warden districts, I regularly patrolled the Missouri River areas for fishing and trapping activities. The Toston Dam area was quite popular with fishermen, with many thinking that the 300-foot area immediately below the dam that was justifiably closed to fishing activities was a great gathering area for trout, and especially for spawning trout.

On one such patrol, I observed a fellow fishing within the closed area and proceeded to contact the man. I notified the fisherman that he was fishing illegal waters and would be issued a citation, and that his fishing rod and the two trout he possessed would be routinely held as evidence, but the man refused to surrender them. Because he refused to cooperate, I took the fellow into custody and brought him to a justice of the peace in Townsend. The man pleaded not guilty to the charge, so a court trial date was set. The fellow was dressed in bib overalls and appeared to be an average fisherman, but I soon learned from the county attorney that he was a state senator!

During the court trial, the fisherman was represented by W.D. Rankin, a well-known Helena attorney. W.D. Rankin was a brother of Jeannette Rankin, the first female U.S. Congresswoman. Attorney Rankin was *very* impressive in the courtroom. After a short period of testimony, Rankin moved for case dismissal. When asked by the justice for the basis for the move to dismiss, Rankin replied, "In the Montana Fish & Game law book, it states that the Missouri River is open to fishing all year. Then, by commission regulation, it further declares that the posted portion below Toston Dam is closed. Now, the law book reads that the river is open all year and as my client followed the Fish & Game Law Book guideline, he should not be charged with a violation!"

Case dismissed!

Will Refund Bachelor Tax

Montana counties must refund the bachelor tax to all those who made proper application therefore, according to an opinion announced by Atty. Gen. Wellington D. Rankin. The poll tax of $3 imposed on all unmarried men in the state by the last legislature was recently declared unconstitutional by the Montana Supreme Court.

(Source: *The Dillon Daily Tribune-Examiner*, March 1, 1922)

Hunter Intrusion into Montana from an Isolated State Line Area

On a rare occasion while patrolling the sizable upper Centennial Valley, I would meet Wardens Sears and Todd afield. We discussed patrolling adjacent stretches of the Montana-Idaho state line, and as I was familiar with a couple state line areas where Montana hunter access was only available from an Idaho backroad, we agreed to patrol one of those areas. When we intersected the Idaho roadway, fresh vehicle tracks were obvious so we followed them, and gave fleeting thought to the possibility that the hunters may do their deer hunting only on the Idaho side of the state line.

I had erected several "Entering Montana" signs along the border as a reminder of the hunting boundary. Almost always the signs had been taken down, probably for an excuse if an Idaho hunter was contacted on the Montana side. As expected, once at the state line boundary, no sign was seen, so we proceeded on and across a sizable mountain meadow well within Montana. On the far side of the meadow, we observed a vehicle with one fellow standing alongside with a rifle. We made contact with the fellow and advised him that he was in Montana by a half-mile or more. Hearing this, he seemed very concerned and nervous, and told us that hopefully his young and ambitious son was in Idaho hunting. The fellow was advised that should his son possibly shoot a deer or elk in Montana, he would be issued a citation. No shots were fired, and when the young man returned after a couple hours, both were advised of their hunting activities. However, due to the circumstances and the possibility of not realizing they were in Montana, and with no visible informative sign at the Idaho-

Montana border, we gave them the benefit of the doubt and no citations were issued.

For good measure, we also informed them that had a game animal been killed in Montana and transported into Idaho, it could fall in the category of a violation of the federal Lacey Act, with serious consequences. My partners were quite disturbed to have left the two Idaho hunters free of citations, but I hinted that perhaps they were just over-eager hunters and did not realize they were in Montana.

F & G Response was Gratifying

Dear Sir: Let me share, with you and your readers, a gratifying experience.

While I have not hunted game for some twenty years, probably due to my inabilities and, perhaps, laziness, nevertheless my interest in same has not waned.

During the last few weeks, we have read numerous articles in letters to the editor that have been highly critical of the Fish and Game treatment of the out of state hunters and some Montana hunters.

These charges, if true and based on facts, are serious and even we non-hunters should be concerned at the treatment the non-resident guest receives, while in Montana.

Also, we have been informed that under Gov. Tom Judge's administration, a new "Service to Citizens—Toll Free Number" is available to discuss state business or activities. Because of the newspaper articles and some of the letters that have been printed in the Standard, I phoned the toll free number (800-332-2272), and as a concerned citizen expressed my feelings on the treatment of hunters, to the young voice that so courteously answered the phone. She assured me that she would contact someone in the Fish and Game Department and that I would either hear from her or directly from them, regarding this problem. Within four hours, Game Warden Wayne Fitzwater spent an hour with me, listened to my gripes and puzzlements, and of course, explained some of the aspects of the specific cases which were not included in the letters to editor and some of the newspaper articles. He also explained the Fish and Game position.

All in all, it was a gratifying experience and I was particularly impressed that "my complaint did not hit file 13" at least until certain remedial explanations were, in length, made to me. I'm sure game wardens and justices of the peace, taken as a group, are no different than store clerks, plumbers, Democrats, Republicans, and even bankers, and maybe we need to be reminded that we are "servants of the People," and should keep our hearing aids turned up to where we can hear the people speak.

I salute our State Administration for providing us with the toll free number and inviting our discussions of the State business in the manner. - PARIS W. ROBERT, Dillon.

(Source: *The Montana Standard*, Butte, MT, November 9, 1973)

Outwitting the Game Wardens

Some years back when my colleague Warden Leonard Secor was working the Sheridan district, he contacted me in Dillon and inquired about some trapper activities which he suspected were those of a couple noted to be sly and crafty. The animal sets he had seen were alongside a creek and very unusual, so Warden Secor wasn't sure if the sets were legal.

We agreed to meet and keep check on the suspected couple to learn of their activities, and what animals were being trapped. The unusual trap sets were blocks of wood with an approximately 2-inch diameter hole augured in about 3 to 4 inches in depth, with a needle-sharp horseshoe nail driven in at an angle at the lower front edge of the hole. A light-weight holding wire was attached firmly to the augured wooden block. The horseshoe nail was intended to impale a mink under the lower jaw once it placed its head in the hole for the bait.

It was obvious to me, as I had once been a trapper, that the trap sets along the stream's edge were intended for mink. Considering the mink trapping season did not open until November 10th, the sets were considered illegal. After some surveillance over a couple days, other more pressing duties necessitated that Warden Secor and I leave the area. As time permitted, Warden Secor would check the wooden block sets and he noted that a couple sets had caught animals, judging from the ground area that was disturbed by a struggling animal.

After a while and with occasional checks, Warden Secor was there when a well-known trapper was running his suspected pre-season trap line. The trapper didn't have any mink in his possession at the time, but Warden Secor advised the trapper that he was issuing a citation for illegal trapping anyway and that it would be necessary to appear before a justice of the peace. The trapper pled "not guilty," and so a trial would have to be held.

Warden Secor kept me informed of the case, and asked if I would appear as a witness at the trial since I had inspected the traps and assisted with surveillance. At trial time, the judge listened to testimony from Warden Secor and me, then asked the old trapper what he had to say. The fellow, being quite talkative and having had numerous contacts with what he termed "two of the finest game wardens he had ever known" stated, "They should be complimented for getting out and doing their job. But, about those kind of animal sets, Judge. I have used them for years, and they sure are simple, do not cost much money, and are the best darned sets I use to catch weasel."

Case dismissed!

Just Short of Getting Caught

While patrolling an area of considerable elk hunting activity, I came across two men who worked for an outfitter that was known to pursue questionable hunting methods. The two men seemed surprised to have come in contact with me and said, "We heard you were in the area."

I noted that both had an appreciable amount of animal blood on their jacket sleeves, shoulders and backs, and both were carrying walkie-talkie radios for contact with one another and the outfitter base. They claimed they were scouting areas for game signs, and the bloody clothing was from previously packing out game earlier that day, which proved to be true. However, no shell casings, rifles, or bullets were found.

Sometime after separating, I went to my vehicle and drove a distance before I parked off the one-lane mountain road and patrolled on foot for a couple hours. Shortly after I returned to my truck, I received a radio message from the sheriff's department that a hunter had found two front quarters and the remains of a moose on the mountainside with no one around. The hunter gave a detailed description of the exact location, which was nearby.

Using his description and my knowledge of the area, I had no difficulty in locating the first set of front quarters because of a gathering of Canadian Jays. I marked the location inconspicuously and then scouted the surrounding uphill areas for the moose remains and found the other front quarters. It didn't take long to find the kill site, thanks to a gathering of flying ravens, and I quickly located the remnants of the moose carcass and gut pile. I spent considerable time going over the remains looking for a rifle bullet, but only found some fragments. I covered the surrounding areas on foot hoping to find the hind quarters, but did not have any luck. Undoubtedly, they had been packed out, and by that time, stashed somewhere else.

I could find no other telltale evidence of significance, but being somewhat familiar with the method that the suspected outfitter and his guides had used to field dress big game animals before, I intended to contact the county attorney for possible issuance of a Fish & Game citation when I returned to town.

I worked until after dark getting the moose quarters to a vehicle access location. Mulling over all the details as I completed my task, I was quite sure that the two guides contacted earlier had been relaying the moose quarters down the mountainside, and when they learned from a couple other hunters that a warden was in the area, they left the scene and abandoned their bounty.

Later, I checked the suspected outfitter's records and learned that an out-of-state hunter had booked a moose hunt with him and was to arrive in a couple days. Undoubtedly, the illegal moose was probably intended for that client, without any actual hunting on his part involved. It was common knowledge in the game warden ranks that occasionally a hunter who booked with an outfitter only wanted to go home as a successful "hunter," and some in that category would rather enjoy partying and gambling locally instead of hunting, so they depended on the outfitter to provide an animal.

Ultimately, the county attorney would not authorize issuance of a citation based on the lack of incriminating evidence, since he had only my testimony to go on. During that era of the early 1950s, the lack of lab procedures to match the dried moose blood with that on the two men's clothes meant the poaching case was lost.

Warden Fitzwater taking a break from patrolling during sage grouse hunting season

One, Amongst Many, That Got Away

While patrolling afoot near a somewhat popular mountain fishing lake, I knew of an occupied osprey nest in the top of a partially dead pine tree, and I was curious to see if there were any changes. A couple hours of hiking later, I arrived at the nest site, and to my sorrow saw a dead osprey nearby. I examined the still somewhat warm bird carcass and found the creature had been shot, so I probed for a spent bullet, which by the lethal wound, was determined to be from a small caliber rifle or handgun.

I resumed my foot patrol, and quite soon contacted a fisherman on the trail. After checking his fishing license and catch of a couple trout, I asked if he had seen any others in the lake vicinity. The man said he had met two young men, one carrying a fishing rod and one carrying what appeared to be a .22 caliber rifle. He also told me that he had heard one gunshot a couple hours ago. When I told him about the dead osprey, he cursed and said he too had observed the osprey for several years. He was amazed at the bird's lake-surface plunge underwater, and the ability to get airborne with a sizable trout and then hold the fish like a torpedo for less air drag in flight.

The fellow then stated he had seen a motorbike with a rifle scabbard on the side on the north part of the lake, but did not know the bike make or the license number. Thanking him for the information, I then set a quick pace to where the bike was seen. Unfortunately, on arriving the bike was gone, and tire tracks in the trail dust indicated the riders were headed toward VooDoo Pass, which was several miles away.

Despite being disappointed in my loss, I still notified the district warden in Ennis and requested he keep watch for a motorbike with a rifle scabbard attached, but never heard a report back.

Game Wardens and Proud Poachers

It seems that in about every game warden district there are certain poachers who make it a game to outwit, outsmart, and outmaneuver the local warden. Some, if caught, take it laughingly and in stride, while others may be plumb ornery, spiteful and downright mean, but it all goes with the badge.

Years ago, my colleague Charlie Price was a game warden when there were very restrictive regulations on beaver trapping, and the prices for good beaver pelts were exceptionally high. That was back when a dollar was a dollar, and those good fur prices were incentive for certain trappers to cash in on a good thing. Between Game Warden Price and a couple old-time trappers, there wasn't the best of feelings, and the trappers delighted in outsmarting the game warden, who had a large area to patrol.

As you may have guessed, Coyote Bill was one of those trappers. He was an expert at trapping beaver, and probably partially because he smelled like a beaver and fit right in with nature. Old Bill located an area where there were lots of beaver, so he planned how he could get in and trap hard and heavy for a while without being aggravated by Warden Price. Before he started trapping at this ideal locale, he planned to set a decoy as a way to distract the warden. So, he went to an area where he knew certain ranchers knew and respected Warden Price, and was sure the ranchers would notify the warden of his presence. He very obviously placed a couple of poorly chosen beaver sets and made sure that he had been seen, ensuring that a report would go quickly to Warden Price.

Sure enough, Warden Price went to the area and stayed at a nearby ranch where he could keep watch on the old trapper's beaver sets, and hopefully catch him red-handed. In the meantime, Coyote Bill didn't waste any time going to the distant prime beaver area and made a haul of good, valuable beaver pelts. The thing that Warden Price didn't know was that Coyote Bill had fixed the traps he had so conspicuously placed for the warden's benefit so they wouldn't trip, and were only bait for the warden to watch while old Bill had a heyday trapping miles away.

Coyote Bill told me this tale and numerous others about his skirmishes and forays with experienced Warden Price. He once said, "I sure miss Charlie being around to keep my wits sharp."

Chapter Four

Rigors of the Job

STATE OF MONTANA
Fish and Game Department
Hunter Safety Program
In Cooperation With the NRA

№ 3957 A

JUNE 30, 1960
Renewal Date

This is to certify that WAYNE FITZWATER

is an approved Montana Hunter Safety INSTRUCTOR and is hereby authorized to conduct Hunter Safety Courses of Instruction in accordance with Chap. 16, 26-202, Sec. 1, Para. 2a RCM Laws of 1957 Session of Montana Legislature and recommend such deserving graduates for Certificates of Competency.

Bob Conlin
Supervisor of Hunter Safety

Rigors of the Job:

Trapping Tales

Guinness Book of World Records Candidate

While stationed at Helena, I was asked on numerous occasions to assist with other Fish & Game projects that were short of needed personnel. Mountain goat live trapping was one such project, so I was asked to aid and accompany animal trapping foreman Jim McLucas to the Holland Lake Trailhead. All the necessary live trapping equipment was packed in on horseback to the Little Salmon Parks area, where we set up tent headquarters.

After setting up camp and getting organized, the next day we went to the trap site, which was a natural salt-lick for mountain goat, and prepared the trap door for proper release when a goat entered the enclosure. We caught five goats the next day, which included a nanny with two kids. While we were subduing the goats so we could crate them for transport, the two kids raced around inside the enclosure. We were very surprised when one kid literally climbed up the sloping netting in back like it was a ladder and escaped. Foreman McLucas said, "We will have to release the nanny, as the lone kid goat would not survive on its own."

I told McLucas that I would try to catch the escaped kid instead, and he laughed as I left the trap and ran toward where the goat escaped. I ran upslope, and not too far above the trap I spotted the kid. I ran after it and for some distance did not gain on it, but finally its pace slowed and I overtook and caught the kicking kid. When I got back to the live trap and McLucas saw me and my catch, he laughed heartily and finally said, "Fitz, you undoubtedly may have made the Guinness Book of World Records!"

Along with the three-man trapping crew was a photographer representing the popular *Life* magazine, and he, being of Japanese descent, was very interested when he learned that once the goat trapping had progressed to a certain point, a couple members of the team would fish the river for a fish feast. When the time came that we could take a break and fish, we caught several bull trout (Dolly Varden) and tossed them on the river bank to the photographer, and then kept right on fishing to ensure we had enough for a fish feed in camp.

I glanced back at one point and was surprised to see that the photographer had made a knife cut along a fish's dorsal fin and was eating it like corn on the cob! We all laughed at his doing and he said, "Try it, you'll like it!" He ate his share of the camp cooked fish, and was hoping we would do the same again before breaking camp.

After our feast, the crated goats were put in a heavy-duty reinforced rubber raft with only McLucas and I as company, due to the weight factor and the need to side-paddle the boat to reasonably safe river channels. We floated the goats down the South Fork of the Flathead River to a nearby wilderness area airfield, where the goats would be picked up and flown to a pre-selected mountain relocation area. When we arrived at the airfield, we uncrated the animals and gave them a shot of tranquilizer to keep them knocked out until the recipients at the goats' destination took over to complete a mountain transplant.

We relocated several mountain goats this way over the course of several raft rides and plane flights. We later learned that one goat had recovered from the knockout shot mid-flight, and had kicked through the side fuselage of the plane and caused a lot of excitement and concern when the plane landed.

Warden Fitzwater and Jim McLucas

Note the black garden hose over the mountain goat's horns, placed there to prevent getting hooked by an aggressive goat. One billy goat escaped with hose still looped over his two horns, only to go back to the surrounding high mountain area. Can you imagine a goat hunter observing the goat through binoculars and seeing seemingly continuous horn growth?!

A Treat for the Trip

In the 1950s and 1960s, when the northern Yellowstone Park elk numbers were at a high level, the extended elk hunts in the Gardiner and upper Gallatin River Canyon areas helped reduce the overpopulation as the elk migrated northerly into Montana. However, the extended hunts weren't always sufficient, and with northern Yellowstone areas still experiencing an overcrowding of elk, a live trapping program at various national park areas was put into effect, with several truck-loads of elk being hauled to several southwestern Montana release sites.

Once at the various release sites, it was required that local landowners be contacted for their approval of the elk release, and what a chore that was! Around some proposed release sites, certain landowners had experienced deer and elk depredations in the past, so they were not very agreeable to having elk transplanted on top of the already present native elk. However, some landowners agreed on the basis that if they should have any winter elk depredation, the Fish & Game Department would extend elk hunting to alleviate their problems.

Warden Fitzwater inspecting the chute of an elk live trap.

Within Yellowstone National Park, I assisted the park rangers with the live trapping at the many stockade-style traps throughout the park. Occasionally the hay-baited stockade traps would have buffalo inside, which were then released and the trap reset. Sometimes the traps ensnared several antlered bull elk. When that happened, one of the trapper crew would try to lasso the animal from a small walkway at the top of the trap, then snub the animal in close and saw off the antlers just above the burr on the bull's skull. What a dangerous job that was at times!

One of several elk live trap enclosures inside Yellowstone National Park.

At one trap site a couple of volunteers, without needing encouragement, helped with the de-antlering efforts. One of the bull elks who had "fire in its eyes" wasn't in a position to easily lasso, so a volunteer had removed his jacket and was trying to use it to get the bull in roping position. As he flung his jacket at the bull's head, the bull hooked the jacket on an antler tine and the fellow was pulled over the stockade top and went headlong toward the ground inside. A park ranger and I grabbed at the falling man, one by his trouser hip pocket and one by a shoe, and finally pulled him back up to safety. The park ranger thanked the volunteer and said, "No more help!"

After the trapping was done, I drove a department truck transporting the elk from several trap sites to numerous transplant areas. To release the trucked elk away from ranch buildings and roadways was very often a problem, and then not knowing in which direction the elk would run made for an uncontrollable situation. Additionally, the elk live trapping was occasionally in progress during the extended late winter elk hunts, and consequently another stockade holding pen was constructed in the Eagle Creek-Jardine area so de-antlered bull elk could be held there until release into the open elk hunting areas early the following morning before the 8:00 AM start of the hunt.

On one trip to an area north of Butte, a bad snowstorm set in, and east of Whitehall heading up toward Pipestone Pass the highway was declared closed. When I arrived at the road closure with the truckload of elk, I was quite concerned because it was very late in the day and there was a group of Butte sportsmen waiting at the elk release site, so I told the highway flagman my predicament and said I would like to get a running start to get up and over Pipestone Pass. I was granted permission, and made it over the pass by keeping the truck in a lower gear and not having to shift and lose momentum.

Due to the snowstorm, the sportsmen at the release site had just about given up on the arrival of the elk, and so were quite pleased when I finally arrived. After the release was completed, I was treated to a Lydia's steak dinner, compliments of the sportsmen group. Having had no lunch, what a treat!

Some of the trapped elk were ear-tagged at the trap site, and during the next couple of big game hunting seasons a few of those tagged elk were killed by hunters rather long distances away, southeast of the release site. It was surmised that the animal homing instinct influenced their lengthy travels. Quite some time later, I was also told that a number of the transplanted elk were poached by Butte hunters, since the released elk were disoriented in an unfamiliar place, and not as wary as they would usually be if they were in their wild home area.

An Air Show of Sorts

During one antelope live trapping project at the Winston Flat area, I accompanied the old experienced plane pilot Jim Stradley in herding antelope by air into the outer ground wings of the trap, and then into the trap proper. To get the antelope gathered and headed in the right direction demanded critical and low-altitude plane maneuvering. On several occasions, Pilot Stradley flew under the many wires from the telephone line near the main Winston-Townsend highway. Sometimes cars would stop on the highway, probably amazed at the plane's maneuvering. Evidently, a couple of viewers were concerned with such flying and called the county sheriff and state highway patrol, who later appeared on the highway to see the erratic flying. I ultimately called the Broadwater Sheriff's Office, and advised them of the live trapping activity, which finally neutralized the concern.

The project was supervised by the Fish & Game Department live trapping foreman Jim McLucas, who was very knowledgeable as to the details of animal live trapping. The animals were released at suitable transplant sites, and at one time Montana antelope were reported to have been shipped to Hawaii for release there. We never received any report whether the transplantation was successful, though.

Beaver Trapped and Relocated

During the early 1950s, beaver could not be trapped except under provisions of a landowner beaver permit, which cost $10.00 for any number of beaver up to ten. This quota was designated by the warden issuing the permit, and included a landowner description by section, township, and range. An explanation of damage being caused by the critters within the permit area was also required.

Problem beavers on public domain lands were either live trapped or steel trapped, and pelted by the district warden or perhaps the state trapper. Howard Campbell worked as the state trapper then, and he was well known for his skills in trapping and skinning beaver. Howard often said, "I'll skin a beaver for fun or money against anyone who thinks he can better my time." I had the opportunity on several occasions to go with him to trap nuisance beavers, and I *never* met any trapper who had more savvy to entice a wise old beaver into one of those bulky and obvious live traps, as compared to a smaller and easily concealed steel trap. He used a very effective scent as a calling card for beaver, and he was quite secretive about the several ingredients included in his proprietary concoction.

I live trapped and transplanted my share of beavers during my many warden years, and a conservative estimate would be between 350 and 500 animals. When beaver populations were at a high level because of poor pelt prices, it was difficult to identify potential transplant sites. The site had to be somewhere where a relocated beaver would be less likely to cause a problem until fur prices were such that trappers were trapping seriously as an income supplement, and consequently reduced the beaver population.

I also earmarked and tagged many live trapped beaver and learned that to release an adult beaver within the same stream drainage, whether trapped upstream or downstream, only meant that, given time, the homing instinct would very likely have that same beaver back in its home area. Most of the irrigation ditch-dwelling problem beaver were adult males that Mama beaver had run out of the colony when she had her young. The summer bachelor beaver looked for easy living, and irrigation ditches and head gate areas seemed tailor-made for effortless dam construction and a fairly shallow-banked dugout den. I took many, many beaver to be transplanted to remote areas with adequate water flows and food sources, but when there was limited time to release a beaver, the Beaverhead drainage animals would go to the Big Hole drainage and vice versa.

Some concerns out of Fish & Game headquarters were voiced about the time and travel involved with assisting ranchers and others with nuisance beavers. However, those assisting efforts served to encourage good relationships with the ranchers that the Montana Fish & Game Department must continuously deal with in wildlife work. Concerns were also allayed when it was pointed out that when a warden was looking into district-wide beaver problems, he was also patrolling and aware of other activities related to wildlife law enforcement.

And so it was with what some might call the "good old days" and "good old boys," that have left their marks and impressions, and will eventually and undoubtedly be forgotten within the Fish & Game ranks.

Damn Beaver Dams

During early winter of 1953, I was assigned to the Helena district, which included the Townsend, Canyon Creek, Wolf Creek, and Boulder areas. Beaver problems were commonplace, and guidelines were quite restrictive for beaver trapping. Complaints were numerous, and I heard them all. Irrigation ditches, canals, and creeks were dammed and causing damaging flooding of croplands, structures, roadways, and trails. Trees cut by beavers and falling across cabins yielded even more complaints. Ornamental and fruit trees could be cut or girdled by the nuisance critters. Low bridges and culverts were flooded, plugged, and washed out as a result of beaver activity. The busy beavers were also known for undermining stream and ditch banks, causing treacherous cave-ins where livestock, fences, and ranch machinery were detrimentally affected. Beaver ponds frozen over in areas of wintering cattle and calves caused livestock loss or injury when the bovines would break through the weak ice and flounder. Complete aspen groves were decimated by cutting or flooding. The list was endless and repetitive.

One complaint came to the Helena office from a known ornery bachelor who lived on a remote homestead near where the railroad goes over the Continental Divide west of Helena. This fellow filed his complaint directly to the Helena office in a very abrupt, demanding, and vocal manner that was quite unfit for the Fish & Game receptionists to hear, so his complaint was referred to Chief Deputy Walter Everin, who was a true gentleman. Everin was a soft-spoken mediator and negotiator, and was a capable representative of the Fish & Game Department.

Chief Everin sympathized with the man's problems and assured the riled, angry, and demanding fellow that the local warden would investigate as soon as possible. Well, this didn't seem soon enough for the irate man and he let it be known by further verbal tirades that there had better be a quick response. Turning on his heel, he left in a huff.

Early the next morning, I showed up at the fellow's cabin and received much of the same exhibition of anger, frustration, and cussin' that took place at the headquarters the day before. While standing in a couple inches of flood water flowing around the cabin, it wasn't difficult to understand the problem. But, it was a challenge to clearly explain to this angry man that I was there to immediately do something to help alleviate the issue.

Since he refused to listen to reason, I couldn't see the gain in any more talking, so I took my leave and surveyed the dams causing the flooding. I proceeded to create holes in them by pulling and tugging willows and debris at positions where the released dam waters would flow down the nearly dry stream channel. I then went to my old panel vehicle and took the three rolls of old woven wire fencing I had brought along to place in the dams after I caught the beaver. I next set the two beaver live traps I had, and after some of the pond waters had receded, I walked the stream channel to see where more work might be done to help relieve the flooding conditions. One larger dam was downstream from the homesteader's cabin and on the upstream side of a fairly low railroad bridge, but it wasn't contributing to flooding at the cabin, so I passed it up for later attention.

To avoid further confrontation with the fellow, I merely advised him that I would be camped nearby and would check the live traps periodically through the night, so if his barking and biting dog raised a fuss in the dark hours, not to come out shooting.

I caught two beaver before midnight, and put them in a holding cage Frank Lancaster and F & G shop foreman Rex Smart had made for me. I reset the two traps and caught two more beaver by daybreak. To prove that some of the damn dam troublemakers were in custody, I showed the culprits to the complaining fellow and informed him I would go release the four beaver in habitable areas away from civilization, then would return later that day to set the live traps again. The man was all for "knocking the beaver in the head," to save time and for his own gratification I'm sure, but I released them far up the Little Blackfoot drainage.

Later that day, I reset the two live traps, but only caught one more beaver that night. The one remaining live trap was left for a couple more nights with no beaver being caught, or any attempted repairs of the narrow openings in the dams, so I placed the old wire fencing to prevent future repair efforts.

With the problem pretty well taken care of, I advised the fellow to check every morning to determine if there were any beaver attempts to mend the dam openings, and if so, let me know pronto and I would place a live trap again. To finish the job, I decided to remove the lower dam at the location of the railroad bridge in a few days' time.

Soon afterward, I met with Federal Game Warden Jim Birch at his Helena office. When I told him I intended to go blast a beaver dam, Birch said he wanted to get away from his office work, and asked to go along. We met the following morning and went to the site at the railroad bridge. In the sizable dam, there were several old weathered and deteriorated railroad ties that seemed to have been well placed in the dam's structure to add to its height and strength. Jim thought that was quite a feat on the part of the beaver and he had many good laughs while he took several photos of the beavers' engineering feat.

After I had just completed placing dynamite charges at a couple key places below the face of the dam, we heard the *putt-putt* of a railroad motorcar, and a section gang stopped to inquire what was going on. We informed the gang boss that we were about to blast away some of the dam as part of the project to solve the flooding problem. Alarmed, he told us we couldn't use dynamite that close to the railroad tracks or bridge.

Unfortunately, the charges were already set and primed, and we didn't wish to try to disarm them under such wet and muddy circumstances. The boss suggested that we had better postpone the plan until he could consult his supervisor at Helena. We tried to assure him that the charges would very likely only cause a muffled *whomp*, with little likelihood of any debris being thrown into the air and onto the railroad tracks. With the day dwindling and his crew's shift about to end he said, "Well, go ahead. But I hope you know what you are doing!"

Luckily, the dynamite charges worked as planned, so the railroad crew went on their way, and the boss's parting words were, "I hope my Super doesn't hear that I was around when you did this, but I guess you saved us lot of miserable work since we intended to tear that beaver dam out."

Before they departed, he clarified that his crew had removed those weathered, deteriorated, and dry railroad ties, and had stacked them below the bridge embankment to be disposed of later. Evidently, the beavers built more on the dam and raised the pond waters until the ties were floating free and had drifted down against the structure. The beaver then proceeded to keep adding willow material around those ties and made them part of the dam.

Beaver Deterrent

While working the Helena area, I received a complaint about beaver damage at a local long-established plant nursery. I took a couple of beaver live traps along when investigating the report, and a nursery worker accompanied me to an area where water was diverted from a nursery creek for irrigating purposes. The worker pointed out several rows of mere stubs where beaver had, with only a few bites, cut young-growth nursery trees and said, "Warden, do you realize the dollar value loss caused by the beaver?"

I investigated further and found a beaver dam in the nearby ditch, made from the trees the animals had purloined from the nursery. As per my usual procedure, I tore out a section of the dam, which allowed for an increased flow of water and lowered the above pond's water level. Knowing that the beaver would return overnight to plug the leak in the dam, I set a live trap, and not long after sundown I checked the trap and found a sizable beaver in it. I set a second live trap, but over a period of several nights caught no more critters. So, I removed the remainder of the beaver dam, and placed a loose roll of old fencing as a deterrent to prevent the dam from being rebuilt in the same spot, which was common.

Some time later, I checked the site again and found that beaver had been there and had poked numerous wood cuttings into the roll of wire, but had no success in building another dam. Pleased with my work, I passed the solution on to my colleagues, should they ever need to discourage any beaver from building another in the same location from where one was removed.

Territory Dispute

Within the fur trappers' ranks, there often arose conflicts over trapping territory rights, and some relied on the local game warden to intervene and settle the dispute. One of the quarrels involved Coyote Bill, who was very protective of his trapping territories, as he depended a lot on trapping income along with a seasonal part-time job.

Coyote Bill contacted me about an intrusion into his claimed trapping area, so I approached the accused intruder. During the course of our conversation, he told me that Coyote Bill threatened him, and then added, "That damned old fool jumped me about trapping in his territory, and considering the area is State controlled, I have as much right there as he does."

He then said Coyote Bill left and came back later with a pistol strapped around his waist, and patting the pistol, he told the fellow, "I'll tell you this just one more time, for the last time, pull stakes or else!"

The alleged trespassing trapper then told me he pulled all his traps and asked me if I thought he should file a complaint based on the threat. I knew that a State official had given the pistol-packin' Coyote Bill permission to trap the spring flow waters in exchange for him doing the work of manipulating several water control structures in order to avoid flooding and redistribute water to adjoining areas. I relayed this bit of information to Bill's opponent, and no complaint was filed related to the assumed threat.

A Last Minute Effort Before Vacation Time

My wife, Alice, and I were already packed in preparation for a long awaited vacation when I received word from a rancher that he was experiencing a beaver flooding problem in an area where he crossed a stream with hay-making implements, and the stream flooding made the crossing impossible.

Even though the situation interfered with our immediate vacation plans, I was never one to shirk responsibility, so I went to the area with my usual supply of dynamite and spent several hours placing the explosives at key areas of the beaver dam. Once the dynamite was primed with detonating caps and fuses and I moved away from the blast area. Then I regretfully remembered that I had left a small keepsake hand axe at the blast site, and when the charge went off, I saw the axe go airborne, along with the beaver dam sticks and mud. I hastily looked for the keepsake, but never found it.

Determined to finish the task at hand so I could get on with my long-awaited vacation, I then set two beaver live traps, knowing the beaver would soon return to rebuild the dam for their own security and livelihood. Before heading back home to Alice, I told the rancher that it would take awhile for the implement crossing the adequately dry up with the dam removed, and that he should check the two live traps the next day and either transplant any beaver caught to another area or do away with them, which was legal for that period of the summer. With that done, I was on my way to start my hard-earned vacation.

Required Pine Marten Tagging: A Long Distance Job

When I was assigned to the Stillwater County district, there were a few old-timers of hardy stock that trapped pine marten during wintertime, as they were quite valuable dollar-wise. I tagged pelts for some local trappers, and soon received word that a couple trappers at the distant Cooke City settlement near the Montana-Wyoming line also had marten pelts to be tagged. At that time, the Red Lodge game warden, Vern Waples, had gone back to temporary U.S. Naval duty, and as Cooke City was within his warden district, I was delegated to take care of necessary duties in his absence.

To get to Cooke City in wintertime was not an easy jaunt. As the Beartooth Pass was snowbound and closed, I had to take the long way around, which added more than 60 miles to my already 100-mile plus drive. I had to meander down through Big Timber, Livingston, and Gardiner, Montana, and then on down through Mammoth and Lamar Valley, which are both on the Wyoming side of Yellowstone Park, and then back up to Cooke City in Montana. When I finally arrived for the quick task after my long journey, I tagged the marten pelts and was fortunate enough to stay at a rooming house with the evening meal and breakfast served for a $5.00 fee. The community, at that time before snowmobiles were in use, had few but hardy occupants and even fewer accommodations.

Bear on the Loose

Over the years, I had numerous experiences that were unusual, and sometimes humorous, in live trapping mostly troublesome campground black bears. On one occasion, a small black bear was making a well-used campground his grubstake. As ordinarily happens, some of the campers were delighted because of the bear's presence. Some went to that particular campground solely because of their interest in the mooching bruin. Still, others complained about the bear's boldness and the possible danger.

To eliminate any threat to campers, I live trapped the bear and took it back to my "headquarters," which was actually my home. Since I returned too late in the day to take the bear to the planned remote release site, I put the trap in a shady location and placed a piece of heavy duty gravel screen over the trapdoor end of the enclosure so the bear wouldn't suffer from excessive heat inside the all metal trap.

Early the next morning there was a knock on the house door, and in answering I found old one-eyed trapper John Burton, a well-known local, standing on my doorstep. Skipping any customary greeting, John said, "Wayne, where did you get the pet bear?"

I replied that it wasn't a pet and warned John not to get too close to the trap. He replied, "Does he just stay around without being on a chain?"

Perplexed, I looked in the direction of the trap and that darned bear was loose and munching on the remains of a sack of dog food! Thinking quick on how to recapture the critter, I thought if I could get some pieces of bacon inside the trap, the bear might re-enter, but I had no such luck. Once the last of the dog food was gone the bear started towards town, which was only about a half mile away.

I hurriedly grabbed my sidearm and a .410 shotgun, got around the bear, and hazed it in a direction away from town. After some more shouting and shooting, I finally got the bear hustled away. Once he was out a good distance I peppered his hide with shot, which really put him in high gear. I jogged in pursuit of the bear for quite a distance, and occasionally it would stop and look back at me. Both of us were getting quite hot.

While crossing an open field with a rather deep irrigation ditch, the bear jumped in out of sight. As I arrived at the ditch, I cautiously looked over the edge of the bank and I didn't see the bear close by, but did see that it had gotten into the water and was in the ditch quite some distance away. After following it in the ditch for a half-mile or so, the bear left the cool water and started up over the opposite bank, and can you guess the next sequence of events?

By chance, there was a fellow irrigating at that location. The bear ran very near the man, who excitedly raised his shovel in a defensive pose, but the bear only hesitated long enough that it obviously scared the fellow. The terrified man quickly turned and rode away on a motorbike in a manner that would have put a motocross rider to shame, riding wildly across the field with irrigation water and mud flying! I would like to have explained what was happening, but didn't have the chance because the guy was gone.

The bear continued into the remote foothills, and I went to a hilltop where I might see if it was continuing in the direction away from the valley fields. Not over a half-mile away, I saw the bear going up an electric power pole. That particular pole was at a jog in the power line, and the hot line and neutral wire were on side brackets close in on the pole instead of on a crossarm. Watching it climb, I thought to myself, "If that bear makes contact with that high voltage wire, there will be fireworks and a dead bear, and probably a power line outage."

I watched intently as the bear climbed up some distance and clung on to the pole while it looked around, probably wondering if he would get his hide peppered again. After a while, I gave up the chase and hiked the lengthy distance back to the house. I later drove out to the pole, and saw that the bear had come down and was not to be found close by.

Tranquil Bear

At one time, the West Yellowstone city dumpsite was regularly frequented by several grizzly bears. When the dump was eventually closed by the state, the bears then caused concern and problems at various area public campgrounds. Game Warden Ken Sears was directed to live trap the bears due to the concern of public safety, and he asked me for assistance.

The two of us towed the newer culvert-type live trap to a campground with known grizzly bear problems, and notified campers to stay inside their RVs and to definitely keep their curious children and pets inside until we notified them it was safe outside. Warden Sears said he had been given a new cookie type of bear tranquilizer, which we tried on the lone grizzly appearing at the campground. The bear scarfed the cookies down, so we waited for it to follow the trail of cookies into the trap, but it only went into a tranquil state and stayed close by in the immediate campground vicinity. We continued to wait and wait, but the bear was only unsteady on its paws. As our voices attracted its attention, it came toward the front of Warden Sears' vehicle and raised up on its hind legs and fell forward over the hood, then slid backwards leaving obvious claw marks. This was very upsetting for Warden Sears, as he always took pride in a clean and undamaged vehicle. Then in a wobbly manner, the bear gained its feet and gradually went toward the nearby willow thicket and out of sight.

As it was nearing darkness, we were in a quandary as to what to do, so I went with my .357 Magnum revolver and a flashlight to where the bear was seen last and only found a bed of matted grass. After notifying all the campers of the predicament and reminding them to stay inside their RVs, we stayed in the area until after midnight with plans to return at daybreak.

When we returned in the very early morning, we scouted the willow thickets and found a couple more matted grass beds, but no bear. That was the last reporting of bears in that campground, but the complaints of grizzlies around other campgrounds and cabin sites continued until winter arrived.

There's No Place Like Home!

Having trapped another nuisance black bear at a sheep rancher's request, I brought the animal back to my home for release the following day in a more remote and relatively domestic sheep-free area. While I had the bear at my house and in the trap, I hoped to mark the bear in some manner so that if it showed up somewhere else after release, I could identify it. I had a few metal ear tags, but couldn't get the bear positioned in the trap to clamp a tag on its ear. After considerable waiting, I took my sharp sheath knife and finally was able to cut off about a quarter of one of the bear's ears. I released the bear later that day, and mostly forgot about him.

A couple months later, a valley rancher contacted me and stated a black bear was in the back area of his ranch, where it had dug down a foot or so to a dead hog carcass the rancher had buried instead of taking to a local animal carcass rendering plant. I told him I would tow the live trap out and try to catch the bear, and get it out of the valley area.

Before I set and baited the trap, I took a hunk of ham from the dead and stinking hog for trap bait. The rancher and I then covered the dead hog, set the trap, and left and stayed away until the next morning. Then, to our surprise, we had caught the bear.

Instead of taking it back to my house for later release, I went ahead and took it directly to a likely release site. Before realizing it, I looked in the trap and was surprised to see the one ear tip cut off! I then realized it was the same bear I had caught and released miles away, and it was probably heading for its original home area. So, to substantiate my belief, after I released the bear I got out an appropriate map and discovered that from that first release site to where the bear was first trapped, it was almost a direct line to this seasonal catch site—so it must have been animal homing instinct!

Bear trapped

Several reports have been filed with the State Game Warden, Wayne Fitzwater, concerning what Fitzwater terms "nuisance bears."

This week the State Fish and Game live-trapped one yearling bear in the Grasshopper area.

The bear has been transported to what officials termed a "remote area." Considerations in the re-location of the animal are "no sheep camps, no summer homes, and mainly getting the bear away from the people it has become dependent upon," said Fitzwater.

The trap used is a barrel type which is made from a large culvert with a gate at one end. The trap is portable, with wheels beneath it for easy mobility.

Bait for the nuisance bear can be anything "attractive to bears," according to Fitzwater.

(Source: *The Dillon Daily Tribune-Examiner*, date unknown)

Rigors of the Job:
Hunting Happenings

A Bull Moose Down in a Swampy Area

One moose hunting area in my patrol district was a huge swampy expanse, and the extensive willow growth within created a moose haven. Most moose permit hunters didn't venture into the swamp, but instead hunted the outer fringes. Keeping this in mind, I hiked up an adjoining steep slope to a high vantage point where I could view much of the surrounding landscape through my binoculars. Scanning the scenery, I caught sight of a moose hunter working his way into the swamp. The hunter took aim and shot a bull moose. The following scene continued to hold my attention as I watched the fellow kneel over the belly of the moose. The man walked around the carcass several times, but there was no indication that he was field dressing the animal. It was even more puzzling that a couple times he sat down on the moose carcass and smoked a cigarette.

Thoroughly intrigued, I decided to leave my elevated position and go check the fellow's activity. After hiking over the frost-heaves and swampy areas, I approached the hunter and it was obvious he had not field dressed the animal. The hunter said his hunting knife was so dull, he had to pound on it to puncture the moose's belly. He told me his kids had dulled it while they used it for their own play.

Fortunately, I had a good, sharp sheath knife and belt saw to cut open the rib cage and split the pelvic bone of the moose. Unfortunately, it was going to be a difficult chore to get the carcass out of the swampy terrain and onto the road. Even quartering the beast and carrying it out in pieces would still require Herculean strength and energy. The hunter, although proud of his hunting success, then realized his predicament.

Since I knew most of the ranchers and settlers in that remote valley area, I advised the hunter that one fellow living a mile or so away had horses he used for logging and firewood cutting. It was possible he may consider trying to retrieve the moose carcass, but would likely charge a hefty fee due to the swamp and distance to the road.

I then left the hunter to his own devices so I could go about my patrolling duties. Before I took my leave, I told the fellow I would check back later in the day to determine the outcome. While making my rounds, I thought of the numerous hunters I had met bagging a big game animal without thinking about where they were, or the very trying job of getting a big game carcass out to a loading point.

Later, on my way back to check on the man and his moose, I came across the settler with his team of work horses. They had just gotten the moose carcass out to the road, and I wasn't surprised to see the horses drenched with sweat and black swamp muck on their legs nearly up to their bellies. Owing to the swampy conditions, they had to use 150-feet of heavy rope to drag the moose carcass out little by little. Overhearing the conversation between the hunter and the horseman, the fee for the work was $100. The hunter gladly paid the horseman in cash, and both were happy, smiling men.

A Method for Hunting Moose

While patrolling an area adjacent to a stream with lots of willow growth, and looking for late fall and early winter fishermen, I came across a hunter. I checked the man's permits, and finding a valid moose permit, we began talking about his experiences the previous day. The fellow stated he had hunted the dense willow bottom the day before, and had seen some fresh moose signs, but thought that kind of hunting was by chance and dangerous due to the dense foliage and inability to see any distance.

I advised the hunter that he might be confronted by a cow moose with a calf, and it could be a risky encounter in the thick willows. The fellow then asked me about the known moose populations for that area, and if any sizable bull moose had been seen during an aerial census of the region. I assured the hunter that the area had a significant moose population and a fair share of bulls. I then suggested that he go up the mountain slope adjacent to the creek and locate a vantage point where he could scan the willow bottom area to locate a moose and possibly shoot one from the slope, or to stalk the moose in the willows.

Taking my leave, I continued to patrol for the day and soon forgot about my meeting with the moose hunter. A couple days later, I received a phone call from the man who said the plan I suggested had enabled him to shoot a nice bull moose. He told me he was very grateful to have had a successful hunt, and very much appreciated the suggested method, which proved fruitful.

Details of a First Deer Hunt

In the various warden districts where I was assigned, I helped with the yearly Montana Hunter Safety program. When at Dillon, my daughter, Lorri Anne, went through the program and was awarded the course completion certificate. As a reward, I promised Lorri I would take her deer hunting so she could use her rifle sighting skills she had practiced.

When the time was right, the two of us got up very early in the morning and went to a mule deer area where we scanned the slopes and soon spotted a four-point buck at an ideal range. At home, she had practiced some sighting using a decorative twelve-inch high bronze horse as a target, which I had marked from the back of the shoulder/spine area down to the heart area, as a vital and quite large target for a killing shot.

As she was zeroing in to fire a shot on the buck, I said, "Perhaps you should hold a little high due to the range."

She fired the shot and the bullet hit the hillside just over the deer's back. If Dad had not made that statement, she would undoubtedly have downed the buck with the first shot. Not long afterward, a forked-horn buck was spotted and, not being unwisely coached, Lorri downed the buck with one clean shot. She was eager to help field dress the animal, and was very interested in the deer's internal organs. Afterward, dragging the buck carcass the considerable distance off the mountain slope, she climbed inside the open cavity for a ride down the mountain to our vehicle.

Lorri is still an outdoor enthusiast, and her successful hunt is a compliment to her hunting ability. I hope that all fathers with daughters are as equally proud as I am of my Lorri. Being "just" a small town girl then, she has since worked over 37 years as a locomotive engineer for the Southern Pacific and Union Pacific railroads, and is now retired.

Documenting My Presence

During the upper Gallatin Canyon extended elk hunts, I put in many snowshoeing hours patrolling in the deep snow, covering hunting areas away from the canyon highway where numerous hunters parked in the turnouts and used binoculars to view surrounding vistas for elk migrating out of Yellowstone National Park. Instead, I regularly patrolled areas where elk migrated to lower country for better foraging. One such patrol was up the Teepee Creek region and then south toward the national park boundary, where some hardy hunters thought it to be a likely place to bag an elk.

While patrolling along the park boundary, I periodically contacted hunters following an animal blood trail to the park edge, as had happened on more than one occasion. However, they were advised to definitely not enter the park in pursuit of an elk with their guns. So when I met hunters in this particular predicament, I would snowshoe into the park following the blood trail on their behalf, and in two instances came across a dead elk only a short distance from the open hunting area. I would then backtrack to the waiting hunter and inform him to leave his rifle outside the park, and the two of us would go and field dress the animal. With much difficulty, we would drag it out whole or one half at a time back to the open hunting area. Certainly, this was against the strict Yellowstone Park rules and a no-no procedure that could have gotten me fired from my job if discovered, but the fact that the elk was shot in the legal hunting areas influenced me to let the hunters claim the animals instead of leaving the carcasses for predators or to spoil.

As a matter of interest, along the park boundary some distance toward Crown Butte, there stands a large old Douglas Fir tree. When I lived and worked in the Gallatin Canyon in the late 1930s as part of the Civilian Conservation Corps, I was there with district forest ranger Vern Edwards. While stopping one day in 1939 to eat a lunch near that big tree, I penciled my and the ranger's name on a scarred pitchy side of the tree trunk, never thinking that at some future date I would be there again. But, as fate would have it, I was there as a game warden in the early 1950s and again in 1977, when I put my name and date to the tree once more.

A Bridge with Limitations

Along the snowy and icy highways near the extended elk hunting spots in the upper Gallatin Canyon, the snowplows made turnouts and many of the "not too ambitious" hunters would park their vehicles and regularly use binoculars to scan surrounding areas. Immediately adjacent to the northwest park boundary of Yellowstone, there was a regular elk migration route across the Gallatin River Sawmill Flat area. It was often an area of overkill for elk, mostly because once any rifle shots were fired, the elk would mill around in a group and a hunter would keep shooting until he was satisfied he had an elk down. After it was evident that more elk were downed than hunters on the west side of the river, it was encouragement for some of the observing hunters settled in their warm vehicles to trudge through the deep snow and hopefully claim and tag an elk.

Having knowledge of the ordinarily deep snow and frigid conditions, I went prepared to snowshoe many areas where hardy and serious hunters were hopeful of getting an elk, even though it meant an arduous task to drag that elk carcass out to the highway. When I arrived for patrol duty one particular winter day, I brought a long roll of highway department wire and slatted snow fence, which I laboriously loaded on my toboggan and pulled the couple or more hundreds of yards to the river's edge. I knew the Gallatin River would be mostly frozen, but would have areas of open water, making it very risky to cross to the west side.

Selecting a frozen over area, I unrolled the fencing on top of the ice, which formed a type of treaded bridge for hunters to safely cross on foot. I put two long stakes at each end and flagged the stakes with strips torn from my red bandana for visual markers. I then passed the word around to several hunters about the safer crossing.

As usual, it snowed for the next couple of days, and early one morning as I had just arrived in the area, I observed a horseback hunter riding parallel to the river. Once the hunter saw the many human footprints crossing the river where the flagged stakes were obvious, he assumed that was a good river crossing. About halfway across, the horse broke through the snow covered slatted fence and was belly deep in the river and floundering dangerously.

I quickly summoned help from several nearby hunters, and with a lot of effort we got the horse free. I then explained the footbridge arrangement to the horseback hunter, who vented his anger very vocally, and openly stated what a "hare-brained" idea it was for such a deceiving structure to be installed. But, no lawsuit was filed!

Negotiated Hunter Truce

As mentioned before, I regularly snowshoe-patrolled an area adjacent to the northwest boundary of Yellowstone Park where, depending on the severity of the winter and snow conditions, many elk were migrating to lower elevations for winter food sources. I had snowshoed a couple of miles to an area where elk regularly traveled down the canyon and soon heard some rifle shots. I headed in that direction and stopped to view the area with my binoculars and it wasn't long before I saw two hunters hurrying as best as possible in the deep snow toward an obvious elk carcass.

When I was somewhat closer, I saw the two men with arms flying about, and in a confrontation with each other, as they were both trying to shove the other. I hastened there while the conflict between the two hunters continued, and I yelled for them to stop their arguing so I might know the cause when both hunters blurted out, "That's my elk!"

Not knowing the exact circumstances, I asked just where each hunter was standing when he shot at the elk, and it was evident that they were quite some distance apart. I then checked the elk carcass for bullet entry holes, and in rolling the carcass over it showed that both men had fired rifle shots that would have been fatal. After getting the two hunters settled down from their quarrel, I advised them that one of the hunters must legally tag the elk or I would confiscate it. I asked them how long they each intended to hunt and both replied, "To the end of the limited hunting period."

With that in mind, I suggested that they split the elk carcass between them. Then, the one with a remaining elk tag could buddy up with his opponent, and if another elk was shot they could also split that one between them. They agreed that this seemed like a reasonable solution. Sure enough, a second elk was later shot and divided. The two men were seen at a local bar that evening once again showing signs of friendship and camaraderie. It was gratifying to realize their confrontation ended in a peaceful and friendly manner.

An Order from Headquarters

While I was called to duty during the upper Gallatin Canyon extended elk hunt, word came down the line to us game wardens that all elk hunters must shoot and tag their own elk. This was meant to warn of situations that were common in larger hunting parties, where it was known that quite regularly one hunter in the group would try to shoot as many elk as there were in the hunting party if he had the opportunity.

For several early mornings, there was an overkill of elk at an area adjacent to the Yellowstone Park boundary. Since I was snowshoeing in the area, I knew I would be field dressing elk most of the day and red-tagging quite a few animals (confiscating on behalf of the state), which would be quite a task before the day's end.

After I had field dressed a couple of elk, I saw that several hunters had left their warm vehicles on the side of the road, and were trudging through the deep snow toward the scattered overkill area. While I was at my third downed elk, a nearby hunter called out to me, "Is there one I can tag?"

Remembering the orders from headquarters for each hunter to shoot and tag his own elk, I told the hunter, "If you want it, then shoot it."

The hunter replied, "Hell, the elk is dead. I'd feel like a damn fool to shoot it."

But, when I explained the circumstances to him, the hunter shot the elk in the head. I then hurriedly explained the dictate to others nearby that each hunter shall shoot and properly tag his own animal to claim it. You can imagine the reluctance and foolish feeling to shoot an already dead animal. In this manner, I managed to effortlessly pass on quite a number of elk that I would have otherwise field dressed and red-tagged for the state. I suggested to the "successful" hunters that they not relate the circumstances of this elk giveaway when at one of the many restaurants and bars in the canyon, but evidently someone did.

Several days later, my regional warden sergeant indicated he had something to discuss with me, and with dread, I knew what it was he wanted to talk about! I well knew my actions were not acceptable or routine. Knowing how many hunters at the end of a day would frequent the several canyon watering holes and spread word of my unorthodox method of managing the overkill, I realized that the procedure must come to an end, and if it did not I would be facing a reprimand of some consequence from the higher-ups in the Fish & Game ranks.

The Making of a Small Avalanche

While on foot patrol duty in the upper Gallatin during the late winter extended elk hunt, I was snowshoeing the fringe of a closed to hunting area. I heard a couple of rifle shots seemingly within the closed area, so I snowshoed the quarter of a mile and finally spotted a lone hunter, and when closer, I saw the hunter standing alongside a sizable bull elk carcass.

The hunter hadn't yet tagged the elk so I checked his license and permit for the special hunt, then advised the fellow that the area was off-limits to hunting and as a consequence, a citation would be issued. The guy shrugged and said, "It was worth it to get such a trophy bull."

He was not at all happy when I advised him that the elk would be confiscated as property of the State of Montana. He exclaimed, "What? There is no way you are going to confiscate my bull!" while I affixed the red tag to the carcass.

After a serious exchange of harsh words, I finally convinced the hunter that our present location wasn't the best place to settle the disagreement. Before we parted ways, I made sure to tell him that he'd be hearing from me at his temporary quarters down in the canyon.

When I returned to district headquarters, I relayed my interaction with the hunter to my supervisor, who decided to go with me to visit the culprit and help further clarify matters. We didn't have much of a chance to get a word in edgewise, as the hunter greeted us with a hostile tone, saying, "I'll see you in court!"

Evidently, his contact with a Bozeman lawyer must have convinced him that the procedure was according to Fish & Game regulations after all, as he later accepted the citation and the Fish & Game Department confiscated his prize bull elk.

The bull elk was shot at a high elevation, and with the very deep snow it was a real hassle to drag it out of the area. The warden captain designated a couple other wardens to accompany me to drag the elk out, and about halfway there one of them said, "How much farther is it?" and added, "Fitzwater, what in the hell were you doing up here?"

Due to the snow depth, dragging the large elk carcass created a small avalanche. At each effort to drag it down the steep slope, a new miniature avalanche would actually bury the carcass, making the drag difficult. Suffice it to say, the two not too ambitious wardens that accompanied me had a good day's workout.

An Improvised Manner of Retrieving an Elk Carcass

While I was patrolling an area of considerable elk hunting activity and the associated nearby hunter camps on foot one day, I had covered quite an expansive range and knew the several vehicle access trails to the area. At one point I observed a vehicle track going around the gentle slope of the mountainside, so I followed it for some distance and soon heard a vehicle engine running at various speeds. As I walked up to the vehicle, I was surprised to see a hunter behind the steering wheel, talking on a portable radio.

When the fellow saw me, he spoke into the radio and said "Hold it, hold it." He then stepped out of the vehicle, and explained the proceedings he and his hunting partners had undertaken. He showed me their method of retrieving an elk carcass quite a distance down the steeper slope below. The three-man hunting group had jacked up the vehicle's rear end, and mounted a wide tireless rim loaded with yards and yards of nylon rope. Two men went down the slope to the downed and dressed elk carcass, then called by radio to the vehicle operator and dispatched orders on when or when not to drag the elk, considering it would hang up at the base of the trees and on a couple wind-fallen logs.

After learning the basics of their arrangement, I went down to the two men and the elk to check for the proper hunting licenses and animal tag. Everything was right by the law, so I made my exit. I knew the retrieval would be a slow undertaking, so I didn't bother to stay until the task was over.

P. O. BOX 33

BILLINGS ROD AND GUN CLUB BILLINGS, MONTANA 59103

February 2, 1970

Frank Dunkle, Director,
Montana Fish & Game Department
Helena, Montana

Director Dunkle:

We, John Michalies and Gary Hjelseth, would like to express our sincere thanks and along with it a word of commendation to one of your personnel whom we met during the special elk hunt in the Gallatin. The person we speak of is Mr. Wayne Fitzwater, a game warden out of Dillon, Montana. We feel that Wayne did us a service above and beyond what his duties would normally prescribe.

We had a large elk down in the Buffalo Creek area, and my hunting partner Gary had walked out to procure a snowmobile to remove the elk from off the mountain. Approximately forty-five minutes after Gary's departure Wayne arrived at my location. He immediately made check of my permit and that I had properly tagged my elk. Wayne then asked if I had a way to remove the elk, at which time I informed him that my buddy had left about forty-five minutes ago to procure a snowmobile.

Wayne then helped me cut open the neck of my elk with his saw, so that I could get the rest of the windpipe out, asked me if I was cold, as I had been standing around in the wind waiting, and offered to build a fire for me. I said it wasn't necessary as I would keep moving around to keep warm. Wayne radioed down the hill to a mobile unit to try and locate Gary, but to no avail as he had already departed the parking area with a snowmobile.

Due to deep snow on the hill it took Gary and the snowmobile operator over two hours to get within 100

"DON'T LET CONSERVATION END WITH CONVERSATION"

P. O. BOX 33
BILLINGS ROD AND GUN CLUB BILLINGS, MONTANA 59103

yards of Wayne and me. Wayne had assured me that he wouldn't leave me until I and my elk were on the way off the mountain. When the snowmobile couldn't get the rest of the way to us Wayne attempted to break trail for it with his snowshoes. When that failed he unhooked the sled, which was attached to the snowmobile, pulled it over to me, helped load the elk, took off his belt, hooked it to the sled and started pulling the elk down the hill to where the snowmobile could meet us. After all of this he left us to go in search of others who might have needed aid. All of this took place from about 2 P.M. until 4:30 P.M. on the 28th day of January 1970.

We would like to say that Wayne is a great credit to the Montana Fish & Game Department. We would like to have this letter placed in his employee file and would request that a copy (enclosed) be sent to Wayne as we do not have his address.

As dedicated sportsmen and members of the Billings Rod & Gun Club we assure you that this incident of unselfishness shall be related to our friends and fellow members.

In closing, we remain

Sincerely yours,

John P. Michalies

Gary Hjelseth

John Michalies
Gary Hjelseth

cc: Commission Chairman
Wayne Fitzwater (copy enclosed)

"DON'T LET CONSERVATION END WITH CONVERSATION"

Exhausting Surveillance

In the community of Dillon, where I lived and worked for the later part of my career, I had received hints over a period of time that a local avid elk hunter had killed elk with "borrowed" elk tags from various college students and then provided the elk meat to the financially struggling pupils. I had this in mind when I observed the fellow traveling toward one of his favorite elk hunting areas. So, along with Warden Secor, we followed the hunter to where he parked his vehicle and took off on foot in the approximately 18-inch deep snow.

Holding back until the hunter was out of sight, we then parked our vehicle. I followed the hunter and Warden Secor stayed at the vehicle. I soon realized it was tough going without snowshoes in the deep snow and steep slopes with dead wind-fallen trees blocking my path. I was surprised at the fast pace of the long-legged and hardy hunter. I was even more surprised at the number of elk the hunter had spooked from their beds, and by their fleeing tracks was perplexed that they were not targets, as I had heard no shooting.

Late in the afternoon, I arrived back at the vehicle quite exhausted, and was advised by Warden Secor that he had checked the hunter as he finished his hunt. The hunter still had an unused and valid elk tag and no indication of any violation, and he stayed by a warming bonfire until I returned to the car wet, tired, and hungry.

After I retired, I worked alongside the suspected hunter, and in our friendly conversations I recanted the details of the unsuccessful elk hunt. The fellow said he was very surprised at being checked by an unfamiliar game warden, and at that time, didn't know that I was on his trail all day. Then he said, "That day I had a premonition that my elk hunting activity wasn't normal, and could be a source of embarrassment for me in the local community."

Considering he was professor at the college where he got his "borrowed" tags, he wasn't wrong!

Truck Stuck, Stuck, Stuck

When I was assigned to the Helena-Townsend district I had a large domain to patrol, which included the Lincoln area. During one patrol, the town's deputy sheriff indicated he was informed that spotlighting was observed on a couple creek-side roads out of Lincoln, so I stayed in the area for nighttime patrol. After several hours of observing vehicle traffic on a couple roads, I saw a suspect vehicle with two occupants and an obvious gun in the pickup cab. When the vehicle turned off the main Blackfoot highway onto a side road, I felt confident the men were up to no good.

Once they had gone a piece up the road, I followed at a distance so as not to be seen and used a special "blackout" light to follow them on the narrow unimproved road. I had also installed a cutout switch on my brake light wiring so they would not be a giveaway when slowing down or stopping. Sure enough, the men soon started using a spotlight to view areas to the sides and ahead of their vehicle, and it was not long before they spotted a doe deer, but did not shoot at it.

A couple miles up the narrow road it split two ways, and I took the left track as it appeared that the two sets of wheel tracks headed the same direction. As I concentrated on watching and listening for gunshots, I had sped up somewhat to close the distance between us, and I suddenly realized that I had unknowingly driven into a swampy area and was completely stuck. When I got out to look at my predicament, I found that the sod covered area was wet and spongy and the front wheels had broken through the surface, causing the vehicle's front end to sink down to the undercarriage.

By then it was late at night, but I decided I would somehow try to get the vehicle back on solid ground. After anchoring the rear trailer hitch to a roadside tree using a type of come-along, I started shoveling and cribbing underneath. I had a high lift jack, and dug under the front bumper and used one of two spare wheels as a base for the jack. Once I had the front end lifted, I cut down some nearby 4- to 6-inch diameter trees for cribbing, and then laid them in lengths that I put under the front wheels in a corduroy fashion. I next used the come-along to inch the vehicle back toward solid ground. I had to repeat this procedure over and over again, which took all night and well into mid-morning the next day. At one point, the high lift jack forced the spare wheel I was using as a base down into the mud at a depth that I couldn't retrieve. It is undoubtedly there yet today!

Throughout my ordeal, I had hoped that the two intended poachers may come back out on that same road and be surprised that a game warden was on their tail, but they must have left the area another way and never realized they were being followed.

A Big Game Hunt with a Questionable Ending

After my retirement, I continued to hunt periodically. On one such occasion, I attended a hunt organized by a friend who had invited a few others to join our party to hunt a rather isolated area for deer. The day did not yield much success for us, unfortunately. Not having bagged any deer, our hunting group left the area and followed a rather indistinct roadway. In some places, this roadway served as the boundary between two separate hunting districts.

The intent of district boundaries was, and still is, to properly manage the deer and elk in the two management districts. Within each separate hunting district the bag limits for elk, deer, and sometimes antelope were different, with the objective of harvesting a particular big game animal to assure perpetuation and proper management of all of them within each district.

While the hunting group was traveling along the rudimentary roadway en route to intersect with a county road, we surprisingly encountered a small group of elk and reflexively shot elk for most members of the hunting group. To have come across elk in that particular region was uncommon, as elk in the two hunting districts were ordinarily back toward the timbered areas that were more generally considered their normal habitat.

When arriving back at our home base, at least one of the hunters in the group stated that he had given it some thought and surmised that the elk kill was in the wrong district. Given my work history, I was familiar with several game management boundaries that were somewhat indistinct as compared to most that used an established and obvious roadway, river, stream, or a mountain ridge top or divide to demarcate the division between two districts. Quite understandably, this revelation left me feeling unsettled, but I knew the elk kill was in the proper area. If I had it to do over again, I would have returned to the questionable area with a Fish & Game Department official to substantiate it to be the proper hunting district by a short measure, if only for my peace of mind.

I had told a couple of the hunters in the group that it would be wise not to repeat the one hunter's claim of wrongdoing related to the hunting area boundary, but it finally became questionable until I accompanied a Fish & Game warden there for verification.

Rigors of the Job:
Making the Rounds

An Uncontrollable Boat on a Windy Reservoir

I was patrolling a reservoir area for fishing and boating activities one time, scanning the area with my binoculars. After a while, a very strong wind came in unexpectedly, and it was obvious that several mid-reservoir boaters were attempting to get back to their launching sites at the marina. The surface wave action had developed into a treacherous category, and several smaller boats headed for the nearest shoreline for safety. Those with inadequate outboard motor power could not make any headway en route to the marina, and finally beached their boats far from their desired destinations.

With all the smaller boats accounted for, I then concentrated my attentions on a pontoon-type watercraft with a lone occupant. Even though the surface waves weren't endangering the craft, the fellow was at the mercy of the wind. Due to the buoyancy of the pontoons, he was being blown toward a rocky shoreline, and finally was pounded onto the shoreline rocks. Once ashore, the fellow abandoned the craft and left on foot, headed toward the nearest road.

Sometime later, I caught up with the frustrated boater. After the man related his reservoir experiences, he said to me, "Warden, my pontoon boat is on the rocky shoreline, and probably beat up. If you will take me to my truck and trailer at the marina, you can have the damn boat! I'll give you the necessary papers to show it's yours, too."

Of course, I gave him a ride and declined the offer of a free boat. I later learned that the marina owner retrieved the boat, and after some repairs to the battered craft, he put it to use.

A Strange and Unusual Find on the River

I patrolled the Big Hole River by canoe quite regularly, checking fishing and trapping activities. Prior to one such patrol, I was told that a truck driver traveling the highway adjacent to the river had lost a large wheel with a mounted tire from his truck bed, and the wheel had bounced off the side of the highway, down a slope, and into the Big Hole River.

Concentrating on my patrol activities, I had nearly forgotten about the report of the lost wheel. But, lo and behold, several miles downstream I saw it had washed up on a river island sandbar. I attempted to load the sizable wheel across the bow of the canoe, but soon realized it was extremely heavy. Eventually, I did manage to get it loaded onto the canoe, but when I maneuvered the boat into the river current, I quickly discovered that the weight made the bow sink quite low in the water. This made the canoe very difficult to handle and the bottom would grind across the rocky river bed in the more shallow parts of the river. After much difficulty getting to my river take-out point, I was lucky to see a nearby fisherman. The two of us really had to struggle to get the wheel loaded into my pickup truck. With the assistance of the Melrose, Montana deputy sheriff, the wheel was eventually picked up by the trucking company.

A Fish Called Ling

Before construction of Beaverhead County's Clark Canyon Dam and Reservoir (Hap Hawkins' Lake), most fishermen were fishing for trout and whitefish during the winter. After construction, the ling (Burbot) population thrived in the reservoir. When caught, nearly all fishermen threw them aside, and many were left hooked on a fishing line and hung on a nearby fence. Only a very few old-timers fished the rivers for ling prior to the filling of the reservoir.

I had worked the Missouri River areas where setline fishing for ling was common, so I knew they were a desirable and edible fish. Therefore, I went to the Dillon newspaper and had an article printed to clarify the value of ling for the growing fishermen activity on the reservoir. The article was a success, and many were pleased to catch ling for eating, especially anglers who did ice-hole fishing in the winter months.

One such group of winter fishermen particularly delighted in fishing for ling, and when I stopped to check their permits, they invited me to join them in their fish fry, buttered bread, and beer outing. They had a propane camp stove, a large vat for boiling water to scald the fish so that the skin could be pulled off the carcass quite easily, and then filleted for deep frying in another container of hot cooking oil. I gladly accepted the invitation and enjoyed the bread and delicious fish, but abstained from the tempting beer—a taboo while on duty!

A Handful of Trout

During summer months, state fish trucks arrived at the Clark Canyon Reservoir to release trout of mostly fingerling size. On one occasion at the south shore of the reservoir, the small trout were being released and soon afterward a large fish was seen offshore literally gulping down several of the small fishes on the reservoir surface water.

There was a shore fisherman nearby, so I approached him and asked the fellow if he happened to have a treble hook in his tackle box. The fellow said he did, but it was on a large lure. I borrowed the fisherman's rod and attached the lure with a treble hook, then cast several times out beyond the gulping fish. Soon the fish was snagged and reeled in to shore.

To the astonishment of all, it was a hefty ling! I opened up the ling's entrails and exposed five of the fingerling trout. It was a surprise to reveal the ling as a predator on live trout.

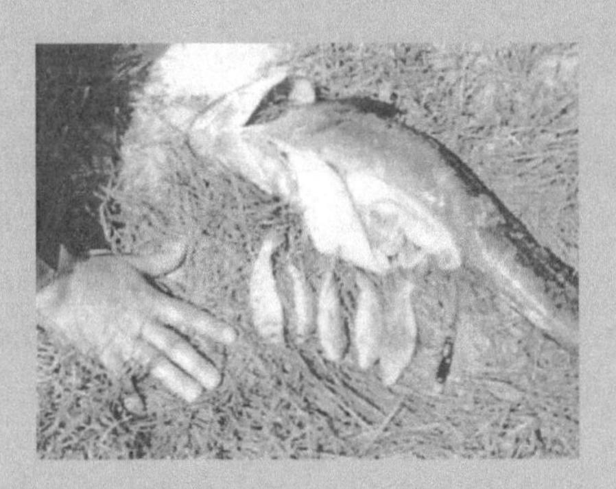

Stubbornly Producing a Valid Fishing License

One mountain lake in southwest Montana was located near the boundary between two warden districts. Therefore, another warden and I shared patrol of the good fishing lake. On a day when I was on patrol duty at the lake, I hiked the trail from the jeep road to the lake shore, and spotted a group of four fishing along the opposite shore. I gradually worked my way over rockslide and heavy wind-fallen timber to check the fishermen. When I asked them to produce their fishing licenses, three did so, but the fourth fisherman refused. I asked him a couple more times, but I continued to get no cooperative response. I then advised him that unless he produced a fishing license, he would be issued a citation for failure to do so.

Apparently he didn't like what I had to say, since he then got quite mouthy and somewhat aggressive. I took one of his companions aside and asked what prompted his friend's attitude, and he replied, "It's booze talking, as he is inclined to be stubborn and aggressive when drinking."

I suggested that the complying fishermen take their friend aside and convince him to settle down and produce the license that they knew he had, or he would receive a citation and very likely be placed under arrest and taken to a justice of the peace court miles away. I also reminded them that to resist arrest or to continue his aggressiveness would be a much more serious violation, with much more serious consequences.

One of the other fishermen said, "Warden, do you know who this fellow is?"

Not impressed by his implied stature, I replied, "No, but that has no bearing on the situation."

"He is a nationally recognized horse jockey, with a stubborn attitude," his friend answered.

After some period of time to think about the problem, the obstinate jockey finally produced a valid fishing license, but without an acceptable or apologetic reply.

An Over Eager Game Warden

A colleague of mine was checking a fisherman at a roadside lake one afternoon. When he asked for the angler's fishing license, the man said it was in his car, parked a hundred yards or so away on the road. As the fisherman left to go get his license, he handed the fishing rod, with baited hook and line still in the water, to his wife. While the man was gone, the warden asked the lady for her license. She indicated that she did not have one, because she didn't fish...so, she received a citation!

Unexpectedly Tipsy-Turvy

Not often, but on occasion, I had help patrolling when there was more than average hunting activity in an area. On one such occasion, Warden Secor assisted me and was driving us along a gravelly road when I asked that he pull aside so I could use binoculars to scan an area of hunter activity. That gravel road lead over the Continental Divide to Leadore, Idaho and had been plowed free of snow earlier in the day.

When Warden Secor pulled the vehicle over, it suddenly tipped over on its side and was embedded in the deep snow, on the downhill side of the road. Secor's vehicle door was buried in the deep snow, so we both had to crawl upward to get out on the passenger side, which wasn't an easy exit. Once up on the solid roadbed, we realized what had happened. The grader snowplow, with its snow blade and extra side wing to force snow farther off the roadway, had picked up road gravel and spread it out and aside so it appeared as part of the roadbed.

We waited over an hour for someone to come by, and then heard the snowplow coming back down from the end of the plowing at the state line. Old John Prohosky, the grader operator, saw our predicament and stopped to offer assistance. With a lot of shoveling to get a log-chain attached to the underside of the vehicle, and more shoveling to clear a path through the deep snow up to the roadway, we finally got the vehicle back up on the road. Not to be deterred by our setback, we then continued on our day's patrol thanks to the helpful efforts of Old John!

Gulley Jumping

During one vehicle patrol with Warden Secor along, I decided to travel a ridge road, which was a shorter route to a small community having a gas station and a small restaurant. The gas gauge showed that we were low on fuel and we were hungry, so we headed for town. The ground was snow-covered and there were no other vehicle tire tracks, but Warden Secor and I had been over that mountain vehicle trail a couple years previously when it was passable.

As we went over a hill, the rough road sloped downward and the road center had washed out somewhat, forming a shallow gulley. A short distance beyond, the washed out center of the narrow road deepened to a couple more feet, then to about three feet. It would have been impossible to back up the distance to the top of the grade so, very cautiously, we kept going, barely straddling the deep washout. After about half a mile, the water had diverted off to the side, but left a washed out trench across one vehicle track, so we were forced to spend an hour or more filling it in with rocks, logs, etc. We then drove safely across and on to the small village for much needed gas and heartily welcomed food. I then phoned the nearby county sheriff's office and advised them about the hazardous road conditions, as the road was used somewhat frequently by hunters and persons traveling that mountain area.

On the Job Sabotage

I made good use of the many old U.S. Forest Service patrol cabins located in various areas around southwestern Montana. While staying at one patrol cabin in a region with considerable elk hunting, I parked my obvious Fish & Game licensed and decaled vehicle alongside the cabin and patrolled the surrounding elk hunting areas on foot, which meant being away in the field all day.

Returning to the cabin quite exhausted and hungry one evening, I immediately went inside for food and rest. The next morning I needed some gear from the driver's side of the vehicle, and then went out for the day's patrol. When I made it back to the cabin late in the day, I was again tired and hungry and went straight inside without noticing something was amiss.

On the third day I patrolled as usual. When I returned to the cabin, I needed an item from the toolbox on passenger side of the pickup bed. It was only then that I noticed that both tires on that side were flat!

I checked and saw that the valve caps with the valve cores had been removed and both tires were completely deflated. However, having had such experiences through the years as a game warden, I always went afield well equipped. I had replacement valve cores and valve caps, and a tire hand pump and vehicle jacks—so the sabotage didn't strand me as intended!

Outside the USFS Divide patrol cabin near upper Ruby River

An Unforeseen Snowmobiling Hazard

One blustery winter day, Game Warden Art Warner and I were en route to a popular snowmobiling area when a blizzard swiftly blew in around us. Thankfully, we were traveling in sight of one another, and I was off to one side and a short distance behind Warner in order to avoid the additional flying snow given off from his machine. Suddenly, Warner and his snowmobile were no longer visible, so I stopped to get my bearings and find my companion.

Off to the side, I spied Warner stuck down in a bowl-like depression that spanned about ten feet wide. I shouted down to him and asked if he was okay, while trudging through the deep snow to him. When I finally reached him, we both checked Warner's snowmobile. Luckily, it had landed slightly nose-first but upright, and was in good shape with the engine still running.

In looking at the fairly steep slopes around the bowl, we grew quite concerned about how to get the snowmobile up and out to continue our patrol. I decided to stomp out an inclined upward trail on one side of the snow bowl. With enough width, it would allow the vehicle to go up without tipping over. It was a tiring and arduous effort, especially with the well-insulated snowmobile suit and heavy underclothing I was wearing. After flattening out a trail for Warner's machine, I then waddled up to my snowmobile for a length of rope to help hold his machine in place while attempting to get it up to a level area. Fortunately, we were successful and were able to continue on for the day's patrol!

Snowmobile Patrol Challenges and Problems

During the time that the Montana Fish & Game Department was saddled with snowmobile patrol to ensure proper licensing and to control machine noise levels, the wardens made rounds in some remote areas of considerable snowmobile activity. Many game wardens didn't readily accept the snowmobile patrol as part of their duties related to wildlife matters, but it was still a requirement at the time.

One such patrol was in the Cooke City area near the northeast entrance to Yellowstone Park, where there was plenty of deep and troublesome snow. As usual, there were numerous enthusiasts gathered there. Some were in the partying mood, causing questionable and unacceptable pursuits for some merrymakers, which was followed by the issuance of appropriate Fish & Game complaints. Quite a lot of snowmobilers enjoying the large expanse of snowy country gave in to the addictive call of the open road and went beyond their abilities speed-wise and safety-wise, which then normally required some manner of rescue. Many snowmobilers attained unbelievable speeds with the forward terrain appearing endless and without obstacles, but the limited visibility due to blowing snow and white-out conditions led to numerous mishaps. Luckily, none were of a very serious nature.

Uncontrolled Snowmobiling

At one time the Montana Fish & Game Department purchased some snowmobiles for game warden use, as the wardens were responsible for snowmobile patrol. The department purchased snowmobiles on a low bid basis, and one purchase was a real lemon since it was heavy and drastically unbalanced.

While I was patrolling an area frequented by some snowmobilers, the snow conditions on the narrow mountain road made it tough going, and at one siding place the snowmobile veered off over the road's edge and down the steep, steep slope to a creek bottom that had a lot of willow and aspen growth. Luckily, and with some skill, I rode the downhill-racing snowmobile and managed to maneuver between the trees in an aspen grove. As there were no trails except cattle paths in that creek bottom, I had to cut downed and dead aspen trees and some willows to finally get to a leveling out location. The undertaking took about seven hours and I didn't make it out until late in the night.

A Sizable Drag of Elk

During one extended elk hunt in the upper Gallatin Canyon area, there was a report of elk overkill in the Taylor Forks and Little Wapiti Creek areas, so I went out to investigate. I ended up field dressing and confiscating several elk. To get the dressed elk carcasses out of the remote and deep-snowed area, I asked for snowmobile assistance. Game Warden Sears, from West Yellowstone, had leased a double track Skidoo and offered to help get the elk carcasses out to the main road.

We dragged three of the elk carcasses to where we could hitch them to the Skidoo, but there was still one carcass down in a recessed bowl-like snow-covered area. Wardens Sears and I went down in the depression to the felled cow elk so we could try and pull it up the ravine. While we were there, a sizable snow slide broke loose upslope without warning, and if it hadn't been for a large fir tree on the upper edge of the small snow bowl that split the fast traveling snow, we both would undoubtedly have been partially buried. After floundering to free ourselves, we realized the cow elk carcass was completely buried under four feet of snow, and we both agreed that it could stay there.

Once we hitched the other three elk carcasses behind the double track Skidoo, and riding double, we realized what a remarkable feat it was for us to have dragged all three elk carcasses the several miles over the snow to a loading point where we could continue the journey by pickup truck.

Frozen Fingers

Many times the Gallatin Canyon and Gardiner area late season elk hunt patrols were during periods of wintery sub-zero temperatures and snow, which could be miserable duty, especially if there was an overkill of elk to be confiscated and field dressed. I had experienced frost-bitten hands at various times in the past, and as a result when my hands became very cold they would not function normally. While patrolling the Gallatin elk hunt area one day when I had been field dressing several over-killed elk, I washed the accumulated elk blood from my hands and lower arms with snow, but then my hands, even with gloves on, continued to be numb and quite useless for some time.

Due to my breakfast coffee, I had the urge for bladder relief so I managed to unzip my trouser fly and do my business, but then could not close the zipper. It was extremely cold and blustery, and the open trouser fly was chilling, so I approached a hunter bundled up good and wearing a knit face mask. Embarrassed, I explained my cold and numb hands problem and reluctantly asked the person if they would zip up my trouser fly and coat. The hunter laughed and pulled down the face mask, revealing that she was actually a lady!

Giggling, she said, "This is quite unusual. I'm not going any further than that!" She motioned for me to follow her, and we snowshoed a distance to her male hunting partner, who also laughed, but did me the favor.

At the end of the day at a warden gathering, one of my colleagues who had been viewing the hunters' and my activities with a spotting scope said to me, “Fitz, after you had dressed the over-killed elk, you approached a hunter. The two of you went to a third hunter, and soon afterward the one hunter knelt down in front of you for what reason, and it seemed to be a joyous meeting with handshakes afterward.” The inquisitive warden then exclaimed, “Fitz, what in the hell was going on?!”

When I explained what had happened, and that my first request for the zipper help was from a lady wearing a face-mask, there was quite a roar of laughter.

Problem on the Snowshoe Trail

While working the Columbus warden district in the wintertime after big game hunting had closed, I snowshoed the Stillwater and Rosebud areas for wildlife census and possible marten trapping. A local outdoor enthusiast told me that he had been in the upper Stillwater and had seen mountain lion tracks at several places, so I planned to go into the area to investigate, as the local government trapper was eager to trap a lion to boost his job standing and self satisfaction.

I snowshoed several miles on a bright and sunny day, and after hours on the trail I started experiencing severe eye pain, which was the result of temporary snow blindness. By holding my hand over my eyes and looking through the slits between my fingers, I finally made it out to my vehicle and back to Columbus. Despite my impairment, I did find the remains of two deer that had been killed by lions. I later went back accompanied by the government trapper, who made steel trap sets but never managed to catch a lion.

Wintertime Patrol and Lost Hunters

During the many years of snowshoe patrol in the late season hunts up in the Gallatin River Canyon and Gardiner areas, I had on numerous occasions assisted in searching for lost hunters. In most instances, it was due mostly to becoming disoriented and losing sight of landmarks during poor visibility in snowstorms. Several times, when I luckily came across a lost hunter, it was pathetic to see their rescue response and hypothermic condition. Several had made an attempt to start a fire, but had waited too long with cold or frostbitten hands. They were not thinking clearly and had unzipped their heavy coat for matches or a trouser fly to urinate, and then were unable to close the zippers. Usually, there would be a pile of burned matches but little fire starting material in the blowing snow. It was a heartbreaking experience for me and a real chore to evacuate some of those lost and suffering from hypothermia and disorientation. I would normally start a warming fire, but had to carefully watch that a hypothermic hunter did not over-do it on warming up quickly, which can be miserable and dangerous if the hunter is suffering severe frostbite, or worse yet, completely frozen hands and feet.

"Pooped Out" Far from Home Base

One winter, I was on patrol duty during the regular and extended elk hunts in the upper Gallatin Canyon and Gardiner areas. It was common for game wardens from outlying districts to be assigned there for patrol duty, and on one occasion a tall, hardy warden indicated an interest in accompanying me for a day of snowshoe patrol. I checked his borrowed snowshoes and harness and bindings for fit on his boots, and then we left en route to an area of regular hunter activity. After several hours of patrolling and checking hunters, my companion showed signs of tiring, so I, who was breaking trail in the less than ideal snowshoeing conditions, took regular breaks so we could both rest.

We eventually reached an area where we could look down below the high bluffs and see the road and river channel. The visiting warden indicated that he would work his way down the steep bluff slope and try to get a ride to the patrol cabin because he was feeling quite fatigued, but I warned him that the steep slope would be hazardous and that the river couldn't be crossed to get to the roadway. About that time several shots were fired nearby and I was quite compelled to go and look into the questionable hunter activities, but the investigation meant considerably more snowshoeing. Not surprisingly, the accompanying warden chose to stay put by a warming campfire while I left to check on matters.

A couple hours later when I returned, he was having very bothersome leg cramps but was eager to get off the mountain. Considering the late hour, the lengthy distance between us and our vehicle, and the warden's serious fatigue, it was a precarious situation. Unfortunately, the remainder of the jaunt was miserable and extended into nighttime. The moonlight was a savior for the snowshoe travel, which necessitated working around deadfall trees, steep slopes, and other obstacles. When we finally got back to the truck, the visiting warden turned to me and said, "Never, never again!"

A Tough and Trying Pursuit

On numerous instances, Warden Supervisor Sherman assigned me duties that were exhausting and somewhat hazardous. One such assignment originated when a Yellowstone Park Ranger named Scotty Chapman advised Sherman that a well-known trapper had a trap line set up to catch American pine marten and Canadian lynx. The problem was that the trap line was suspected to go inside the Yellowstone National Park boundary.

Sherman knew I excelled at snowshoeing and had past experience as a trapper, so I was assigned to secretly follow the old trapper on his line so I could observe his route and activities. The snow depth and condition at that high elevation wasn't ideal for snowshoeing, but I accepted the duty and waited in the Jardine area for the trapper to run his line. I intended to keep out of sight following the trapper, but soon realized that the old fellow seemed to be watching his back trail. Due to the blowing snow conditions, it was risky and arduous staying concealed.

At several sites, it was evident that the trapper was within the park boundary, but the white YNP squared posts with blowing snow sticking to the them surely made it questionable whether it was an intentional intrusion. Once the trapper was at the end of his line, I hurriedly backtracked on the already broken snowshoe trail and stayed well ahead and out of sight. I later filed a summary with a rough sketch of the trap line route but never received a report as to what, if any, action was taken.

Patrolling the Hard Way

I was sometimes the center of jesting about my regular snowshoe patrols during periods of deep snow and oftentimes miserable weather conditions, when it was a less arduous task and much simpler to check hunters as they dragged an elk carcass out of a snowed in hunting area to a highway loading point. My thinking was that the activities and acts of hunters back in quite remote hunting areas was often in the illegal category, which was not evident once an elk carcass was dragged out to a roadway loading point.

Through my many years as a Montana Game Warden from 1950 through 1978, I had covered *many* miles. By checking through my accumulated warden diaries, I finally arrived at a conservative figure of approximately 3,800 miles, which for my 25+ years of service was not significantly impressive. When asked at the age of 60 and facing mandatory retirement I said, "I wouldn't wish to retrace those many miles, and under the same weather conditions!

Rigors of the Job: *Animal Anecdotes*

An Unpredictable Bucking Cayuse

While my colleague Warden Milholvich was temporarily ill, I had occasion to patrol a portion of his district. I was loaned a horse by old-timer Bruce Neal, and I horse-packed my camp gear to a site off a trail to the east portion of the south fork of the Flathead River. After about a week of patrolling and checking hunter camps on foot, I packed the horse for the trip out and hadn't gone but a few miles when the horse started bucking and shed all the camp gear, with its lash ropes trailing.

The scattered gear was retrieved, and the then calm and seemingly gentle horse was again carefully packed and led down the trail. After going a few more miles, the horse broke free of the lead rope and bucked until all the camp gear was thrown off a second time. So again, I gathered the dispersed gear off the trail and went down to where the horse had stopped and was eating the trailside grass with no sign of shyness or nervousness.

I led the horse back to the pile of goods just as an outfitter came down the trail. When I told him about the bucking

Impatient Horse Wrangler

While patrolling the Gardiner area late elk hunt, I was directed to check on the activities of a local outfitter suspected of illegal pursuits. I snowshoed to an area where I could watch the outfitter when he left his makeshift ranch base soon after daybreak. As the outfitter and a guide were gathering horses for the day's work, the horses were unruly and reluctant to be caught or saddled and the outfitter was cursing a blue streak in frustration. After failing to catch any of the unruly horses that were being led by a dominant one rebelling at being caught, the outfitter yelled, "Shoot the S.O.B.!"

As the rodeo continued, the outfitter did exactly that, much to the surprise of the on-looking warden!

sprees, the outfitter said he would pack the animal and, for sure, the jughead horse wouldn't buck it off. To be safe, I checked the pack saddle blanket and saddle before the outfitter loaded up the horse, and didn't find anything to cause the bucking.

After completing his task, the outfitter continued on down the trail with his pack-string, and I consoled the horse and continued down the trail too. I didn't make it far. Almost within sight of the trailhead, the horse bucked again and all the gear went flying. Now beyond irritated, I decided to retrieve the scattered things and backpack it to my vehicle, instead of trying to load my equine companion one more time.

When we arrived at the trailer, I had no difficulty loading the horse for the journey back to Bruce's. When I returned the horse and trailer and told him about the bucking incidents I had had to endure, he laughed and said, "I should have mentioned that the cayuse has a tendency to act up occasionally!"

Sometimes Horses and Bears Don't Mix

On a pack trip with other wardens into the Bob Marshall Wilderness, everything was going well. Early one evening our intent was to stop at a forest cabin for the night instead of roughing it out with our bedrolls and an open fire. The weather was somewhat threatening, so the cabin would be shelter if it rained and the small wood cook stove made meal preparation more convenient.

As the pack and saddle horses were a hundred yards or so from the cabin, a couple of the cayuses became somewhat nervous and skittish, so we agreed that there must have been a bear around. This skittishness became worse as we drew nearer to the cabin, so we dismounted and led the horses as we approached the hitch rack beside the cabin. Before we even had a chance to drop the reins or utilize the hitch rack, the horses bolted as a bear came charging out the cabin door and hesitated to see what had interfered with its trashing fun inside.

To say the least, man and beast were surprised! As the bear woofed at our sight, there was quite a rodeo as the horses spooked and tried to go in different directions. It took some cowboying to get things under control before we could check the cabin interior. The door to the cabin had been badly damaged by the bear, and apparently other bears too, and the interior was a sad sight. After spending some time tidying up as best possible and trying to salvage the door to block the entrance, we decided to continue on the trail to a small meadow to camp for the night and give the pack-string time to settle down.

Horses can tell a man a lot if he has the savvy to read the signs.

Camper's Surprise!

Many years ago, I was working the Helena area and a call came through that a troublesome bear was at a campground near McDonald Pass. I quickly proceeded to the campground to determine the extent of the problem and if the bear should be live trapped. It just so happened that shop foreman Rex Smart and I had just built a black bear live trap with two 55-gallon fuel drums, and we were eager to learn if it would work.

Arriving at the campground, I noted that there was only one out-of-state trailer camper present. No one ventured out of the trailer, but I spotted a person peering out of a window, so I went to the trailer's door for information. It seemed that after breakfast, the elderly lady in the camper had gone to the garbage pit, which had a sheet metal cover plus a round cast iron lid with a foot pedal lever meant to open the lid. Evidently, someone had broken off the pedal end of the lever, which allowed the lid to go back over center and stay open unless closed by hand.

As the woman dislodged some food from a pan on the edge of the already open lid, there was a loud growl and something struck the pan. Needless to say, the woman was frightened and ran to the shelter of the trailer to tell her husband. Being an old but brave man, he went to the trash pit and tried to convince her she was overreacting and that it may have been only a small, harmless creature. As he stood there feeling certain his wife was unduly excited over nothing, a bear's head came periscoping out of the round pit.

The old fellow hastened back to the trailer and the two decided they should hitch the trailer to their vehicle and leave, but not knowing much about bears they decided to stay safely inside and wait for someone else to arrive in the campground. After a while, another trailer camper pulled in alongside them, so they promptly shouted at the new arrivals to inform them about the bear. The newly arrived vacationers agreed to pull out immediately and inform the proper authorities about the intruder, which is how I came to be there.

As I approached the garbage pit, the bear's head again peeked out of the round opening, and I could see that the bear, by sticking its head out first, could not escape because its shoulders were too wide for the space. Had the bear tried to get out with his front legs first, he may have squeezed through the opening the same as when he entered.

I proceeded to dig around the sheet metal cover, and then tied a rope to the stub of the lever on the lid, and threw the rope over a tree limb. I then fastened the rope to my vehicle bumper, and slowly backed up to pull the garbage pit cover up in the air.

Soon afterward, a small black bear scampered out of the smelly pit and ran toward brush cover. Just before going out of sight, the bear stopped, gave a woof, and shook like a wet dog to rid himself of the clinging garbage, then disappeared, never to be reported again at that campground. The old couple immediately hitched up their camper and left. Undoubtedly, they have told and retold about their bear experience in Montana.

Puzzling Demise of a Bull Moose

Over the years, I experienced a few instances where a big game animal was killed or died due to unusual or strange circumstances. One such happening occurred in a forested area where there was an old cattle driveway, used in the past by ranchers herding many head of cattle to mountain summer pastures. The several cattlemen normally had a range rider at a cow camp who rode the huge pasture areas checking cattle distribution among other things. During one pasture season the rider, Austin Parcell, who was an old-time and effective range rider, was following the old cattle driveway through a timbered and somewhat swampy area when he came across a moose carcass which was still quite warm. The surrounding area showed evidence of a struggle between two animals. He noted many cattle and moose tracks surrounding the dead moose and was puzzled as to what had caused the moose to be killed.

After studying the surrounding area, he got off his saddled horse and partially field dressed the moose to stave off spoilage. He then traveled a few miles by horseback to the nearest ranch phone and notified the county sheriff office. He also asked the sheriff that I be notified and given directions to the spot.

Fortunately, I was available and hastened to the area, which I knew well. When I arrived at the nearest vehicle accessible jeep-like trail, I hiked to the moose carcass and proceeded to complete the field dressing. I then quartered the carcass, leaving the hide on. I backpacked a couple quarters out, minus the heavy lower leg bones and minus the considerable bloodshot and broken rib areas. I planned on dragging the heavier quarters on a ground tarp, and little by little get the four quarters over the half-mile or so to where I had parked my truck.

Quite soon afterward, range rider Parcell arrived and offered to assist me with use of his horse. The animal was somewhat shy of the exposed and bloody moose quarters, but Parcell managed to handle the skittish horse. It was after dark before we had all four quarters to the vehicle loading point, and I was very grateful for the help provided. I have forever wondered what really took place to have caused the moose's death, but it was just one of many strange and curious events during my job as a Montana game warden!

A Bothersome Day

During a patrol of the upper Red Rock River, I continued on above Lima Dam to contact a rancher about reported beaver damage. I parked at a roadside turnout overlooking the Lima Reservoir waters and saw a loon apparently battling something on the water surface. Closer observation with binoculars showed that the loon had captured a ling fish, and as it was quite large, it seemed that the loon had "bit off more than he could chew." I continued watching as the ling became less active. The loon finally positioned the fish and partially gulped it down, but not entirely, as one-third of the fish was still hanging out of its mouth.

Once again resuming my drive along upper Lima Reservoir, I spotted something protruding out of the exposed bottomless reservoir mud on the shoreline. Binocular viewing revealed the thing to be a domestic cow's head and neck, and it was obvious the animal was struggling to get free. I went to the nearby ranch to report the distressed cow and the rancher stated that he had lost several head of livestock in that same manner and rescue would be a futile attempt, due to the endless and seemingly bottomless quicksand-like mud. Bothersome, bothersome, bothersome—so I went back to the edge of the shoreline mud, and with my holstered revolver shot the struggling cow to end her misery.

Observing an Animal Preparing for Winter

En route to Morrison Lake high in the mountains, I stopped at the base of a large rock slide and saw a small pika scurrying up the rocks with a mouthful of grass, so I sat for quite some time watching the little critter. It turns out that I wasn't the only one that took notice of his actions for I soon spied a fox that was also watching the pika, who was readying a cache of food for winter under deep snow and cold.

It appeared that the fox would certainly catch the pika, but when he made an onrush toward the little creature, the pika dived into a rock crevice and let out a warning call. It was a relief to me to see the little fellow escape, but the fact remains that the predator versus prey rivalry is a constant and continuing struggle for the survival of predators. It still doesn't make it any less bothersome to witness it firsthand!

A Bumper Crop

Early on one late October morning, a school bus driver on his student pick-up route struck a deer, and the animal was mortally wounded alongside the backroad. Of course, this was troublesome and stressful to many of the students in the bus, so when the driver made his next stop at a nearby ranch, he explained to the rancher what had happened and asked him to call County Sheriff George Paradis. The rancher called the sheriff, who authorized him to kill the still alive and suffering deer. Meanwhile, the sheriff radioed me to report the incident and ask for my advice.

By chance, I was in the area checking a report of a troublesome beaver on the A. Reider ranch, but it would be a little while before I could make it to the deer carcass. Since it was too late in the year to live trap and relocate the beaver, I opened up a small channel in the sizable beaver dam and placed a loose roll of wire fencing in it to alleviate the serious adjacent flooding. After my work was completed, I directed a licensed trapper to take over the problem and then headed over to investigate the struck deer situation. Once I arrived at the scene, the rancher had already put the wounded animal out of its misery, so I field dressed the deer with the help of the rancher, and then donated it to the Boulder River School and Hospital. In appreciation, the school superintendent invited me to stay for a meal with him and his some of his staff, who wished to visit and acknowledge other donations I had made to the school.

Crashing Experiences

While working the Helena area, the Fish & Game office received a phone call that a mule deer was feeding on various shrubberies in the south end of town, and being chased by a couple dogs along the way. I searched the vicinity and found the deer in an area later known as "Last Chance Gulch." At that time, I was not equipped with any tranquilizing devices, so I hazed the deer toward the nearby mountain area. I was making good headway with my hazing when a couple of dogs ran straight after the deer, which spooked it, so it turned and came back toward town and the street-side businesses.

The damn dogs continued their barking pursuit and the deer was dodging around vehicles and pedestrians, finally crashing through a large plate glass store window. It ran around crazily inside, causing a great deal of havoc and damage. The two dogs were right outside the window, and still barking furiously, so a couple of onlookers helpfully shooed them away.

A Helena policeman arrived on the scene, and said he knew a local veterinarian who had a tranquilizer gun. He went and got the gun from the veterinarian, and came back and tranquilized the buck deer, which finally collapsed. With plenty of onlookers and help, the police officer and I loaded the deer in a pickup bed and took it back into the mountains to be released.

Another time, a disoriented bobcat was loose in the area, and a couple of gutsy dogs pursued it. One of the dogs got a bobcat swat, which required a veterinarian's patching. The bobcat then climbed a transformer power pole with electrified wires, and fortunately didn't get electrocuted or cause a power outage. With quite a gathering of curious spectators, I kept people at a distance with help of the city police. After a lengthy wait, the bobcat finally backed down the pole and scurried away to the nearby hills.

Illegal Category, but Excusable

On a patrol when Warden Secor came to Dillon to lend a hand making the rounds, we were leaving town by way of a back road and I observed the top of a fellow's head above a ditch bank. As Warden Secor and I watched through our binoculars, we could see the man going from below a large ditch head-gate with two buckets toward the Beaverhead River. Being very interested in the man's actions, we hiked down to the area. When we contacted the fellow, he turned out to be Steve Logan, and he said, "Fitz, you are just in time. I am tired out from rescuing the trout trapped in that pool of water below the head-gate."

The water from the running irrigation canal was shut off suddenly and several large trout were trapped in an isolated pool of water, where a few had died and others were barely surviving. Logan had rescued some by carrying them in buckets to the nearby river. We assisted with the rescue of numerous trout, and noticed that a few dead but still fresh ones were up on a grassy ditch bank and covered with moist grass.

We told Logan that the dead trout must necessarily be confiscated, and he said, "I'd sure like to have them to give to some local needy people."

This gave us pause, so after a discussion between us two wardens, I stated that to avoid confiscating the trout I would give Logan a certificate of sale to allow him possession of the dead fish. This procedure was questionable at best, and definitely not by the book.

Later, Warden Secor told me, "I wouldn't have thought to handle it that way."

At month's end, I sent my regular monthly report and the accompanying few dollars for the so-called sale.

Rigors of the Job:

Critter Control

Elk Hunting Pressure Influencing Elk Movement

Due to elk numbers in excess of winter range capacity and in conflict with the area cattle grazing allotments in the Snowline and Lima Peaks areas one year, I recommended an either sex elk hunt with a provision that the hunt could be closed on 48-hour public notice. This was an agreed hunt by the Helena Fish & Game Department headquarters, but with considerable concern of a possible overkill. I tried to assure the Helena game management personnel that a game checking station would be established at the only Montana highway outlet from the hunting area and elk hunting success would be monitored at the station day and night. The recommendation was accepted, and my plan was put to use.

It was surprising the number of hunters that checked into the area, and in just a few days the hunt was closed down as agreed. The number of elk killed was about half of the previous winter's aerial census of approximately 400 head. I quickly realized that the unusual and popular either sex elk hunt was a drawing card for many elk hunters, but felt assured the checking station tally would be a safeguard. The situation seemed okay until the following two winters' aerial elk censuses only tabulated about fifty elk total. Needless to say, the Helena big game management personnel were very concerned and I felt the heat, with my job seemingly in jeopardy.

After the winter census, a cooperative meeting was held between the Montana and Idaho Fish & Game Departments. A couple of Idaho big game management employees revealed that their elk census figures on the Idaho side of the Continental Divide, which also serves as the state line, was about 150 or so more than usual and indicated they had numerous Montana elk on their Idaho side. I assumed that clarified the low winter elk census in my controversial area, and realized the excessive hunter activity in Montana had literally pushed many elk into Idaho. However, there was still an ongoing concern whether the elk would return to Montana and their "home" area for summer grazing and cow calving.

Now, I remember several elk hunters later saying that they had seen a long line of many, many elk traveling into Idaho through a state line pass near the Red Conglomerate Peak. Fortunately, the significant return of elk was confirmed the next winter when the census proved that the elk had returned home. Recognizing that the hunt went as planned, my concerns were put to rest. It was definitely a learning experience for me and the game management officials!

"Hope You Are Done Tagging, Because Here We Come!"

While assisting with the elk and moose calf tagging project in the Gravelly Mountain Range, I was on a horseback crew of three or four that worked as a team to achieve the sometimes challenging task. Once a cow elk was spotted the team would closely observe the actions of the cow, specifically the direction she was intently watching, which invariably was toward her calf lying hidden on the ground. Thanks to our sly approach and football-like plunging tactics, our success rate of finding the calf was surprisingly high and many elk calves were ear-tagged for study purposes in order to determine the extent of their range of movement in the surrounding mountain areas.

With a cow moose and her calf it was a different situation, as the cow was very protective of her nearby calf and would stand her ground, with threatening ears laid back and very reluctant to leave. One team rider would whoop and yell and make a rush toward the cow, and it proved to be an effective way for the remainder of the tagging team to ear tag the calf. Even so, a mature cow moose may be hazed off aways, but occasionally challenged the cowboy rider who would be chased back to the calf, yelling, "You better have that calf tagged and get saddled up, because here we come!"

As a side note, I never did get trampled by an on-rushing cow moose. I did, however, fracture my pelvis when I was bucked off a Tennessee Walker cayuse when we were leaving our USFS patrol cabin lodgings for the day. My one-man rodeo-style bucking event sent me flying through the air, and when I made contact with the ground, it was with my hip – landing squarely on top of a boulder with my holstered .38 caliber revolver directly underneath me. That landed me in the hospital for nearly a week!

Elk Kill Permit and Results Ends Elk Damage Complaint

A local rancher called the Helena Fish & Game Department headquarters to issue a complaint about elk damage to his haystacks, and the resulting loss of much needed hay for carrying his cattle through the seemingly endless winter months. He indicated the culprits to be nearby wintering elk. The rancher indicated he had already lost a couple or more tons of hay, and pleaded for our help.

Warden Supervisor Sherman convinced his superior that issuance of an elk kill permit was undoubtedly the best way to handle the complaint, as the deep snow and problem of getting paneling material to the haystack wasn't practical. So, Sherman called me because of my known gun marksmanship. A probationary warden in the district that was close and available was also called upon to help.

Before daybreak, the three of us went to the problem area and trudged through the deep and crusted snow to position ourselves behind some shoulder-high sagebrush along a fence row. After viewing with binoculars in the moonlight, we could plainly see a group of approximately a dozen elk. Once the oncoming daybreak caused the elk to leave the haystack in single file, we agreed who would aim for which targets—front, middle, or back—and proceeded to shoot until our rifle magazines were empty.

Afterward, Sherman asked us how many elk we felt sure each of us had downed. Sherman indicated he had downed five. I had zeroed in on the middle line of elk and said I had also downed five. The recently hired warden informed us that he wasn't sure how well his rifle was sighted in and probably downed just one. At that point, there were only two elk running away toward the timber about a quarter of a mile away.

We trudged to the haystack to inspect the dead and dying elk, and found one who had only been injured and still needed to be killed. It took quite some time to field dress all the animals, and when we were finished we went to the rancher's house to report the kill. While were doing the field dressing, the new warden said he didn't have a knife, except for a small pocket knife. It was then that I knew quite definitely that the somewhat inexperienced warden would probably be relieved of his probationary warden duties—which was true!

Luckily, the rancher offered to hitch his team of horses to a sizable sled-like piece of equipment he called a "rock boat." It took him four trips to haul the carcasses to his ranch barn, where they would be protected from magpies. It was a tough haul for the horses in the deep snow. A day or so later, the eleven elk carcasses were trucked to Bozeman Region Three Headquarters and sold at public auction.

Fencing Hay

On the north side of the Centennial Valley, the Les Staudenmeyer Ranch had the Metzel Creek place when "Slim" Johnson built a cabin for ranch use. old-timer Les trailed cattle there in early summer and hauled hay for their livestock in the event of lagging winter and snow, which was commonplace in the Centennial.

I hadn't been in the Dillon area very long as a game warden when Les contacted me about elk seriously damaging the much needed hay. There wasn't an easy way for me to handle the problem, but as there was a good stretch of decent weather, I towed my own flatbed trailer to Price Creek and cut about two dozen pole-size lodgepole trees and hauled them across the valley to the ranch site. I had heard that the Fish & Game Department had access to six-feet high snow fence, so I went to Helena and loaded six rolls and took them to the Metzel Creek place to put around the haystack, too. I leaned the poles against the haystack and then rolled the fencing around the sides. Thinking that drifted and possibly crusted snow might enable elk to get above the six-foot tier of fencing, I decided to double tier it, and with rope over the top of the haystack and pulling with my chained-up vehicle, I managed to get it done after hours and hours of continuous day- and night-time effort.

I was told that Les was an ornery old dutchman and hadn't the kindest feelings toward Fish & Game people, but I'm proud to say Les and family have been good friends all through these many years.

Scarecrow Deterrent

Depending on the severity of Montana winters and other contributing factors, game damage complaints were common and solutions varied by the district game warden implementing them. Suggested remedies included a recommendation for reopening a limited hunt for deer or elk, the possible use of a propane operated scare gun, erecting high paneling around haystacks, and hazing by horseback or snowmobile away from the game damaged site. With continuing snowy and cold, cold winter conditions, the hazing was many times only a temporary solution.

On one occasion, I received a complaint of moose within a paneled haystack yard that spooked the rancher's team of horses so that he couldn't get hay for his cattle. I tried hazing the moose away from the ranch area, then used a loud blasting scare gun with little success, so as a last resort I borrowed a couple incessantly barking dogs and built them a baled straw dog house. The moose gained the victory, however, because they became accustomed to the barking and stayed at the stack yard, knowing the dogs would not chase them away.

Remembering the value of a scarecrow as a farm kid, I then constructed a wooden scarecrow frame and stretched the dirty, smelly beaver and bear live trapping coveralls I wore in the field over the frame with the sleeves waving in the wind. Then I peed on it. On my next contact with the rancher he said to me, "I don't know what you finally did to keep the moose away, but it seemed to work best!"

With the seasons changing from winter to spring, it was more likely the troublesome moose left for another foraging spot.

Verification of a Rancher's Complaint

Another complaint in my Dillon district involved a federally allotted cattle grazing area high up the headwaters of Nicolia Creek, so I accompanied the grumbling rancher, riding horseback the several miles upstream to the area in question. When we arrived at the site at about noon, we sat and ate a sack lunch and talked. During our lunch break, the rancher said, "Fitzwater, you can see all the elk droppings and the overgrazed grass."

I acknowledged what he saw, and noted the Continental Divide mountain Ajax Peak was visible at the head of the drainage. After pondering a while, I said, "I realize your concern, but actually, where would you have the elk go?"

The rancher, munching on a sandwich, was quiet for some time and finally, somewhat laughingly, said, "I really never thought of it that way! Let me say that is the last complaint you'll get from me."

Still wanting to help alleviate his concerns, I assured the rancher that a few elk hunters would be directed to the problem area with the hope that the hunter and his gun might relieve some of the pressure on the limited grazing.

The Migrating Buffalo of Yellowstone National Park

The migration of buffalo from Yellowstone National Park to adjacent Montana would seem simple but was both complicated and controversial, even today. Some years ago, the Montana Fish & Game Department had the responsibility of handling the yearly problem through opening buffalo hunting, but unfortunately certain anti-hunting factions opposed and interfered with the hunt. Consequently, stockmen were concerned about the spread of animal-to-animal Brucellosis disease.

Despite hunting in severe winter conditions, there is no lack of hunter interest and participation by those interested in the challenge, desiring an alternate food source, and seeking hunter pride. Such a buffalo hunt can be compared to the successful yearly extended elk hunts in areas adjacent to the northern park boundary. Before those hunts were initiated, the elk migrating out of Yellowstone caused very severe damage to foraging vegetation in the Gallatin River Canyon, and also had a detrimental effect on the native elk in the areas.

It is pathetic to me that certain animal rights organizations regularly oppose such meaningful and necessary animal control methods, and are a hindrance to necessary and proper game management and recovery of overused animal foraging areas.

An Era of Mule Deer Problems

During the 1950s, mule deer populations had increased and numerous areas were overpopulated, with deer winter ranges being severely overused. When I worked the Stillwater County district, the Horseman Flat area was recommended for an extended deer hunt, along with a couple of ranch areas experiencing damage by mule deer.

Later, when I was assigned to the Helena district, the deer depredation problems continued, and certain areas were opened for extended mule deer hunting. Additionally, numerous ranch haystacks were paneled with high fencing to prevent the mule deer from foraging on the ranchers' winter livestock feed.

Then, when I was transferred to the Dillon district, where mule deer populations were still at a high level, extended hunts were opened in several problem areas. One regional biologist, Phil South, also stationed at Dillon, established deer study areas in overused deer wintering ranges at Scudder and Lost Creeks and Axes Canyon. He erected fenced enclosures for comparison of unused plants within the enclosures to the same types of plants in the outside areas of overuse. In conjunction with the study, a couple deer were killed every month so that the animals' general condition could be diagnosed and internal organs inspected, along with stomach paunch samples collected for study. To aid with the progress of the ongoing investigation I assisted in killing several deer, and with the severity of the cold and winter snow during those extended hunting seasons it wasn't always an easy task.

Some F & G game managers had heard from colleagues that the mule deer overpopulation in the northern Arizona Kaibab plateau was an example of the need for some states to put into effect deer population control measures. Unfortunately, wild animal depredation control measures can be time consuming and laborious, and are often unpopular with local sportsmen clubs and individual hunters.

Golden Eagle Depredation

One spring, I received a report from local sheep ranchers Helle and Rebish that they were experiencing lamb depredation by golden eagles. They were open range lambing, instead of shed lambing, which was less stressful on the ewes and resulted in better survival of newborn lambs, so long as they weren't being snatched up by eagles.

Because golden eagles were (and still are) a federally protected species, I had to notify the S.W. Montana U.S. Fish & Wildlife game agent, Federal Game Warden Ash Brann. He was doubtful of my report, but quite soon a couple of representatives from the U.S. Fish & Wildlife Department and a recognized eagle expert brought in from Texas by the name of Mike Lockhart arrived and acknowledged the serious lamb depredation. The sheep kills were obvious by the surrounding animal blood and signs of struggle, and posed no problem to substantiate the eagles' kills.

After surveying the ranch, expert Lockhart stated that the lambing area was below a northbound eagle migration route and, due to cool weather conditions the widespread gopher population had not emerged, which was a primary food source for the migrating eagles. Federal Warden Brann and Lockhart determined that live trapping the eagles was the best solution.

To accomplish this, sizable leg-hold steel traps were used. The traps' springs were weakened by hammer blows to the ends of the spring and then tested for jaw holding strength, followed by padding the trap jaws to eliminate injury to an eagle's legs. Next, the steel traps had a length of heavy wire attached but were not staked down. This served as a drag that would allow a trapped eagle to get airborne, but would hinder the bird from flying a great distance. Jackrabbit carcasses were then staked to the ground as bait, with two or three traps arranged around the bait.

Amazingly, we caught 145 golden eagles, and two bald eagles. The captured eagles were then taken to a nearby old log building on site, which had elevated horizontal pole roosts and large chunks of butchered meat for food and, of course, a container of water. Lockhart cautioned all those assisting to exercise caution when handling an eagle, as the leg talons, if clasped on one's hand or arm, could cause serious and painful injuries. Quite often, many of the handlers would carry an eagle under their arms with secure grasp of the legs. The threatening open beak of the eagle was, although worrisome, an unlikely threat.

Once the eagle migration flyway tapered off to fewer birds, and the many gophers emerged out of their burrows, the eagle trapping crew proceeded to leg band and feather paint-mark some of the many captured eagles. We put them in crates to be transported to selected release sites, with the adults and juveniles going to different locations for record keeping considerations.

This was quite an unusual circumstance regarding migrating eagles, and a significant and costly depredation for the rancher.

Ring-Neck Pheasant Habitat Alteration

Before the Beaverhead Valley land was altered by the construction of a dam and irrigation canals to serve an adjacent farming bench, it was fair habitat for ringneck pheasants due to a variety of farm crops, like grain, on which they could thrive. Then, with the valley's land crops being switched mostly to hay and the widespread use of pesticides and herbicides, the pheasant population dwindled. The organization Pheasants Forever attempted to better the valley habitat through various projects in cooperation with agreeable landowners, but without much luck.

Another problem that ground nesting birds faced was the railroad lines that ran through their domain. At a time when the valley pheasant population was at an all-time high, railroad right of ways, with their tall grasses and cattails, provided good bird cover and nesting areas. This all seemed well and good until the yearly right-of-way maintenance began. Under close supervision, the right-of-ways were burned as a snow-catching deterrent, and to prevent the grass fires that are sometimes caused by railroad locomotives from endangering adjacent private holdings. I notified the Helena Fish & Game headquarters of this burning practice and the consequential habitat destruction. Thankfully, over a period of time and in cooperation with railroad officials, the procedure was stopped to the benefit of ground nesting pheasant, partridge, meadow lark, and other birds.

A Poisoned Lake

During a period when the spruce budworm infestation was killing many conifer trees, an aerial spraying project was being initiated. On a summer day during the treatment project, a military-type plane took off with a heavy load of insecticide spray material. The pilot gained altitude with the intent of spraying down the mountainside, but as he banked the aircraft at that high altitude, he lost the plane's lift and out of desperation crashed in the nearby mountain lake. Perhaps the pilot failed to take into account the extenuating flight circumstances, but the hot day and high altitude were the likely culprits behind the unfortunate event. Sadly, the toxic spray killed the fish and other aquatic life in the lake.

Over a period of several years following the crash, I took water samples to the Fish & Game lab, and finally received the report that the lake was clean of toxic material. Because of the long-awaited favorable result of the lab report, plans were made to restock the lake, and it was determined that California golden trout would be aerial planted. I knew this was a bad choice for a high mountain lake, given the cold waters and limited food source. The presence of brook trout in the inlet waters and the future incompatibility of the two species was another concern. The plan was carried out anyway, and the golden trout never did attain any desirable size, with the population ultimately dwindling over time.

Rigors of the Job:
Public Relations

A Helping Hand In Tough Times

One September years ago when I was working the Stillwater district, I received word through the sheriff's department that a rancher at a remote, small ranch was having serious beaver problems and wished to contact a game warden. Answering the call, I proceeded up a rough and rocky road to the homestead. Upon arriving, I could readily see that the beaver problem was serious because water was flowing out of two creek channels and around the ranch house. The dam (or was it damn?) builders had the entire area flooded, and efforts at diking and diverting water hadn't helped very much to discourage the busy beavers who were preparing for winter.

I learned that the man, his wife, and two children lived there, and had pioneered through two summers and a winter with a few head of cattle, cutting poles and posts, and raising a sizable garden. When the beaver moved into the creek area, the rancher thought steel trapping them would bring in added income and solve his flooding problem. Hearing this, I advised the man that a landowner beaver permit cost $10 for any amount of beaver up to ten, and the fellow answered, "By golly, we just do not have $10 to spare just now."

It was evident that the flooding would be a problem once winter arrived, and being too late for live trapping it would make the area a sheet of ice. So, I decided to issue the permit on the spot and would stand good for the fee until the rancher was in a position to pay. After this was settled, some quick pointers on how to trap, pelt, and stretch beaver pelts were given, along with a couple steel traps loaned to help the fellow.

I intended to leave immediately after, but the rancher asked me to have a cup of coffee and consider eating with the family. I gratefully accepted the cup of coffee, but declined sharing a meal with them, as I regularly carried camp groceries. But, as usual, the visit lasted longer than intended, so the fellow again asked me to eat with them as the meal would be ready about then and the missus had homemade bread. Not wanting to be impolite, I agreed to have another cup of coffee and a slice of that delicious smelling bread. The man called his wife into the room and introduced me as the game warden, indicating that I would eat a bite with the family. The woman's face immediately flushed, and her nervousness was very obvious as she left the room and went back to the kitchen.

Soon she returned, and as we all sat at the table the lady seemed unusually uneasy with the presence a warden, and her husband soon followed suit. But, the food looked delicious, and as I ate a slice of warm bread the man offered a slice of meat from a well-browned and tasty appearing roast. Noticing that there was more than enough meat for all present, I decided I would make a sandwich with a slice of meat and bread.

After finishing the meal, I thanked the lady for the good food, and as I left the house the man followed me outside and said, "I didn't know the wife was having a roast. I know as a game warden you certainly realize the meat was venison, so I guess I'll owe you much more than the $10."

"I'll say this, you have done a good job of keeping the deer meat since last hunting season," I quickly answered, and then I promptly left. I experienced some uneasy feelings as a game warden, but other, better feelings prevailed.

Years ago, during the Great Depression, the local justice of the peace jurisdictions and county attorneys, who gained office by political votes, had a tendency to view some categories of poaching with less seriousness due to the hard times and their "can use the meat" attitudes. Today, with the availability of certain modern facilities for investigative purposes and procedures, many poaching cases can be successfully and rightfully concluded. However, in court with a jury trial it can very possibly, and not surprisingly, end in a not guilty verdict!

Aspirations for Kayaking from Montana to New Orleans

Some time ago, I was contacted by a young New York state man saying that he intended to kayak from the farthest reaches of the Mississippi and Missouri River drainages, and head downstream to the mouth of the Mississippi River. The man asked where his starting point should be in southwestern Montana to attain his goal. I pulled out a map and pointed to the extreme headwaters of Hell Roaring Creek, accessible only from a primitive road on the Idaho side of the Continental Divide.

I had traveled the road on many occasions because I periodically patrolled Blair Lake from the Montana side for fishing activities. It was most often fished by visitors from Idaho and Utah, usually without a Montana fishing license. Since I had already planned to patrol the lake, I offered to transport the fellow and his floating equipment to the starting point at the extreme headquarters of the drainage.

Over the course of my 28 years as a Montana game warden, I had canoed all the continuous waters from Red Rock Creek, just above Refuge Lakes, to Holter Dam on the Missouri River. Relying on these experiences, I suggested to the young fellow that to start the float, he would need to carry his kayak and meager equipment down the creek, through a rocky canyon, and into Alaska Basin. Here the stream intersected Red Rock Creek, which could be floated intermittently until it flowed into the Red Rock swan refuge and upper Red Rock Lake. I also told the man that there were about six reservoirs in Montana to traverse downstream on the way to the North Dakota state line. The floater stated that he planned to follow the reservoir shorelines to avoid windy conditions mid-reservoir. For the most part this plan was okay, but I advised him that to follow the Fort Peck Reservoir shoreline wouldn't be feasible due to its irregularity and distance.

Before parting at that very remote and distant starting point, I asked the fellow to contact me when he arrived on the Beaverhead River in Dillon so that I could accompany him by canoe for a day, and give him a packet of self-addressed postcards to be mailed at various stops along the way.

Quite some time later, Warden Secor in Glasgow, Montana notified me that the man had arrived at the Fort Peck Dam and had swamped his kayak several times, losing a considerable amount of equipment, including the postcards. That was the last report I received, and I have often wondered about the outcome of that long, long float! Eventually, I wrote to the man's family in New York, and inquired whether the young floater managed to complete the trip, or gave it up somewhere along the way. I never received a reply, and I still wonder what became of the man to this day.

Shelter in a Winter Blizzard

One cold day in the 1950s, game biologist Ralph Rouse asked me if I would accompany him to a north Centennial Valley area to assist in collecting some biological data related to elk and their wintering range; I agreed to join him and provide whatever assistance he needed. Mind you, this was wintertime, and I well knew that the open treeless valley could quickly change from a calm winter scene to a blizzard condition in a short time. Realizing this, I packed some camp grub, extra winter garments, fire starter and split wood, and, for good measure, I threw in snowshoes too.

We two Fish & Gamers, towing a trailer with two horses and gear, managed to get into the valley 16 miles or so before we encountered snow drifts that halted further progress. We unloaded our horses and proceeded on horseback for a few more miles to an area where some elk were known to winter. I shot one of the elk so Rouse could collect rumen samples and other biological data. When Rouse was pretty well satisfied with what he had accumulated, we headed back toward the vehicle.

Along the way, we had both remarked that it seemed to be getting much colder, and within a half-hour it was getting very windy and bordering on a ground blizzard. We rode steadily on, but had to keep our heads down and faces protected with neckerchiefs because of the driving snow. It wasn't long before the horses literally balked at facing the driving snow, so I walked ahead breaking trail, which encouraged the horses to follow. Very often, we encountered snowdrifts that were tough to break through, especially with some being crusted on top. When we couldn't determine how long a snowdrift might be due to the complete lack of visibility, we would continue to break through the crusted snow heading for the vehicle in the most direct line possible.

After sundown, and in some moonlight, we finally arrived at the vehicle, only to find that it was badly drifted in. We started shoveling but quickly discovered that snow had drifted under the hood, completely covering the engine except for the air-cleaner. Before leaving earlier, Rouse had raised the hood and placed the keys on the air-cleaner in the event that we were separated during the day. Unfortunately, he had failed to securely snap the hood down, which let snow drift in on top of the engine.

After it was evident the vehicle couldn't be freed or started in such a storm, and being well acquainted with ranch buildings in the valley, I decided it best to head out for an occupied ranch three miles or so away. We tied our bedrolls with some camp groceries rolled inside across the saddles and proceeded to hike and lead the horses to bachelor Walt Sperry's ranch.

On arriving, no one was in the ranch house but it was warm inside. While Rouse stoked the fire, I took the horses to the log barn where I found rancher Sperry doctoring a couple critters. I explained our predicament with the vehicle and hoped he could offer us shelter for the night. Graciously, Sperry helped tend to the horses. Knowing me very well, he seemed anxious to jibe me and said, "Leave it up to a couple dumb game wardens to get lost in a blizzard. Where in the hell did you come from?!"

As we walked back to the ranch house, I shared that we had some camp groceries to fix a meal with, but Sperry said, "How about a couple steaks and some spuds?"

Music to our ears! He already had a large pan of boiled potatoes, so we went to a cold room where three hefty steaks were sawed off a hind quarter. How lucky to have gotten to the ranch where the weary horses and we were fed and rested. The next day after the blizzard conditions subsided, it took a couple hours of shoveling before our vehicle was freed and started.

About a year later, I came across rancher Sperry in Dillon and treated him to a restaurant dinner, but we both had to agree it didn't equal the steak and spuds at the ranch. During our meal, Sperry seemed compelled to blurt out, "Did you get indigestion that night? Those steaks were from one of your elk that was feeding on my haystack!"

At that late date, I really didn't care if it was elk, legal or not, remembering the miserably cold experience and good food and warm shelter in the remote Centennial Valley, but I did keep in mind the killing of an elk under such circumstances.

A Fisherman's Tragic Demise on a Lake

Within a couple areas that I patrolled in Silver Bow County, there were several rivers, lakes, and reservoirs. Sadly, due to weather conditions and poor boating procedures, many people drowned over the years in those and other waters. On one particular lake, some bank fishermen that had just arrived soon observed an unoccupied boat afloat on the lake. This immediately puzzled them, as they hadn't seen another vehicle in the area. They thought that perhaps there was an occupant laying down in the boat bottom relaxing or sleeping in the warm sunshine, since there was an anchored fishing rod with line out in the water. However, the boat wasn't anchored, and moved with the wind. Eventually, it drifted to the shoreline and the bank fishermen hiked around the lakeshore and discovered the boat was empty, which of course caused them much concern.

As there was not a phone facility in that area, one of the men drove to a residence some miles away and notified the county sheriff's office. He then returned to the lake. As the trio of fishermen then had an inkling that the situation was a tragic one, they refrained from fishing while awaiting the arrival of someone from the sheriff's department. After a couple hours of waiting, a deputy arrived. After a conference with the group of men, the deputy notified the search and rescue unit who, within a couple more hours, arrived to begin searching the lake for a possible drowning victim.

Several hours of searching later with no success, a vehicle arrived. It was learned that the driver had dropped off his fishing friend earlier, and agreed to come back later in the day to pick him up, which was his intent when he arrived at the scene. The fellow was devastated to think his friend had undoubtedly drowned in a puzzling manner.

The initial search efforts were not successful, but the team intended to stay and consider other search methods. It was suggested that some type of net towed slowly by two boats might be a good method of dragging the lake bottom. I had just arrived after receiving word of the drowning on my two-way-radio, and listening in on the discussion a bit, I suggested that the local fisheries biologist had large mesh gill nets that might be used.

The next day the net was tried. After numerous attempts in different directions, and with the net snagging several times on the lake bottom, the body of the drowned fisherman was recovered. What a stressful and heart-rending situation for the numerous relatives and friends who had gathered at the rescue site!

"It's Sacrilegious!"

While I was working the extended upper Gallatin Canyon elk hunt, a report was received of a missing hunter in the area I regularly snowshoe patrolled. Another hunter had come across the body of the missing hunter and relayed the description of the area, which I recognized. Later, a county sheriff's deputy arrived at the district headquarters and informed me that he must get authorization from the county coroner to move the body from the mountain area, which was at least three-and-a-half miles from the highway.

Knowing the area very well, I offered to assist with the retrieval of the man's remains when the authorization was obtained. The deputy was pleased to accept the offer since he was not an experienced snowshoer. With a hardy volunteer accompanying me, we took a canvas tarp and snowshoed the distance to the deceased hunter. We positioned the now very rigid body, wrapped it in the tarp and bound it to drag it in the snow. We had proceeded a couple miles out toward the highway when another hunter was met going into the hunting area. After some conversation the fellow said, "I see you are dragging out some game."

When he didn't seem to understand our reply that it was a dead body, he said, "What did you say?"

We repeated that it was the body of a hunter that had died, and he pointed at the tarp-wrapped body and said, "Fellows, this is sacrilegious!"

We asked if he knew of a better way of getting the body out over the difficult snow conditions, but he had no reply and was openly disturbed.

Upon our return, I was asked to roughly sketch the area surrounding where the body was found, and it was later determined that the deceased hunter had a history of heart problems.

Denied Montana Outfitter License for Lack of Proper Equipment

A local college professor by the name of Ken Hunter was a friend of mine, and had an obsession for hunting trophy-size buck mule deer. I had received a couple reports of possible illegal pursuits related to Hunter's yen to hunt frequently during the approximately 30-day open season. I also heard tell of the questionable and unusual manner that he field-dressed deer. Hunter was a brute of a man who once backpacked a heavy wood stove out of an abandoned cabin in the Alaskan wilderness, and who jockeyed around a collection of very big, heavy boulders until he was satisfied with his home's landscaping.

When he applied for an outfitter license, I was obligated to interview the hardy and skillful deer hunter and determine what variety of equipment he possessed to meet the guidelines for issuance of the license. Unfortunately, he did not possess the necessary trappings essential for the licensure, and I had to deny his application. When Hunter was informed that certain equipment was required, he said he would cater to hunters interested in trophy bucks since he did have the equipment for that specialty hunt. He was confident that once his hunting skill in locating big buck deer was known, he would have many clientele inquiries on a regular, good paying basis. However, I did not relent, and refused to issue the license. Hunter was quite upset due to my denial, but we remained friends.

All the same, Hunter was an aggressive and dedicated buck mule deer hunter, and pursued the hunt at a difficult and demanding pace, which I experienced the two times I unknowingly followed him during his pre-dawn to afternoon hunts where a sizable buck was killed and properly tagged. The fellow was very adept at removing the hide in the carcass areas of an animal, where he would then take the meat, minus any bone. He would next open enough paunch to remove the heart and liver, and put all the meat in a couple pack sacks. Hunter had a large German Shepherd dog, and it was suspected that the dog was well fed on venison. Admittedly, the man was a fellow of questionable, unusual, and skillful traits, and put his educational abilities as a college instructor in jeopardy for want of a different life.

After about three years, Hunter had several mule deer antlers mounted and displayed for the local newspaper, which exceeded the number he could have legally killed for the period of time he taught psychology at Western Montana College. When I approached and questioned him about the antler excess, he stated that he had antlers mounted of those animals he killed legally and then quite a few were mounted for "enthused hunter friends." Following the interview, I contacted the county attorney to determine if Hunter's display of too many mule deer antlers would justify issuing a citation, but as expected, the answer was NO! Still wondering if Hunter was poaching, I had to remind myself that a game warden cannot solely concentrate his efforts and patrols on sportsmen suspected of poaching, due to the vast districts each was responsible for monitoring. So, I had to make my peace with moving on to attend to my other warden's duties.

After living and teaching in Dillon a while longer, Hunter went back to Alaska and worked at the fish netting business in the Bristol Bay-Egegik area. While there, a friend and fellow worker, Richard Mason, had a serious falling out with Hunter.

Later at the net fishing site, the serious disagreement developed into a gun confrontation with Mason and another worker by the name of Michael Sattleen being shot and killed, supposedly by Hunter.

Then, the story goes that the dead men's bodies were wrapped and weighted in fish-net and dropped in the current of the Egegik River, never to be found. Hunter claimed the people in the Egegik community had a grudge against him to the point of being threatened, since they were friends of the deceased. The state prosecutor of Alaska brought charges against him, and he was found guilty of murder with a lengthy prison sentence, where he eventually died.

Rigors of the Job:

Strange Finds

An Unusual Find out in the Boondocks

One fall season during the yearly antelope hunt, I was patrolling a huge expanse of country, mostly sagebrush rolling hills and wheat fields in the adjoining dry land grain areas. To get a better view of the region and monitor for possible antelope hunters, I drove my vehicle upslope, then proceeded to hike higher up to a good observation point where I could use binoculars to scan the lower areas.

A couple antelope hunters were visible far out in the vista, so I tried to determine the best access route to meet up with them later. While sitting at my observation point I had heard and seen ravens in an area higher up the slope, so I decided to check in their vicinity to determine what was attracting them. After hiking a considerable distance, the foul odor that greeted me indicated something was dead and I soon saw the deteriorated carcass of a Rocky Mountain sheep. Further checking didn't reveal any evidence of a gunshot, so I continued on.

In scouting the surrounding areas, I came across an old, old hillside dugout cabin with a caved in roof, and mostly rock front walls. I threw aside some of the rotted roof material and soon saw some metal protruding out of the caved in debris. A considerable amount of digging finally revealed wrought iron from the base of an old sewing machine. What a surprise to find such an item out in such a remote area, far from any dwellings or any road or trail!

I had in mind to return and do some more digging out of curiosity, but never did. The remainder of the day I traveled back the lengthy distance and checked the antelope hunters' permits and bagged game.

Several days later, while contacting the Jefferson County attorney and sheriff, I told the sheriff about finding the crude old cabin. After some thought, the sheriff said that several administrations before him there was a report of a wanted man in that general area, but no case had ever developed and was forgotten over a period of time.

Old Stage Road Discovery

The sage mountain grouse hunt was in progress and I was patrolling an area that was used by many not-too-serious vehicle hunters. As I was hiking a section of the old, old Virginia City-Bannack stage and freight wagon road, I observed a small metallic item protruding from the center of the road bed. With a sheath knife and some pointed sticks, I spent about an hour digging the item free. My efforts were rewarded, and I was quite surprised to find an old rusted revolver that still had a full cylinder of cartridges, but so rusted that the caliber couldn't be determined.

I have very often wondered about the revolver's history. During that era of road agents and gold prospectors, nearly all men wore a side arm out of necessity. Considering the value of wearing such a piece, I have wondered if a victim of the road agents was waylaid on that spot, and his revolver left behind to be eventually covered with road dust and embedded in the ground.

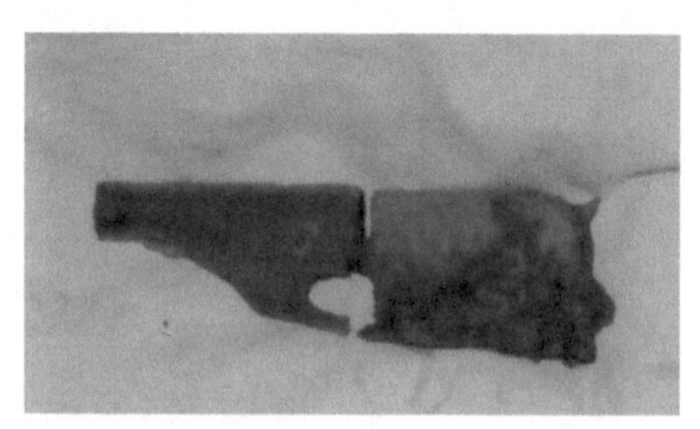

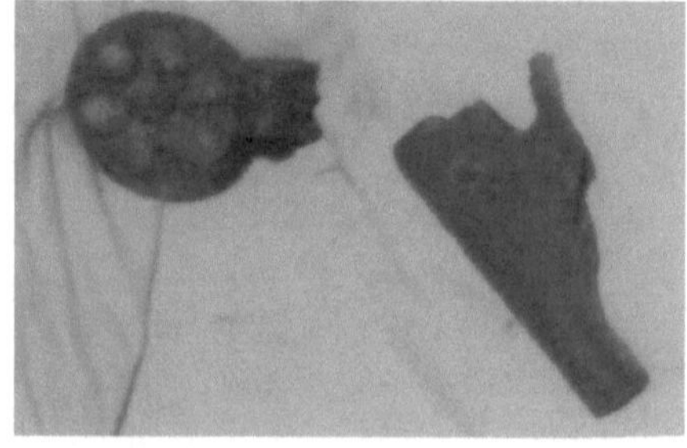

Remaining Evidence of Old Homestead Hardships

During the many years working in several districts, I came across numerous old homestead sites with remnants of old, usually caved in and deteriorated log cabins or hillside dug-outs with front or complete stone-work walls. Usually, there was a hand dug well, or a path to an invaluable nearby spring, sometimes with a surviving Virginia creeper vine and currant berry bush.

Many homestead claims had no trees close by for firewood or other needs, and it is difficult to imagine trying to heat a badly perforated cabin with dry cow chips and sagebrush for fuel! Also, if a metal stove wasn't part of the cabin furnishings, a crude fireplace constructed of mud mortar and rock must have left a lot to be desired for needed heat and cooking.

The normal 160-acre homestead wasn't adequate to make a living, and after barely surviving the extreme hardships, many who filed for homestead ownership abandoned their once proud piece of land, or sold it to someone more fortunate nearby.

Many of the old homestead structures showed evidence of a woman's touch with remnants of shaggy curtains and occasionally inside wall coverings of cloth or paper. The cabin roofs were usually soil and sod over logs, which also left a lot to be desired.

What an ordeal it must have been for the so-called "weaker sex!"

A Strangely Afflicted Moose

In a distant valley within my district, a rancher on horseback was riding along to check his cattle and discovered an adult cow moose who was circling while standing in a small area. He surmised that the animal was blind as it would face his horse as he maneuvered from side to side. After receiving a report from the rancher, I went to the remote grazing area, which had rolling hills below the base of a mountain. The rancher's description of the area was accurate with scattered trees and brush, and I had no difficulty locating the moose. Watching for a moment, I had to agree with the rancher's assessment that the moose appeared to be blind, but with no apparent injuries.

Back home, I contacted the regional Fish & Game headquarters, who advised me to kill the moose and take it to the Bozeman lab for diagnosis, so I returned to the ranch and carried out the orders. I then had to undertake the demanding and rigorous chore of dragging the moose carcass by horseback quite a long distance to where I could load it into my truck for transport to the lab.

Some weeks later the lab technician reported that a kind of insect had bored through the skull and into the moose's brain, which caused the strange and unusual circling movements. The moose would have died a miserable death had she not been humanely dispatched by me instead.

Prey's Escape from a Predator

While patrolling the Beaverhead River by canoe, I had occasion to tie the canoe to an overhanging willow bush below a river cut-bank. Sitting and eating a sandwich in the shade, I was surprised to see a mink pursuing a muskrat on top of the river bank. 'Lo and behold, the muskrat plunged off the bank and landed in the bottom of my canoe with a thud. The mink lingered momentarily then scurried away. I quickly grabbed the confused muskrat and tossed it in the river.

Later, floating over a shallow riffle area, I spotted an object protruding out of the river bed. I tied the canoe alongside the river bank and waded to the mysterious thing. It appeared to be a horn of sorts, so I took my G.I. entrenching shovel and dug around it. After some time digging in the compacted gravel, I was surprised to see it was the greater portion of a buffalo skull. Wouldn't it be of interest to know the circumstance for that buffalo skull to be there for many, many years? A couple of Dillon old-timers had once stated that there was a buffalo crossing on that portion of the Beaverhead River, so perhaps that is the answer.

Chapter Five

Close Calls

COUNTY OF BEAVERHEAD

KNOW ALL MEN BY THESE PRESENTS, That I have this day appointed and by these presents do appoint Wayne Fitzwater to be Special Deputy in the Sheriff's Department of the County of Beaverhead, State of Montana, giving him full power and authority to act in my name the same as I would in law be empowered to do, if personally present.

IN WITNESS WHEREOF, I have hereunto set my hand, this 31st day of December, 1974

R. L. "Buzz" Davis
Sheriff's Signature

SHERIFF DEPARTMENT - County of Beaverhead

Oper. License #0057446 Chauffeur
Badge #Special Comm. #
Birthdate: Nov. 9, 1918
Hgt.: 5'-5" Wgt.: 130
Hair: Brown Eyes: Grey

Wayne Fitzwater
OFFICER'S SIGNATURE

Thumb Print

Scare Gun Scare

In some areas during severe winters, elk feeding on haystacks can cause real problems for ranchers. It is often difficult to keep the elk away from the stacks without resorting to expensive fencing or paneling, and occasionally a re-opened restricted elk hunt is necessary.

In the early 1960s, the F & G Department began to use scare guns in an effort to keep elk away from the haystacks. A scare gun looks and works much like a small cannon. They operate on an explosive gas, such as carbide or propane, and are detonated by a sparker mechanism. The sparker is activated with a gas powered timer. Gas from a storage tank slowly fills a chamber until the pressure reaches a critical point that triggers the sparker, which then fires the gun. It sounds about like a 12-gauge shotgun. By adjusting the flow of the gas, the gun can be made to discharge more or less frequently.

After receiving a game damage call from a local rancher one day, I decided I would give the new contraption a try. Due to the deep snow, I had to snowshoe the gun and the propane tank to the haystack on a toboggan. The temperature that day was about 15 degrees Fahrenheit, with forecasts calling for much colder temperatures. The haystack was surrounded by a stackyard fence to keep the

Warden Fitzwater setting up a scare gun

cattle out. The fence did an adequate job of keeping the cattle out, but it was not much of an obstacle to the more athletic elk, who jumped over it with relative ease. I placed the little cannon near the stack and adjusted the timer so that it was discharging about every 10 minutes, figuring that this would be a good rate to cause the elk to keep their distance. After setting up the gun, I snowshoed back to my vehicle and left.

The rest of that evening and the first half of the night were spent patrolling a nearby deer wintering area where I had been receiving reports of jack-lighting. Around midnight I drove to the haystack area and looked across the meadow in the moonlight with my binoculars to see how things were going. I was somewhat surprised to see that the herd of elk had returned and was inside the fence eating hay. At this point, I concluded that the scare gun must not be working, so I unloaded my toboggan, strapped on my snowshoes, and was preparing to go and repair or remove the inoperative gun. It was much colder now and as I shivered and prepared to leave, there was an earsplitting blast from the haystack. The cannon had fired. I grabbed my binoculars and looked at the stack and elk were stampeding in every direction. They were falling all over themselves trying to escape, so I decided to wait and see if they would return, but after a considerable period of time, it appeared that they weren't coming back. During the entire wait the scare gun never fired again, so I decided to check on it.

Upon my arrival at the haystack, I just stood and stared at the wreckage. The elk herd had been inside the pole fence when the gun fired, and in their haste to depart they had neglected to jump the fence and had just crashed right through it. Poles and fence posts were everywhere, so I knew I wouldn't be dealing with a happy rancher in the morning. There wasn't much I could do then, except to take the gun back to the shop for a check-up. I disconnected the fuel tank and dragged the gun back to my warm truck on the toboggan.

When I reached the truck, I placed the gun on the front seat, closed the door, and proceeded to remove my snowshoes and load the toboggan. I had just opened the driver door to climb inside, when I was nearly deafened by an explosion. The cannon had managed to fire one last time, even though it was disconnected from the fuel tank, due to the built up pressure in the chamber. But, I didn't know it would do that, so after I re-gathered some of my senses, I stood there and thought about other possibilities. Suppose the thing had delayed another couple seconds until I was in the truck with the door shut before it went off, or suppose it had really delayed the discharge until I was back in town driving in traffic! With these thoughts in mind along with the severe ringing in my ears, and the unpleasant prospect of explaining the haystack situation to the rancher, the trip home was rather unpleasant.

Over the years, I came to understand the little quirks of scare guns a bit better. It seems they are somewhat temperature sensitive. The gas fills up the firing chamber until a certain amount of pressure is achieved, then it fires, and if you set the flow of gas when it is warm so that it will fire every 10 minutes or so, it may only go off every hour or so under extremely cold conditions. I also discovered that disconnecting the fuel tank does not release the gas already in the firing chamber, and if the chamber is quite full and you jar the gun or warm it, it could fire unexpectedly. Sometimes one learns to use equipment by merely reading the direction booklet, but other times it's just a case of trial by error.

To help ease the ill feelings of the rancher, I assisted in rebuilding the stackyard pole fence with the thought, *it all pays the same*, knowing it would also help better the public relation aspect between ranchers and the Fish & Game Department.

Buried In Snow

During the upper Gallatin elk hunt, I made it a point to snowshoe some relatively isolated areas where a few of the dedicated and hardier hunters ranged in search of elk, which were not always out near the highway or easily found. On one such patrol, I had snowshoed back near the head of a relatively short drainage where a couple hunters knew that a few elk congregated in their quest for winter forage on steep slopes, and their pawing for feed was somewhat easier.

I had seen a couple hunters on the opposite slope of the drainage and later heard a couple gunshots from that direction, so I started to snowshoe across the steep slope of the small, treeless basin. About halfway across the basin I sensed an unusual movement of the granular snow, and was conscious of a swishing kind of sound. I was immediately caught in a small snow slide, which tumbled me downslope. When all was quiet, I found myself deep in snow, though thankfully in an upright position with my head at the surface and my legs straddled apart. In fact, I was doing the splits and was really hurting because of the extra stretch!

I nearly always used ski poles when snowshoeing, and so had them strapped around my wrists like usual. The straps made it quite difficult to get my arm to the surface, but the granular snow allowed me to work my arm free enough that I could clear the snow away from my head, one handful at a time. It seemed to take an eternity to finally get my other arm and nearest leg free, and the snowshoe harness off my foot. Thankfully, I always had my snowshoe harness rigged so that one pull on the heel strap would release my foot. Once that snowshoe was worked free, I tried to use it in a shovel-like fashion to dig myself out, but the snow either flowed or blew back in on top of me. To avoid this, I threw the snow upward and the wind would blow it aside. After the hole around my upper body was large enough, it was much easier to free myself, but retrieving that lower, buried snowshoe took more digging.

After I managed to extricate myself from my snowy confines, I eventually caught up with the two hunters later that day and told them of my earlier predicament. One of the hunters said that he had indeed seen a lone person coming across that open basin, and then not long afterward saw no one, and wondered where the person had gone so quickly. I often think how very lucky I was to have been partially buried with my head up at snow level instead of the opposite direction. Even though they were cumbersome and binding, the fact that I was wearing heavy woolen trousers and shirt with a heavily lined duck-type shell coat kept me relatively dry and warm.

Avalanche Spectator

During the early 1950s, quite a number of fur trappers were putting out considerable effort to trap pine marten, which necessitated extending their trap lines up into the higher elevations of the mountains. One winter day, I snowshoed along one trapper's line, checking his methods to determine if everything was within legal bounds. It had been reported that this particular trapper regularly used mountain grouse and deer meat as bait for marten and lynx. My patrol efforts had taken me far up a drainage to a high, treeless basin that extended up to a rocky rim. Stopping to take a short breather, I used binoculars to scan the area and noted some ravens were high up near the rocky rim on the far side of the basin. After watching the birds for awhile, I decided they were feeding on some kind of animal carcass.

I decided to snowshoe there and determine what kind of animal the ravens were attracted to, so after starting across the deep snow basin I zigzagged back and forth to gain the elevation necessary to get to the carcass. I still don't know why I stayed on the south side of the basin instead of heading across the center, which would have been the shorter and more direct route, but it proved to be a good decision. Once up high, but still below the rocky rim, I maneuvered around the mountainside toward where I had seen the birds. About halfway there, I saw snow movement about fifty feet below, and as I watched I realized it was the head of an avalanche. The sight that followed was breathtaking, as the whole center area of the snowy depression literally roared down the slope, toppling several trees at the lower part of the basin. The utter silence that followed was unsettling.

After regaining my composure, I continued on to my destination and found the animal carcass was that of a mountain goat, but the cause of its death couldn't be determined because of the deteriorated condition of the skeletal remains. Around the carcass were numerous Canada lynx tracks, so there was the possibility that a lynx could have killed the small mountain goat.

During the course of my career, I witnessed other avalanches, and the memory of that sight and crashing sound has a way of coming back to mind, almost like a bad dream. How fortunate it was that I was high up on the slope instead of down in the snowy basin!

The Smell of a Grizzly Bear

During foot patrol duty in the Hoadley Reef area on the south fork of the Flathead River, I observed a mountain goat hunter stalking a goat on a rock ledge with a drop off far below. The hunter finally shot the goat and ever so slowly worked his way down to the goat carcass. Due to the lateness in the day, I decided to hike the distance back to my camp and planned to go to the goat carcass the next day. Previously, at a hunter camp that I had checked earlier in the day, I learned that one of the hunters intended to hunt for a goat, so I assumed that was the fellow who had shot the animal and was certain that it would painstakingly be retrieved by horse.

The next day I hiked the long distance to the goat carcass. Once I was only fifty yards or so from it, I was sure I smelled grizzly and soon saw grizzly droppings. The odor grew stronger, which put me on alert with an uneasy feeling. I continued to the goat carcass and saw that a grizzly bear had indeed fed on it so I didn't linger, as I thought that the bear may be bedded down nearby with a full stomach.

Later that day I hiked to the hunter camp I had previously visited, and advised the hunter who had killed the goat of the grizzly and the sad condition of the goat carcass. I warned him that he should use extreme caution when he arrived at the scene, and that if the carcass wasn't salvageable, he could just take the head and cape.

A Surprise Meeting

At one time, I was authorized to patrol hunters' camp areas and activities in the Strait Creek and Danaher areas, along with the south fork of the Flathead River. I would often go before my patrol duty and scout out an advantageous campsite. On one occasion, I hiked miles in on the trail, which took all day, and I was quite late hiking back out to my vehicle. At dusk I realized that my revolver, an old .38 Colt with a butt lanyard ring, had bounced out of my holster, probably while I was jogging at one time or another.

Even at the late hour, and with a bright full moon, I went back the several miles to look for the gun. At one bend in the path, I saw a sizable grizzly on the trail ahead. As the bear stood its ground and raised upright looking at me and swinging its large head from side to side, I backed off just far enough to keep the bear in sight. After quite a long time in standoff, the bear finally left the trail.

After spending so much time waiting for the bear to move on, it was getting quite dark when I was at last able to continue looking. The darkness, combined with my fatigue from a long day's hike, followed by the several miles I had already backtracked made the decision to resume my search in the morning an easy one. When I returned the next day, I did ultimately find the missing firearm, albeit several miles in on that long trail.

A Broken Boulder

I well remember an incident that nearly cost me my life. While hiking to a couple of high mountain lakes on a patrol with the intent of camping out three nights or so, I chose to camp out of sight of the trail so any fishermen going to those lakes on the weekend would not know of my presence. I chose a campsite for its huge granite boulder, with the front face sloping back. It formed a natural shelter that made a nearly perfect place to bunk down, and would reflect heat back from a campfire. I built a larger than average campfire that night so it would leave an ample bed of hot coals for cooking, and especially for warmth through the very cool night.

While the fire was going, I placed a pole lengthwise under the overhanging boulder and filled in the space between the pole and boulder with pine needles. Pleased with the arrangement, I thought I might use that campsite again sometime when on patrol in the area. I spread my bedroll on the mat of pine needles and laid my small pack sack aside. After watching the campfire settle down to hot coals, I decided to go to the nearby creek to wash up and get water for camp use.

On my arrival back to the campsite I could hardly believe what I saw! The heat from the campfire had caused a huge, heavy slab of the granite boulder to fracture off, and it had fallen down on the prepared bunk and completely covered my bedroll, except for a small portion on one end. The slab of granite was so heavy that I couldn't budge it even a fraction of an inch, and had I been on my bunk, it would certainly have crushed me. It seems that such close calls in a person's lifetime have a tendency to stay in memory and surface occasionally as a reminder of how lucky a man can be to still be living at the ripe age of 97 years.

Lightning Encounter on a High Mountain Slope

Out on foot patrol one day, I hiked to a high-elevation mountain lake to check for fishing activity and there was a vehicle parked at the trailhead. The trail crossed a grassy slope several miles from the trailhead, and while I was making my way across that grassy range a thunderous lightning storm developed overhead. To keep from getting dampened by the scant rainfall, I took shelter under a small limber pine tree. Not long afterward, several lightning strikes were visible in the area. One bolt struck a large dead pine tree very close by to my hideout and literally blew dry pitchy chunks of wood all around me. Having served in WWII battle areas, I was somewhat shaken, as the blast reminded me of artillery or mortar strikes.

Airplane Mishaps and Two Lucky Landings

Through the years, several Montana game wardens and game warden managers died in plane crashes pursuing their duties, conducting aerial game censuses and mandatory law enforcement patrols. As sometimes happens, pilot error in the high altitude conditions ended up being fatal mistakes.

When I was assigned to the Helena district, I experienced two close calls with light plane engine failures while flying alone, and luckily landed safely both times. I had been coached by an instructor that in such an event, quickly choose a landing spot, and even if the choice is not the best, do not "stretch the glide" of the plane and possibly stall airborne.

The first close call occurred when I had an engine catch fire. I remembered my instruction, so I chose a hayfield for the "dead stick" landing, and with the hay growth about halfway to cutting time the lateral irrigation ditches were not very obvious. On landing, the gliding speed was enough to skip over the first ditch at a 90-degree angle and the height of the hay slowed the plane quickly. As I struck the second ditch, the plane nearly nosed over, and in what felt like slow motion settled back to a three-point position—lucky, lucky!

The other engine failure ended by landing on a graded area alongside some highway department gravel stockpiles. Due to the short landing area while descending powerless, I put the plane in a "slip" by cross-controlling to lose altitude faster and slow forward flight. This time a wire fence was about fifteen feet ahead when the plane stopped! Naturally, I hiked to the rancher's domicile to report the stalled plane in his field, and my plan to remove it with the least damage to his hay crop.

Flying High

When I occasionally flew over certain areas of considerable fishing and hunting activities, I would fly above several high mountain lakes, especially during holiday periods. One such flight took me over the Tizer Lakes in a pocket below the surrounding Elkhorn Mountains. As I circled over the lake, I was conscious of a down draft, and when deciding to leave the area, I could not gain the necessary altitude due to the gutless Aeronca light plane. Stuck circulating over the lake, I finally noticed a slot through the conifer trees at the lake's outlet. It seemed the only choice to get out of my predicament, so I flew through the tight confines of the many tree branches, and I managed to go downstream and gain altitude, then fly back to the airfield with bothersome memories of that close call.

Airplane Hopscotch

On a winter day in the mid 1950s, Refuge Manager Winston Banko, at the Red Rock Lakes Refuge in the upper Centennial Valley of southwest Montana, sent word out to me that he wished to discuss troublesome beaver dams on Red Rock Creek above Upper Red Rock Lake before springtime. His concern was that the many beaver dams on the creek would interfere with the spring spawning run of Montana grayling.

While flying winter game census in the north and south Centennial areas, I mentioned to the pilot, Gene Sherman, that I planned to go to the refuge once the south-side road was passable by vehicle. Sherman kindly offered to land near the refuge, as we still had quite some time left on gas reserve and several hours of daylight, which would save me a snow-plane trip. Sherman's plane had skis for snow landings and wheels for bare ground landings, so he made a ski landing in fairly deep snow in a comparatively small nearby pasture field. With a stiff headwind and upslope terrain, it was a good landing with some clear area still ahead once the plane was stopped. I expected Sherman to taxi that extra distance nearer the fence and road, but he didn't.

We trudged through the snow to the refuge headquarters. While having a cup of coffee and homemade cookies (good too!), I discussed the beaver dam situation with Refuge Manager Banko. Plans were made to dynamite many of the obstructions the following spring, and to also have a West Yellowstone trapper with decent trapping skills, but not the best reputation, trap as many beaver as possible so there would hopefully not be much interference with the graylings' spawning come springtime.

It was soon mid-afternoon and still windy, so Sherman and I made it a short visit and went to the plane to take off for Dillon. Because of the snow depth and wind, the ski tracks from the landing were barely visible, so I mentioned to him that perhaps a trail should be broken on the path of the take-off, but he indicated there would be no problem. I expected him to taxi the plane the extra distance to the upper area of the field to provide more runway for take off, but Sherman said he would turn the plane by hand instead and then for me to get aboard.

Once aboard, Sherman went full-throttle downwind and downslope and I could see the dense willows at the far end coming at us much sooner than I wished! I had flown about 70 hours myself by then, and didn't care for that downwind take-off in deep snow and in that short runway area, but it didn't seem appropriate to coach the pilot who had many more mountain flying hours than me to his credit.

The plane's ski drag in the snow was obvious and when there wasn't any more take-off area ahead, and the willows were closer and closer, Sherman brought the control stick back and we finally became airborne. The plane soon shuddered and mushed and then settled down so that we hopscotched over the willows. Sherman dropped the nose of the plane and kept full throttle as we brushed the willow tops and were finally airborne and clear. Nothing was said by either of us, as though it was an everyday occurrence.

The plane's skis had a system so they could be raised for a wheel landing or lowered for a snow landing, so en route to Dillon, Sherman hand pumped the hydraulic system for the skis to raise for a wheel landing, but for some reason the skis wouldn't lift. After several repeat tries, he asked if I would take the stick while he went out and gave the skis a kick or two to try to free them from their stuck position.

Sherman was a big man so, because of my small stature, I offered to do the kicking instead. As we opened the upper and lower cockpit doors, the wind was darned cold but I went out on the plane's wing strut and sat on it so I could kick the landing gear. After a couple hefty kicks, the problem was temporarily corrected and the skis were raised for a wheel landing. We proceeded on our flight path over mountainous terrain and made a normal landing at the Dillon airfield, calling it a day.

Sherman checked the landing gear and later that evening called to tell me that everything was a "go" for another game census flight the following day, weather permitting. I thought at the time, "Knowing Sherman, we'll go if it's anything less than a blizzard and we can see the ground!"

The experience was truly a close call!

A Bad Drop Off

While on patrol one day, I came upon a group of snowmobilers riding along a trail on the ridge between two mountain drainages. After checking their compliance with state regulations, I followed them for a while before moving on to monitor other riders in the area. Before parting ways, I observed one of the riders go off the trail to an overlook to take in the spectacular view. He rode out onto a large area of accumulated overhanging snow, but from the trail it looked to be part of the mountainside.

Shockingly, when I crossed that way again later in the day, I discovered that the snow had broken away and caused a small avalanche below. The "mountainside" snow was actually a snow cornice created by snow drifting over the ridge. It was a dreadful thought to realize how tragic it would have been had the cornice broken away while the rider and his snowmobile were atop it.

About to Sink in a Lake

Warden Art Warner and I got together occasionally to do some snowmobile patrol at a few lakes that were fished through the lakes' surface ice. As we approached one lake, we didn't spot any fishermen, so Warden Warner left the trail above and dropped down to the lake shore and out on the surface ice, which had approximately six to eight inches of snow cover. I stopped on the trail, but still within voice contact of Warden Warner. After breaking for a cup of coffee, I noticed that a huge area of ice was slowly sinking with Warner and his snowmobile on it in about in the center of the lake, so I yelled out, "Get the snowmobile off the lake quickly! It is slowly sinking! Quick, quick!"

Fortunately Warden Warner heeded my directions. Once he was back on the trail, we sat and could see by the water line in the snow that with the weight of the snowmobile, the sizable circular piece of ice was still slowly sinking. We shuddered to think of the near tragedy.

High-Stepping Warden

While working in Broadwater County and the surrounding area in the early 1950s, I was occasionally assisted by Sheriff Jack Thompson, who had at one time also been a state game warden. On one such occasion, Sheriff Thompson had received some reports of night hunting and shooting in an area where livestock was present. I told him I would go to the area and put in some night patrol, and he offered to accompany me.

Upon our arrival at the site, it was agreed that I would climb to the top of a nearby rocky outcropping, which would serve as a vantage point. If any spotlighting activity was seen or any gunshots were heard, I was to radio Sheriff Thompson on his walkie-talkie and guide him to the location or, if needed, rejoin him to investigate the situation.

After a couple of hours on the peak, I saw a distant spotlight and heard a shot—then nothing, so I radioed Jack and we agreed it would be better for me to rejoin him and we would head in the direction of the light and shot and see what we could find. As I started bounding down the hill, hopping from rock to rock in the moonlight, I heard it, and the instant I heard it, the hair on the back of my neck stood up. It was one of those sounds that if you've ever heard it, you never forget it...RATTLESNAKES!

In the daylight they are scary, but at least you can see them. At night, all you know is that they are right under you somewhere and rattling. They seemed to be all over the hillside and due to the steep angle of the hill and my forward momentum, I couldn't slow down without planting both feet and coming to a virtual stop, which could have meant a snake bite. Every time I landed, I just hoped that I wouldn't twist an ankle, or land on a loose rock in the dark for it wasn't a good place for a fall. The entire run probably only took a couple minutes, considering the speed at which I was cannon-balling down the hill.

Once at the vehicle, I slid into the patrol car and wheezed out the story to Jack. Jack told me that he did recollect that this hill was supposed to be a denning area for snakes, but that he thought the snakes would have been denned up by this chilly, fall date. Evidently the snakes found it more comfortable to snooze on daytime, sun-warmed rocks at night rather than in a damp underground den.

After catching my breath, we took off in pursuit of the poachers but didn't find them in the darkness. The next day we found one empty cartridge in the area, but no sign of a drag trail or blood.

Rattlesnake Strikeout

I was checking fishermen's licenses and their catches near a campground that was close to a river one afternoon. I had traveled quite a distance along the rocky river bank while making my rounds, and was quite far from the campground by then. Out of the corner of my eye, I saw some movement by my leg and was rather surprised to see a rattlesnake, with its fangs caught in the jeans down over my boot.

Having handled numerous rattlesnakes through the years, I caught it and took it back to the campground with me. I found a container at the campground's trash disposal area and put the snake in, with plans to take it home at the end of the day. Considering the number of people around the area, including children, I went around the campground notifying visitors about the rattlesnake, and that there could be others in the area. Naturally, that ruined the enjoyment of camping for many there.

I took the rattlesnake home that evening, and the next day I examined it. On closer inspection, I learned it could not rattle due to an obvious, old injury. Later that fall, I scouted the rocky outcropping and south slopes of the area adjacent to the campground where the snake had been, and located a rattlesnake den with quite a gathering of snakes in the warm late fall weather. I suggested to the campground manager that it would be wise to put up a couple signs informing visitors of the possibility of encountering a rattlesnake, but he said it would probably discourage campground use.

The hill out of Radersburg, MT that Warden Fitzwater used as a vantage point to observe for illegal nighttime spot-lighters in High-Stepping Warden.

Another Close Call with a Rattlesnake

One fall season when the sage grouse hunt was in progress, I was patrolling a sagebrush basin. After scanning the area for hunters, I decided to hike to a rocky outcropping to get a better view with my binoculars. I worked my way up to the top of the outcropping's rock ledge. As I was just short of the top of the ledge, I managed to get a foot and handhold and kind of bounced upward to help hoist myself up. To my surprise, there on the ledge in front of my face was a sizable rattlesnake stretched out full length in the daytime sun. As you can imagine, it was fortunate that I did not extend my arms above the ledge before I looked over the top, because it would have undoubtedly caused the snake to coil into striking position. That incident caused frequent bad memories and even today, many years later, it comes to mind and is still troublesome!

Flooded Out and a Surprise Strike

While patrolling a lake area where there was a creek crossing en route on the access road, my engine stalled mid-stream in the creek. The engine wouldn't start, so the water current gradually washed the stream-bottom sand away from the wheels, and water was soon flowing above the floor boards from door to door. Considering there was very little fishermen traffic to that particular lake, I had a long, long hike to the nearest ranch for help. In a hurry to get to the ranch, I took a shorter route across a rocky, dry sagebrush covered area, and at one point I stopped for a break. As I sat on a flat rock, I immediately heard a rattlesnake's signature sound, and the snake struck my boot just above the boot heel. When I arrived at the ranch and told the rancher about the snake, he said that they had killed more rattlesnakes than usual that year in the hayfields adjacent to the rocky hills.

A Failed Idea

In the late 1940s and 1950s, numerous mule deer areas were opened to after season extended hunts due to overpopulation in deer wintering areas. The overpopulation of deer on the Northern Arizona Kaibab Plateau was used as an example of the need for deer reductions, and the hunter and his gun were the tools needed for the necessary decrease in the mule deer population. While I was assigned to several southwestern Montana areas, I worked many districts with mule deer overpopulations, such as the Stillwater Horseman Flats, Broadwater Limestone Hills, Beaverhead Scudder Creek, and Little Sheep Creek areas, all of which were re-opened to extended deer hunting.

While out patrolling the Little Sheep Creek area during severe cold and blustery conditions, my vehicle defroster and heater weren't functioning properly, so I had an idea to try to defrost the windshield. I raised the vehicle hood and then found a small round stone alongside the road. With my right hand, I held the stone in place so the engine heat might defrost the windshield. As I was forcing the counter-balanced hood down with my left arm, the stone tumbled into the engine compartment and the hood snapped down and latched, painfully trapping three fingers and thumb of my right hand. Being trapped just so, I couldn't free my throbbing fingers while stretching upward due to my short stature, and so I was in a serious predicament. Unfortunately, I had left the vehicle cab with my coat unzipped and the below-zero cold was quite chilling. What an embarrassing situation if by chance a hunter had come by!

I momentarily thought that the only possible option would be to pull my fingers free and suffer the damaging injury, but looking at the snow covered ground I saw a small stick extending above the snow. I used my left foot to work it toward my legs and after several tries, I managed to get it where I finally worked it upward and within reach of my left hand via some painful stretching. Luckily, the wooden limb was strong enough to enable me to pry the crushing hood up to free my injured and discolored fingers. Another close call!

A Wild, Wild Ride

Out on patrol one day, I was driving in a popular deer hunting area when I observed that a vehicle had gone up a long, steep slope which led to an excellent plateau area known for sizable bucks. I had chained up my vehicle because of the wintry, snowy conditions, and figured the truck could make the journey up the treacherous road.

I started up the long, long, steep slope following the well worn, snow covered, deeply rutted and frozen jeep trail. When I was nearly to the top of the long grade, the trail was quite rough and the vehicle stalled because of improper carburetor float level adjustment. I held the vehicle with the brakes while trying to re-start it. Slowly, it started to skid backward, so I intermittently applied the brakes, thinking if the tire chain cross links were positioned right it would probably hold the vehicle. Instead of slowing, the vehicle gradually gained more speed backward down the slope! So, I did the only thing I could do and held the steering straight and steady while I kept braking for whatever good it might do. Truly, it was one of those wild rides no one would wish to experience.

Near the bottom of that snowy grade, the jeep trail veered off at an angle. My vehicle jumped out of the rutted tracks and kept going until crusted snow and taller sagebrush slowed it before, as if in slow motion, it tipped over on its side. I then climbed out the top door window and surveyed the damage, which appeared minimal.

Feeling slightly relieved things weren't as bad as I thought, but still shaken, I unloaded my high-lift jack and spare tire. Using my jacket as padding at the top of the door on the ground, I managed to lift the vehicle enough to position the upright spare under the lifted vehicle so I could get a good base, then continued to jack it up until the vehicle landed back on all four wheels. Once upright, it then skidded for several yards until it stopped by some clumps of sagebrush.

After again checking the vehicle and finding no serious issues, I determined that if the engine would start I would continue patrol for the remainder of the day. It started, so I continued on, but I never, never want to live through such a helplessly wild, wild ride backward down a mountain slope ever again!

"Timber-r-r-r, Look Out!"

While working the Butte area, I received a report that some illegal hunting might be taking place in a remote area that was accessible only by four-wheel drive vehicles. At that time, old-timer game warden Howard Larsen had retired and his winch-equipped jeep was transferred to me as the incoming warden, so I made good use of it to patrol such areas.

While proceeding over the very rough jeep trail on my way to investigate the illegal hunting, the vehicle became stuck in a deeply rutted muddy area. I climbed out of the jeep and pulled out enough winch cable to go around the base of a nearby and fairly large dead tree, then I engaged the winch to slowly pull the vehicle forward. Considering the winch was geared very low, I watched off the side of the jeep for forward movement but saw none, so I got back out of the vehicle and checked the engaging lever and cable. Determining that everything was okay, I assumed there must have been considerable slack in the winch cable. Again I proceeded to slowly winch the vehicle forward, and was looking off to the side for even the slightest forward movement, but saw none. I stopped the jeep engine and was about to get out again when I looked ahead and saw that the large tree was very slowly tipping over toward the jeep.

There wasn't time enough to do anything but duck sideways on the seat while that tree came crashing down and barely missed the vehicle! Having lost my primary anchor point, there wasn't anything else close by to again fasten the winch cable, so a steel bar carried for just that purpose was driven into the ground. Thankfully, it held enough to get the vehicle free.

As I had already had my fair share of vehicle casualties through the years, I was very grateful that the good little jeep escaped what could have been a vehicle disaster. Undoubtedly another close call.

A Wild Ride Down the Mountainside

While night patrolling for people spotlighting deer and elk, and driving only with military style black-out lights, I was following a vehicle using a spotlight. I stopped my vehicle at a curve in the unimproved mountain road to get a better sight on the spotlighter, without paying much attention that I was parking at the edge of a roadside precipice off a high, steep grade. I leaned over the steering wheel to look through my binoculars at the vehicle winding along the road below. I was so engrossed in my duties that I had not set the emergency brake, and unbeknownst to me, the vehicle was slowly moving forward, until it finally tipped over the steep road embankment. The vehicle went once end-over-end, then rolled twice sideways, then backward, and ultimately landed in a creek channel, with all my gear and supplies in the front seat next to me.

I was lucky—I only ended up with a gash on my head and one ear injured, plus some bruises. After gathering my senses, I looked for my flashlight and realized it was after midnight. There were no ranch residences for miles and miles, and I thought about the long, miserable walk out. I found my flashlight and was surprised to see the headlights of an oncoming vehicle up on the road, so I waved the flashlight at just the right time, and after the vehicle bypassed the area for a short distance, it then backed up and a fellow yelled, "Is someone down there?"

I answered by name and there was silence while I slowly climbed the steep slope to the road above. When I got there, I was surprised to see it was a local fellow that I had issued a Fish & Game citation to only weeks before. The guy jokingly said, "Fitzwater, I should have left your ass down there!"

What a stroke of luck to have the fellow see my flashlight and stop to give me a ride to the Dillon hospital.

Surprised by Reservoir Gale Force Winds

I was occasionally asked to assist the regional fisheries and game biologists in pursuit of their work projects afield. On one occasion, the fisheries biologist asked if I would assist in putting out gill nets for his study of reservoir fish populations. I agreed to lend a hand, so we went out and set the nets at the appropriate reservoir locations. Being occupied with our tasks, we failed to see an oncoming storm, but we hurriedly set the last gill net as the wind increased suddenly. Since we were midway out on the reservoir, we quickly started for the nearest shoreline, which was rocky. The wind increased to gale force, and in desperation to get off the water we had no choice but to land on the shoreline rocks. It was really a chore to pull the boat up over rocks, and then drag it quite a long distance to the boat launch site. The reservoir has a history of surprising boat fishermen with sudden winds and has caused numerous mishaps.

Unexpected Dunking

During wintertime, I would periodically patrol certain frozen-over lakes for fisherman activities, and usually did so by snowmobile if snow conditions were appropriate. On one patrol, there were only a couple of fishermen present, so I walked with ice-cleats on my shoes toward an angler who had just hooked a fish in the area of open water beyond the edge of the ice. The fellow was quite excited, as it appeared that he had caught a sizable trout. As I made my way over to him, I stopped to check another fisherman who had augured an ice hole back on the deeper frozen ice. As we talked briefly, we heard a couple loud yells and looked to see the other fisherman floundering in the water. A section of ice had broken away and tilted downward, sliding him into the water. The fisherman, with his snowmobile suit zipped up, was quite buoyant, and he continued to hold onto his fishing rod while yelling, "Help! Help!"

I ran to my snowmobile and got a rope, and then ran out toward the edge of the ice. I got down on my belly, and heaved the rope out but it landed short of the fellow. So the guy, still floating on the water's surface, arm-paddled in closer where he then grabbed the rope. The other fishermen and I had difficulty pulling the frightened fellow up on the ice, but we managed to get him up on the thicker ice edge. The dunked fisherman tossed his fishing rod out on the ice surface as he clambered out of the water, and we were all surprised when later a sizable trout was reeled in!

Once the big trout was reeled in, all the fishermen and I moved back to shore to warm up by a fire that I had built to help dry out the doused angler. Amazingly, he was only wet at his lower neck, lower arms and lower legs, because the tight-fitting and zipped up snowmobile suit had sealed out most of the water and kept him buoyant, and undoubtedly saved him.

A Hazardous River Float

At a specific time of year, depending on weather and other conditions, the renowned Big Hole River has a significant salmonfly hatch which draws many fishermen, with many floating the high runoff waters. It was common for trees along the riverbank to be washed out and float downstream in the turbulent river flow, and occasionally such floating objects posed a threat to boaters.

Accompanied by neighboring Warden Secor one day, we were boat patrolling the river during a high water time. As we were going downstream, there were a couple washed out whole trees floating ahead. Unexpectedly, one tree stump end was held on the deep river bottom and the tree top lifted out of the river surface and went upright, then slammed downward with a huge splash. Luckily, we were not dangerously close, but another boat with two fishermen was quite close and they were visibly shaken.

Along that same stretch of river there was an old cable anchored on both river banks. With significant high waters and the sag in the cable running bank to bank, it was at times low enough that a standing fisherman in a midstream boat would need to duck under the cable to clear it. I later returned to the cable while on canoe patrol, and tied some fluorescent yellow ribbon on it to warn fishermen who were otherwise engrossed in their angling activities of the cable's presence. A person had to be quite cognizant when floating that part of the Big Hole River.

White Fish and Shelf Ice

While assigned to the Stillwater County district, I was out one wintry day making the rounds along the sometimes treacherous Yellowstone River, where a few hardy fishermen were after whitefish for smoking. Old "Swede" was regularly out fishing, and on this particular day there was considerable shelf-ice which jutted out into the river, and in places was helpful in fishing a good whitefish hole.

Swede had a small bonfire along the river bank, and was thawing out his fish line while warming his hands when I asked to check his license and catch. Swede told me that he had some fish in his fish sack, which was out on the ice, away from the bank. So I went out, knelt down, and proceeded to check the fish. While kneeling down, I noticed that water was slowly coming up on my foot and the packs, and then looking toward the bank, I could see that a large chunk of shelf ice had cracked off at Swede's bank fire and was slowly tipping toward the fast flowing open water with me on it.

I hastily started toward the bank, but with water covering the ice it was too slippery. I quickly sat down in the water, tossed Swede's fish sack toward the bank and called to Swede for his help. Slowly and casually, the fisherman extended his long solid length cane pole out to where I could grab it, and I literally went hand-over-hand up the cane pole to the safety of the bank.

I still occasionally have bad thoughts about that experience, and feel very, very lucky that Swede was using a solid length cane pole instead of a jointed one, which would have certainly come apart and sent me out into the surging river and then under the surface ice a short distance downstream, meaning doom for me. Or, it may have been doomsday for Swede if he had been the one out on the ice after I left!

Chapter Six

Entertaining Encounters

MONTANA SHERIFFS
AND PEACE OFFICERS ASSOCIATION

This is to certify that WAYNE FITZWATER
STATE GAME WARDEN, DILLON, MONTANA.
is a member of the MONTANA SHERIFF'S and PEACE
OFFICERS ASS'N. and has paid dues to 1-1-77
Dated this 28th day of May 19 76

Secretary-Treasurer

1361 Wayne Fitzwater
Member's Signature

Entertaining Encounters:
Comical Critters

How Not to Discourage a Nuisance Bear

While working the Helena warden district, I received word through the main Fish & Game office that there was a black bear problem at the Gates of the Mountains campground, which was accessible only by boat. I went to the boat landing and rode the excursion boat to the campground, along with a boatload of sightseers and picnickers. At the campground, several people from a previous excursion trip were picnicking and had been chased away from their picnic table by the bear, who was not far away.

I told the excursion boat operator that I was compelled to live trap the bear due to the dangerous possibility of it chasing people. The boat operator said that wouldn't be necessary, and he offered to coach picnickers on how to avoid a confrontation with the bear. After his speech, the bear came right back to a picnic table, so the boat operator took a long willow switch and said, "I'll show you how to discourage the bear," and proceeded to switch the animal. The bear left the table and, with ears laid back, came at the fellow, who gave ground. The bear pursued him down the pathway between some laughing, excited, and frightened people to the excursion boat, then ambled off while chomping its jaws in anger.

Having a sudden change of heart, the boat operator said, "Warden, that bear was good for my boat business, but I agree you should live trap and remove it."

Quite a few people had gotten in the boat by then in a rush for security, and one man in the boat was calling, "Women and children first." After the situation had quieted down somewhat, the boat operator advised the passengers that he was obligated to first transport those who had made the first excursion trip that day, and allowed some of them to board the boat along with a few others that were very frightened that the bear would return. However, I was concerned that the boat was overloaded and without adequate life preservers, so I had some people stay behind to wait for the next sailing. I stated I would remain at the campsite and keep the bear away until the last of the visitors were transported back to the boat landing.

As part of my regular warden dress, I carried a .38 caliber revolver and one fellow asked, “Would you really shoot the bear?”

To reassure him, I said, “Only if the bear returned and was seriously endangering anyone.”

Meanwhile, the fellow who called out that women and children should be allowed to go first aboard had a couple of admirers who were holding his arms up in praise of his stand. Upon return of the boat, the bear had not made another appearance and I suggested to those who had planned to picnic that they not open their picnic food at the campground tables. Quite a few of the people awaiting the arrival of the excursion boat were very skittish during the wait, and continued with loud sound making as a deterrent to prevent the bear's return.

The next day I took the live trap to the campground and soon caught the bear, with plans to release it in a remote area the following day. The local Federal Game Agent learned of the planned bear release and wanted to accompany me to the release site to get some photos of the bear. At the site, I opened the door on the live trap and the agent was off to one side with an old

Brownie box camera. Yet, the bear didn't immediately run off, and instead started toward the game agent, and I had to call to the agent to get aside as the bearing was coming right at him. As some may recall, the old style box cameras' view finders put the photo subject out at a greater distance than the reality.

Welcomed by an Aggressive Dog

A rancher contacted me about nuisance beaver building dams on the ranch creek, which flooded the hay meadows to the extent that he couldn't cut his hay due to the flooding and saturated ground. When arriving at the ranch, I was welcomed by two ranch dogs. As I was walking toward the ranch house, I realized that one of the dogs was very aggressive. This dog had come in behind me and quickly snapped at my leg. At the time, I was wearing a metal leg brace due to a WWII combat injury, and the brace had mercifully prevented a flesh wound.

Later, I paid another visit to the ranch in order to notify the rancher that the beaver had been live trapped, that the dams causing the flooding had been removed by blasting, and that some of the willow stick dam materials may be in the adjoining hay fields. In anticipation of this meeting with the rancher and his dog, I exited my vehicle with a lead-head blackjack in hand. Sure enough, as I walked the distance to the house the aggressive dog slyly approached from behind. Just as he was about to bite, I quickly whacked the dog's head and the dog fell to the ground. By the time I reached the rancher's front door, the dog had recovered and was on his feet.

Answering the door with a crude napkin in hand, the fellow said, "You caught me at eating time."

I didn't want to keep him from his meal, so I quickly spoke my piece about the doings with the beavers and their dams, and he thanked me for my "extremely helpful" efforts. Almost as an afterthought, he then said, "I should have told you that the one ranch dog will bite."

During a couple of my later visits at the ranch, the dog barked at me but never attempted to bite me. Perhaps the whack may have been a lesson well-learned.

A Wrong Kick in the Butt

I visited and checked numerous big game hunter tent camps through the years, and when visiting one camp, one of the hunters asked me how best to treat embedded porcupine quills and the punctures they left behind. It seemed that one of the hunters had an unwelcome dog in camp, and the dog had gotten into some of their food in the cook tent on occasion. One of his hunting mates was at the makeshift table in the tent writing a letter when he saw movement on the ground near the entrance flap and readied himself for a kick in the dog's butt. He said, "My foot was about halfway there when I realized too late that it wasn't the dog, but a damned porcupine."

He had quite a lot of quills throughout his slipper socks, and his hunting partners tried to remove them as best as possible. One guy said he had heard that vinegar would soften quills and make them easier to remove, but the damage and pain were plentiful and persistent.

A Surprise Revelation

I was again working with a couple wardens, patrolling and checking hunters' tent camps. After checking one of the camps, a warden approached one of the resident hunters about their success. The hunter replied that they had not had any luck. Questioningly, the warden then said, "It appears that you have deer or elk heart or liver in those plastic bags out back of the tent."

The hunter laughed, and then replied, "Those are bags of poop from our porta-potty. That's how we keep animals from chewing through the bags, which we will properly dispose of later."

Cowboys Shouldn't Rope Bears

Out in the rugged Montana wilderness one day, two cowboys saw a black bear in an open field and foolishly decided they would test their team roping skills. They managed to neck-shoulder and heel catch the bear well enough, but their horses didn't particularly like the catch. They had their own rodeo going for awhile, and could have caused their cayuses some real hurt with spooked horses and slack in their ropes.

They were hoping to get both lariats free at about the same time, but had their hands full just staying clear of the bear, so one of them went around a tree trunk and tied his lariat hard and fast. His partner then tried to keep a tight rope on the bear while he cautiously approached the beast. He intended to bash him over the head with a sizable rock, in hopes of getting their lariats loose, then quickly remount and get in the clear.

Amazingly, the cowboy did manage to wallop the bear upside the head with his rock. The blow momentarily stunned the bear, but he managed the get only his partner's lasso loose, so now they had a roped bear tied to a tree! The cowboys stayed around awhile, thinking the bear might climb the tree and the lariat might work itself loose enough that they could get in and untie it from the tree trunk and quickly ride away.

It was about this time that I received a call about the cowboys' antics, so I took the bear live trap out to the scene. The bear had climbed the tree, but still had the rope over its one shoulder and neck. I baited and set the trap, and since it was late evening by that point, I decided I would check the trap the next morning.

Sure enough, the bear was in the live trap the following morning, and luckily the rope was off, so I drove the trap and bear back home with the intention of releasing it somewhere more hospitable later. Along the way, I noticed the bear was bleeding slightly from either the nose or mouth. With the bear's best interest in mind, I decided to observe it a couple of days to try to determine if its injury was of any seriousness. In the meantime, my wife Alice and I provided food and water and numerous tidbits of Alice's good goodies, which the bear readily devoured.

A few days later, the bear seemed to recover from the cowboy's rock-bashing, so I transported the trapped bear to a remote mountain area for its release. I raised the live trap door and went to the cab of my pickup truck, expecting to watch the bear make a hasty getaway. The bear didn't get out! I could hear the bear's claws raking the bottom of the live trap, but still no bear came out. So, I backed down the slope, then applied the brakes to try and gently jostle the bear out and saw just its hind legs on the ground, but then the bear went back into the trap. I repeated the procedure again, and when I looked around, the bear immediately jumped back in again. The next go-round put the bear on the ground again, so I immediately went forward upslope, and after a moment's hesitation, here came that damn bear behind the trap. Determined, I sped up and finally the bear stopped with a futile look around, then ambled off towards the nearby timber.

Alice thought it was her kitchen goodies that brought about the bear's reluctance to leave a good thing!

A Mother River Otter's Challenge

When I worked the Helena, Lincoln, Townsend, and Boulder areas, I had been issued a Grumman canoe, which I made good use of in patrolling the Missouri River areas for fishing, trapping, and boating activities. At that time, the Canyon Ferry Dam was being constructed, and the river area in the Canton valley was part of my patrol district. Some deer hunters floated the river during early morning and late evening hours when it was open season. In the early 1950s, landowner permission for hunting wasn't an issue and in floating the river, private land ownership determination was almost impossible. During summertime setline fishing was common, and catching ling was the main goal.

To patrol portions of Lake Helena, Hauser Lake, and Holter Reservoir by canoe had its limitations. On one patrol above Gates of the Mountains, I was paddling along the west shoreline and was surprised to see a river otter swimming toward the canoe and making a threatening sound. She came alongside the canoe and bit at the paddle, leaving teeth marks still visible today.

After going on and checking a few shoreline fisherman, I later canoed back to where I encountered the otter and once again was charged. Looking around the shoreline there were some fish heads and crayfish shells in the water above the surface rocks, indicating it was undoubtedly an otter den. To see a river otter denned up in a lake was quite unusual!

Entertaining Encounters: *Fishing Follies*

Emergency Field Surgery

When the stonefly (salmon) hatch happens on the Big Hole River, many fishermen show up for the better than average fishing, and many fly fishermen use the rather large artificial stonefly to better their chances of catching the trout, which gorge themselves during the yearly hatch. To monitor the busy fishing season, I patrolled the river frequently by canoe, paddling along the bank areas.

On two bank patrol occasions, I came across two fly fishermen who were hurting due to the large fly hook embedded in the right ear of the one fellow, and in the right shoulder of the other. Both fishermen intended to cut the fly line, and at a later time go to a restaurant close by for food. However, the thought of being embarrassed at the restaurant in front of the other fishermen was troublesome for both men, of course.

I saw their predicament when I approached them to check licenses and catches of trout. Once I was informed that they had planned to go to the nearest restaurant, which was a popular watering hole for local fisherman, I offered to remove the embedded hooks. Before getting started, I went the half-mile or so to my vehicle and grabbed my first aid kit and a pair of needle-nose and side-cutter pliers. I hiked back to the sportsmen, and explained what I intended to do: first, I would use a cotton swab saturated with Anbesol to somewhat numb the pain, then I would cut the hook eye off, and use my pocket knife to cut away the fly body material. Then, I would use the needle-nose pliers to further drive the hook barb out of the flesh, and extract the hook shank.

Naturally, it caused some additional hurt and bleeding, but in both instances the men were elated to not have an audience and stated the numbing lotion really made the hook removal bearable. As thanks, I was invited to an evening dinner with the 'hooked' fishermen with the hope that other fishing friends wouldn't learn of their surprise cast.

The Big One That Got Away

While patrolling a lake area and observing fishing activities from a high vantage point, I could hear the voices of some fishermen from a distance. A man and boy fishing from a rubber raft and slowly trolling stopped on the lake. As the man's fishing line tightened, he yelled, "I think I have a big one on!" and told the boy to have the retrieval net ready.

The man kept the line taut, and from my vantage point I could see the rubber boat was being blown around at different angles. The man's fishing line stayed down at the same angle instead of moving about like a fish would, so I was quite sure that it was snagged on the bottom. However, the feeling of the line being pulled, even though it was actually from the wind blowing the raft, made the fisherman certain he had hooked a sizable fish. After some time battling his catch, the line slackened and the fellow said, "Damn, I just lost him!"

Undoubtedly, the experience was the basis of a fishing story of how the big one got away!

Kid Honesty

Game Warden Howard Larsen, truly an old-timer, and as tough as leather, had many tales about fishermen and hunter reactions when he had contacted them afield. He once told how a father fishing with his small son said to Warden Larsen, "All the fish we have are in the creel," which turned out to be a full legal limit. After some discussion, the innocent young son said, "Dad, how about those other fish under the car seat?"

"Damn That Game Warden!"

When I was assigned to the Butte district, I came in contact with many people that had had experiences with ex-game warden Les Barton, and vividly remembered him. One old fellow told me the following account, but first a little backstory. This fellow and his usual fishing and hunting partner didn't have much use for game wardens and particularly not Warden Barton, who they claimed was plumb ornery and unreasonable. It could be said that their sentiments were "piss on Les."

So, one time the old fellow and his friend planned a fish-fry. They went out to a favorite stream immediately alongside a backroad where they could see some distance in both directions, and were illegally netting fish in a couple good holes. They had quite a few trout in a bucket when a vehicle appeared down the road and one of the fellows said, "Here comes that damn game warden."

The one fellow, who intensely disliked Warden Barton, grabbed the net and bucket of fish and backed himself in under the clump of overhanging willows near the road, while the other fellow picked up the fishing rod he had in readiness and proceeded to begin fishing in a normal and legal manner. Warden Barton stopped, so the legal-appearing fisherman waded across to the road and produced his license. After checking the fishing license and glancing in the pickup truck, Warden Barton casually walked over to the clump of willows and took a pee!

The poor guy under the cut-bank and willows didn't dare reveal his presence with the illegal net and bucket of fish, so he withstood the worst of indignities—to have that damn game warden do that to him!

The fellow who posed as a legal fisherman said that when the warden left, his partner came out cursing and stripped down and bathed in the cold creek water. He rinsed his clothes out and put them on wet. Seemingly somewhat relieved, they resumed their fishing and continued to net more fish for their big fry-up.

Montana Piranha

One evening at dusk, I was returning from a day's patrol south of Dillon. At a slough along my route that was popular for fishing, there were a couple vehicles parked, so I proceeded to stop and check fishermen. As I made my way down the slough, I spotted one fellow in particular that I had been meaning to contact for business reasons that were associated with the local sportsmen's club.

I passed up a couple fishermen in favor of making contact with the sportsman's club individual before dark. As I approached the fellow, I noticed that he was squatting down alongside the water's edge and all at once he quickly jerked his arm upward and a sizable trout went airborne. I assumed the fisherman just threw a trout back to be caught another day, which was a common practice with the man.

As I came within talking distance, the fisherman said, "Hey, Fitz! Did you see that?"

I replied, "It looked as though you threw a nice one back to be caught again."

Then the fisherman said, "Oh no, and you will not believe this. I was cleaning this smaller trout and was rinsing it in the water when that big fellow came up and grabbed the cleaned fish, and got my fingers too!" He proceeded to show me the teeth marks on the back of his fingers and said, "It sure scared the dickens out of me! I darned near threw the big fish out on the other bank."

About a year later, one of the fishermen that I had bypassed that evening told me that he appreciated the break I had inadvertently given him by not checking him that time, because he had hurriedly closed his Dillon shop to go fishing with a persistent friend, and he had failed to get his license. He was one of those fellows who believed that the local warden knew all those who had purchased licenses, and was convinced it was a friendly and considerate gesture on my part to have bypassed him that particular evening.

"Hardly!" I laughed.

A Bird Dog Retriever of Sorts

"Give a...dog a fish, and he'll...stash it away?" That's not how the saying goes, but it's what I happened to observe one day while patrolling along the North Boulder River. Earlier, I had been occupied with assisting the fish hatchery truck in distributing catchable-sized trout alongside the riverbanks. I noticed several fisherman keenly watching the happenings, and knew that many would be returning to the release sites for easy fishing, so I decided to return too.

At one release site, a fellow was fishing in the company of his retriever-breed dog, and I observed the two for a spell. The man was doing quite well fishing, for the fish were easy to catch. Each time he caught a fish, he'd toss it back up onto the grassy, bushy bank and cast his line again. So engrossed was he in his fishing, he didn't notice that his "bird dog" was repeatedly making off with his catchings, and stashing them in different spots among the bushes.

Seeing that the man was really reeling them in, I approached him and said, "You seem to be doing quite well, so I'll ask you for a fishing license and check your fish."

The fisherman replied, "I really hit the jackpot catching fish! My fish are here on the river bank, as I don't have a creel." Turning to show me his catch, he was quite surprised to discover that his bounty had been pilfered by his four-legged friend.

I shared that I had been watching the dog do this for a while now, and asked if he had any idea how many fish he had really caught. The fellow wasn't sure, so the hunt began for the missing fish. All told, the fisherman and I retrieved sixteen trout—one over the catch limit. Smiling, I said "Keep better count of your fish, and better watch on your dog," and let it go at that.

"They're Catchin' My Fish!"

Some hunters and fisherman who fit into the poacher category often resent any intrusion into their poaching territory, and so it was with Charley, an old-timer who bached alone, and paid no mind to open and closed fishing seasons. He fished whenever he had the urge and wanted some fish for the frying skillet. When in the area on patrol, I made it a point to visit with the old fellow because he was very observant of any unusual or questionable activities in "his" area, and therefore was a decent source of information. During one such visit, Charley complained that some ornery kids were up the creek fishing, and he reiterated, "I don't like that because that's my stretch, and I look after it and throw the little ones back, because they don't fill the skillet."

After I sat for awhile and accepted a cup of his very black and strong coffee out of a rather old discolored coffee-stained porcelain cup, I drove up the road, parked, and hiked up the well-worn game trail alongside the creek. Up about a mile or so at some beaver ponds I found a couple small cutthroat trout lying on the ground, then I found another and another as I proceeded upstream. Soon, I could hear a couple boys calling to one another when either caught a fish. One said "I got one that's bigger than the rest."

I watched their activities for a while, then approached them. When they spotted me, the one Huck Finn like kid put down his fishing pole and it appeared he was about to run when I called his name, which seemed to change his mind. The other boy was immediately trying to hide the stringer of fish, so I went and retrieved a willow-stringer with a couple dozen miniature sized trout. It was evident why several fish had been found along the game trail as the weight of all those fish on the one willow stringer were stripping some off the bottom, unbeknownst to the young nimrod.

The two young culprits were directed to go to my vehicle, and then we would go to Charley's cabin, but the one boy said, "We don't want to go down there because old Charley will be mad because he thinks he owns this creek."

Nevertheless, we stopped there and Charley immediately climbed their frames and said, "You kids are ruining my fishing, and keeping those little fish is against the law."

The boys offered him the fish as a sort of peace offering and Charley replied, "Okay, but you can clean them for punishment."

I intervened by saying, "I'm sorry, but any such illegal fish are the property of the State."

Both boys were very nervous because they hadn't been informed what would be done about their fishing during closed season and catching more than the legal limit. I told them they must appear before the local juvenile officer, who would determine their fate. These two young fellows and another local lad were suspected of shooting a young buck deer with a .22 caliber rifle, so I thought a follow up might help straighten out their unruly acts. One of the kids showed concern and said, "The first thing he'll do is tell my dad and make me do some cleanup work around the school, and then everyone will know it!"

Considering I was en route to a remote area of my warden district for a few days' patrol, I couldn't very well keep the fish, so

I made out a certificate of sale for the confiscated fish, indicating they were sold to Charley and then I "donated" the $2.00 fee to be submitted with the sale report. The two boys and I went to the creek bank and cleaned the 28 small trout to be given to Charley. Before leaving, Charley asked me to stay awhile and we'd have a skillet of fresh fried fish and a cup of coffee, but the thought of that last cup of coffee was enough to influence a hasty departure.

Entertaining Encounters:
Peculiar Patrols

A Booming Puzzle

In the springtime one year, I received a call from a rancher who wished to lodge a complaint about elk damaging his mountainside pasture. He valued the pasture as a place to graze his cows and their newborn calves, but instead he found he was unwillingly grazing elk. Following up on the call, I investigated and saw at least a dozen elk grazing there in the very early morning hours.

The Fish & Game Department had recently acquired a device commonly referred to as a scare gun. The scare gun could be set up in a desirable location and programmed to discharge cracker shells at prescribed intervals to frighten unwanted wildlife away. So, I packed one up on the mountainside, and activated it so the loud discharge would boom every thirty minutes or so. The only problem was, I forgot to notify my colleagues in the Boulder Sheriff's Department of my plans.

Not long after putting up the scare gun, someone heard the booming and thought for sure that some poacher was after elk. He advised Boulder Sheriff George Paradis, who, along with a deputy, went to the area and investigated, considering they were dedicated big game hunters. Owing to his affinity for hunting and fishing, Sheriff George asked me to cooperate with the investigation to ensure there were no Fish & Game violations. Still, it didn't occur to me that the scare gun was the culprit.

When the sheriff and his deputy arrived in the vicinity of the booming, there was no one to be found. Not to be deterred, they hiked up the mountainside and began scouting the area for the offender. They were given a good surprise by the booming scare gun when it discharged as they came near it. Feeling quite perplexed, Sheriff George and his deputy hiked back down the mountain and headed over to see the rancher who had spoken with me earlier, not knowing that we had talked. The rancher told Sheriff George and the deputy that I had placed the scare gun up on the mountain to deter the elk that were destroying his valuable pasture land, which was certainly news to them.

When the sheriff returned to his office, he called me. He was not at all pleased with me for not informing him of my plans to install a loud, booming scare gun that could easily be mistaken for a poacher. I apologized, of course, and the booming puzzle was solved.

Cabin Sleeping Interference

Occasionally a couple of wardens would buddy up for patrol duty and many times, the two wardens stayed in a Forest Service patrol cabin near where they were working. After a strenuous day of foot patrol, it was a welcomed arrival at the cabin for eats and night time rest, which was really just an early siesta. On one overnight stay, I was quite antsy and got up several times during the night. This constant up and down was understandably irritating to my fellow warden, who said, "Dammit, why don't you settle down and get some sleep?!"

I quietly tried to heed my roommate's request, but didn't have much success. The problem was, my bunk was next to the log wall that was part of a runway for a couple mice that would regularly jump from the wall onto my bedroll on their way elsewhere in the cabin. Fed up, I pulled my cot out away from the wall, and the mouse route was detoured.

Early the next morning, my accompanying warden griped about the interference with his sleep. As we were dressing for the day, my partner was surprised to find one of his boots with oats inside. They came from a wooden horse feed container inside the cabin, which the mice had chewed a hole through, and they were stashing the oats in his boot for future sustenance. Considering the patrol was for several days, I fashioned a mouse trap by cutting a jagged hole in an empty food can, which solved the problem, though only temporarily. At least we were able to get some sleep!

Surprise Critical Visit to Patrol Cabin Outhouse

Before the Fish & Game Department arranged bunking and eating at Gallatin Canyon lodging and restaurant facilities, the several patrol wardens used the old Cinnamon, Sage, and Porcupine U.S. Forest Service cabins. These cabins provided crude living and eating quarters with wood stove heating and cooking. Wood fuel was a problem along with the limited creek water use. The chilly outhouse was located some distance from the creek, as required. In addition, the roadways from the cabins to the main canyon highway would often be snowed and drifted in, which required shoveling before daybreak for the day's patrol.

At the Cinnamon cabin, the path to the outhouse was kept open on a daily basis. As steady snowfall was common in the upper canyon, it was not unusual to have three or more feet of snow shoveled to the side. Early in the morning, when all of the several patrol wardens were up and stoking up the heating and cooking stoves and preparing for the day's patrol, the sometimes urgent trip to the outhouse was based on a "first come, first served" system, and it was helpful that the outhouse was a "two holer."

One of the newer hired wardens headed for the outhouse, and soon came excitedly back to the cabin and said, "There's a damn moose bedded down in the outhouse path! Now what do we do?"

Along with another warden, I went out and pondered how to handle the hair-hackled and ears-laid-back cow moose. I decided to fire a pistol shot in the air and throw some snowballs, but the moose didn't leave to buck the deep snow.

As a result of the outhouse path blockage, a couple wardens hurriedly went to shovel out the access lane to the highway and then quickly drove on to the Almart Lodge, which provided the needed toilet facility. After some patrolling, a couple wardens checked the moose situation and reported by radio that it was "all clear."

A Puzzling Question with a Plain English Answer

After several years of the wardens cooking meals at the U.S. Forest Service Cinnamon Cabin while on patrol in the upper Gallatin area, and in better times when warden monthly wage increases rose above the beginning $150 monthly, the men ate at the nearby Almart Lodge, where this funny little occurrence took place.

A vehicle with New York license plates was parked outside, and a couple was at the service counter paying their bill. The well-dressed, petite lady showed an interest in some unusual type of jewelry. After looking at some black, shiny earrings, she asked the proprietor just what they were. He replied, "Plastic covered elk droppings."

She evidently didn't understand and asked him again. The proprietor laughed and repeated his clarification. The lady was still puzzled, and a cowboy waiting to pay his bill said, "Elk shit, lady. Elk shit."

The lady immediately dropped the earrings on the glass-topped showcase and said, "I simply abhor such things!" Needless to say no sale was made.

Perhaps that was the origination of an offensive bumper sticker I've seen occasionally in later years: "SH.. HAPPENS!"

Thievery with Contempt

During the patrol duties of several game wardens at the extended late season elk hunt in the Gardiner and Jardine areas, many elk were confiscated due to hunters' fish and game law violations or as the result of overkills, which were quite common. Outside the crude old Eagle Creek patrol cabin in the 1950s, there was a big elk carcass rack that held the carcasses up off the ground.

When the wardens had put in a cold, snowy, and many times laboring day and returned to the cabin for the evening meal cooked by the more chef-oriented wardens, some went to bed dog-tired and others usually played poker. Naturally, things outside were quiet, and at a late hour one of the wardens went outside for a toilet call and came back in the cabin and said, "Did someone take one of the elk carcasses from the rack for one reason or another?"

Of course, no one had done so, and some of the wardens were asleep. A few of the wardens went outside and it was evident that a vehicle had backed up to the rack and loaded an elk without being caught in the act. Through the many following months and couple of years, it was never known who the gutsy, thieving persons were.

About 1953, I was transferred to the Dillon warden district. Having worked in the Gallatin Canyon before being hired as a game warden, I was quite surprised to meet a Dillon resident who had previously lived in the Gallatin Canyon also. Over a period of time in exchanging experiences and information related to the canyon, this fellow, Walker, said, "Fitzwater, is Sherman still your boss?"

And as I replied in the affirmative, he laughed and said, "I had a couple run-ins with him when I lived in the canyon, and I hated his guts!"

I asked what prompted his ill-feeling toward Warden Supervisor Sherman, and Walker said, "It's all water under the bridge now."

Sometime later when talking to rancher Walker, he said to me, "I have a tale for you, and it's old and probably forgotten by now." Then he said, "Have you worked the Gardiner elk hunt?"

When I told him I had for the last couple winters, Walker said, "Was there ever any talk between wardens of an elk being stolen at the Eagle Creek cabin?"

I told him I was indeed at the cabin but probably asleep, as I was tired from a long snowshoe patrol and turned in early. Walker laughed and laughed and said, "You're looking at one of the thieves along with Taylor, who also hated Sherman."

In due time, I told Supervisor Sherman about Walker's confession and that he ranched in the Beaverhead area. Sherman said, "If you get a chance to catch him poaching, sock it to him!"

Unacceptable Duty

At the old Gardiner, Montana Eagle Creek patrol cabin during the 1950s, the living conditions were quite crude for the several game wardens assigned for patrol duty there. The local old-time district warden, Red Burke, pretty well officiated over the patrol assignments in the absence of the region warden supervisor, Gene Sherman.

Red awakened very early and stoked up the old wood cooking stove, and started a rib-stickin' breakfast. One morning he called out, “One of you lazy ass wardens get me a bucket of water,” so a recently hired probationary warden was directed to the nearby Eagle Creek water hole through the ice. Not long afterward, he came back in the cabin with the empty bucket and asked if there were two holes for water. When Red said, “No,” the warden said he wasn’t about to bail a bucketful out of that waterhole with horse droppings all around it, so he put the bucket down and didn’t stay around for coffee or breakfast that morning, or for a couple more cabin meals.

When asked where he was eating, he replied, “In Gardiner,” and added, “I’m not about to eat at the cabin, where that creek water is used for coffee, cooking and washing dishes.” The couple horses in the small horse barn were watered at that same waterhole and that was the first time there was any controversy about it. That probationary warden stayed around for patrol for a couple days, then by request went back to his assigned warden district and, as I remember it, he never completed his one year probationary term.

Beer Guzzlin' Sailors and a Boat Mishap

Every July there is an annual Yellowstone River float trip that was called the Mayor's Float, but is now known as the Yellowstone River Boat Float. Back when I was a game warden, it started at Livingston and ran to Big Timber the first day, then on to Columbus the second, and Billings the third. I was assigned that river patrol duty on three occasions, and checked boats and floaters for proper gear at the first day's launch, then during all the days' floats for unsafe practices, littering, and life-preserver requirements.

At the Livingston launch site, I noticed that four Navy guys' large rubber raft did not have much freeboard out of the water, so I said, "Fellows, you are sinking before you start!"

One sailor laughed and said, "Let me show you something!" and proceeded to throw a tarp aside, revealing a hefty supply of beer and ice. He then said, "You will see the raft floating higher through the day, as we are dedicated beer drinkers."

I cautioned them about littering, and as one brawny sailor had just emptied a can of beer, he said to me, "This is what we'll do with the empty beer cans," and proceeded to crush it down to a mere disc.

Somewhat satisfied, I then told them I would do them the favor of coming alongside their raft in the morning and afternoon and pick up their empty cans. Needless to say, those four Navy men had a very enjoyable float, particularly by having water fights with the numerous boats carrying young women. I heard report that during that first Big Timber layover with dancing and partying, the sailors had many fun dance partners.

The second day's float saw quite a number of additional floaters and we two patrolling wardens had been assigned a jet boat, which made it possible to go up and down the river with ease. The river split into a couple of channels at various places, but there were no markings to designate the best channels to boat. At one place, there were three separate channels, with one flowing considerably less river water. As we drew near the channel, we heard excited calls downstream and quickly went to investigate. Upon our arrival at the scene, we saw where a rubber raft had overturned and its occupants were in the water, clinging to driftwood that had floated there during the springtime high waters and had completely blocked the channel.

With the jet boat going over very shallow riffle waters, we knew the water intake of the jet system would pull in gravel and stall the boat. Instead, we went around the river's island and then up the channel to the location of the capsized raft. Due to the swift current, the four floaters were still clinging to the front edge of the pile of driftwood. Luckily, they were wearing life-preserver vests, which helped keep them afloat and from being sucked under the driftwood.

My colleague and I securely tied the jet boat to large pieces of driftwood, and eased out on top of the stable pile of wood. One by one, we assisted in getting all four boaters to the jet boat. The rubber raft was being held tightly against the driftwood, and was bottom side up so it was difficult to wrench free, but we finally managed to pry it loose and dragged it to shore. There was no apparent damage to the raft, and the air pockets were still inflated and solid. Since their watercraft was in good shape, we told the boaters they they could continue with their float to Columbus and complete their trip.

Before setting off, one of the fellows said that they took the smaller river channel because they were looking for a likely place for a pee call. One of the women in the party said, "I've already been relieved!"

With that, my partner and I went up-river to where the small channel started, and placed a red flag and a wooden arrow to indicate that channel should be avoided.

When You Gotta Go!

I had a couple vantage points around a popular fishing reservoir where I would observe the activities of both bank and boat fishermen. On one occasion, a man and woman were fishing from a boat and were off quite some distance from the others. After a while, the woman stood up in the boat, obviously preparing to lower her slacks to urinate over the side of the boat. The man shifted his weight to one side to balance the boat and just as the woman positioned herself to pee, the fellow quickly grabbed a fishing rod that evidently had a fish strike. When he stood up, the boat tipped and the woman went backward over the side and momentarily went completely underwater. She came up flailing her arms and floundering at the same time the man was reeling in a fish, so he didn't immediately assist the woman. Having landed the fish, he then went to the other end of the boat and extended an arm to the woman. She grabbed the side of the boat and nearly swamped it, so the man then helped her to the stern, but their efforts to get her aboard were futile despite several tries.

After some pondering, the man took the oars and with the rather heavy woman paddling behind, they went a few hundred yards to where it was shallow enough for her to stand upright on the muddy reservoir bottom. As she made her way in, she was trying to pull her slacks up so she could walk toward more shallow areas. When the boat bottom was finally grounded, the wet and muddy woman managed to get in, though I can't imagine she was very happy.

I checked them later for proper licenses and fish counts, and the man said, “Warden, you will not believe what happened to us!” to which the woman hastily replied, “Never mind!”

I didn’t reveal that I had seen it all!

Moose Butt Surprise

In patrolling a river by canoe for fishing and fur trapping activity, I had covered several miles of river and maneuvered around the many meandering channels. As I quietly paddled around on the sharp riverbed, I was surprised to see a large cow moose standing in mid-channel. The moose's hind legs and rear-end loomed like a bridge, so at close quarters I slapped the water surface with the canoe paddle. The cow quickly turned, the hair on her back and neck was flared up, and her ears were laid back in an ominous way. I quickly back-paddled and, after some hesitation, high stepped it out of the river. For a moment, I even thought about overturning the canoe for shelter.

On that same canoe patrol, a small group of ducks was on the river waters ahead. As they quickly took to flight, two of them treaded water upstream into the wind. Since they were extremely low, they flew right overhead and I extended my paddle upward. One duck hit it, and fell stunned in the canoe. It caused me an ill feeling due to my foolish act, but the duck soon recovered and was put in the river to fly away.

Just One Of Several Embarrassing Happenings

I patrolled umpteen southwestern waterways by canoe over the many years working as a warden. On one such patrol down a portion of the Beaverhead River, I saw a group of people by an entanglement of exposed roots. As I approached, a woman surrounded by several children said, "Oh, look children, a game warden canoeing the river," and with a certain feeling of game warden pride I checked the young fishermen's licenses and catch of fish.

The woman and children were interested in the canoe so I explained the various paddle strokes needed to control the canoe on winding river channels, and the dos and don'ts of canoeing, due to their tendency to tip over under certain conditions.

Having finished my impromptu lesson, I walked toward the secured canoe and caught my boot toe under a tree root, causing me to fall headlong in the aluminum canoe with a loud metallic bang. Needless to say, I hurriedly untied the rope to the canoe and hastily paddled downstream.

"Warden, You Can Have My Stalled Vehicle!"

On one patrol of the by then vehicle-accessible Hidden Lake, I checked several fisherman and then heard the sound of a revved up engine. One of the fisherman said, "A guy is stuck on that steep grade down to the lakeshore."

Once I made my way around the lakeshore, I was confronted by an agitated fellow who said, "I'll give you that damn cab-over truck lock, stock, and barrel." I of course turned down the offer, and the disgruntled fellow asked if he could get a ride to town as it was late in the day and I was leaving soon. Once in town, I was treated to a dinner as thanks for the ride. I later learned that a local man had accepted the giveaway offer and, with assistance, had gotten the vehicle up the steep grade and happily to town!

Stash of Outlaw Henry Plummer's Gold?

While I was patrolling areas of Big Sheep Basin on foot, I got caught in a rain shower and sought shelter up on a nearby side hill, tucking myself into a shallow cave. As I waited out the rain, the smell in the cave indicated the workings of a packrat, and in close proximity was a large packrat nest, with various items attractive to the little creature on display. Out of curiosity, I took a nearby stick and dug into the midden. After some poking about, I noticed what appeared to be a rawhide thong. I dug deeper and was surprised to see a weathered and time hardened rawhide drawstring pouch. I took a closer look and found the bottom lacing was gone and the pouch bottom was somewhat open.

I had heard stories that Henry Plummer's outlaw gang had robbed and killed many gold miners leaving the Bannack gold diggings, and rather than get caught with a pouch of gold, the outlaw would stash it in a place where he could find and retrieve it later. I have often wondered if that was the circumstance related to this unusual find. I even thought I might return and chance digging deeper in the midden and perhaps find some gold, but with no water source nearby for panning, I never bothered.

Entertaining Encounters: *Trapping Trials & Tribulations*

Quickly Gained Rep

While I was working the Broadwater area, a rancher complained of nuisance beaver, so I went to the area to set live traps. It was late afternoon, and the rancher was working in a field with a tractor, so he pointed out the problem irrigation canal and I proceeded over there. I had set one live trap at about dusk when the rancher and his son stopped by, as they were curious about the live trapping procedure. There wasn't an appropriate place to set the second live trap, so I took it down the ditch a few hundred feet to a likely spot as the two curious ranchers watched. At that time it was nearly dark, and as we stood visiting, I heard the familiar sound of the first trap snapping closed, but it seemed too early for beaver activity. I told the two ranchers that the gob of mud with beaver scent must have dislodged and fallen on the trap-pan, and said we had better go check. The three of us walked to the live trap and, lo and behold, there was a young beaver in it!

LIVE TRAPPED—State Fish and Game warden Wayne Fitzwater of Dillon

Having no holding pen, the rancher and I carried the live trap complete with beaver contained inside to my vehicle. We continued to visit for awhile, and about the time we were ready to leave, we heard the second trap snap shut. When we checked, there was another young beaver harmlessly caught in the cage of the trap. So, we gathered that trap up and carried it to my vehicle too, laughing about the trapping success.

At such times, I believe that such success should be chalked up as skill, instead of luck. I fully realized that the animals caught were two young, dumb and curious beaver, but didn't say so. It wasn't but a week or so that there were comments around the town of Townsend that "the game warden really had the know-how for trapping beaver." In fact, Sheriff Jack Thompson, who was known to be a good trapper, commented to me about the rancher bragging on my trapping skills. Sheriff Thompson even asked about the ingredients in my beaver scent, which was indeed a compliment coming from Thompson.

For Fun or Money

While working in the Helena game warden district, the Fish & Game headquarters office received word from the county sanitarian that the beaver at the city water supply reservoir should be removed because their presence was polluting the waters. Their complaint was passed on to me, but as the beaver trapping would take major effort and time during a busy time of year for wardens, the department law enforcement chief determined that the state trapper, Howard Campbell, would be called in to do the job instead.

When Campbell arrived, I offered to assist him when I was able and had the time. During that fall season, it was decided to steel trap and pelt the beaver, which was time consuming. I had been a trapper as a farm kid, and had trapped, skinned, and stretched many nuisance beaver pelts, and knew it wasn't an easy chore. Being familiar with the process, it was evident to me that Campbell was truly an expert in that regard. I was amazed at his skill in skinning out a beaver, and I told him so. Campbell replied, "I'll put my skinning skills against anyone—for fun or money!"

I timed him skinning a large beaver, and in less than five minutes the job was done, with little hide flesh left afterward. When I asked what he used as a scent or attractant, he stated it was his own secret formula of beaver castors and additives. After the trapping was completed in a week or so, Campbell gave me some of the scent, which proved to be very effective.

A year or so later, I heard that a Blackfoot Indian challenged Campbell's beaver skinning skills but did not win, by quite a margin.

A Prankster Prevails

I had issued a late spring trapping permit for ten beaver to a rancher in the Stillwater district, and at a later date I received a phone call indicating he had some beaver pelts to be tagged prior to selling them. I asked how many pelts needed to be tagged, and the man said he had fourteen, which was four over what the permit allowed. I informed the rancher he was over the limit on the permit, but all the guy casually said was, "That's ok, Warden. Just come on out and tag them."

I thought it was somewhat gutsy for the man to be so unconcerned. I hadn't worked the area very long but had heard that this particular individual was somewhat ornery, which influenced my thinking that I might for darned sure file a complaint as way to demonstrate that I was serious about game laws and regulations, even when rather trivial.

On my arrival at the ranch, the man was busy, so he told me to leave the metal tags and he would put them on the pelts later. Of course, this would have been unusual, because the warden was supposed to affix the tags to the pelts. Irritated with the rancher now, I explained the correct tagging procedure and that I had to be the one to affix the tags. Finally the rancher lead the way to an outbuilding where there were ten adult beaver pelts, plus four very small unborn kit pelts, neatly stretched in the usual round fashion.

The rancher's manner immediately changed to friendliness as he showed off his bounty. He laughed and said, "I had you going didn't I? And I bet you thought you had a live one!"

The beaver kit pelts were confiscated and turned over to the Fish & Game Department for disposal. The man continued to be a prankster over the years, and seemed to thoroughly enjoy doing so.

A Lucky and Rewarding Find

I received a phone call from both a stream-side property owner and the State Highway Department about a flooding problem on a stream emptying into the Big Hole River one morning. As the problem was on the boundary of two warden districts, I contacted my neighboring warden, Leo Secor, who offered to assist in alleviating the flooding problem. We managed to remove the entangled beaver dam of sticks and mud with some difficulty, but for the time being, solved the flooding problem. I then set two beaver live traps knowing the beaver would later return to repair the dam.

At lunchtime, we headed off to a local eatery. As we walked into the restaurant, Warden Secor realized he had lost his wallet, so we cancelled our lunch stop immediately and returned to the creek to look for his billfold. There was little hope of finding the lost wallet, due to the fast-flowing stream which emptied into the Big Hole River just a short distance below where we had extracted the beaver dam. We were about to give up the search when just a short distance downstream, we spotted the wallet. It had lodged against an underwater willow branch. With the fast flowing Big Hole River waters only yards downstream, it was sheer luck to have found it!

Everyone Should Know What a Bear Live Trap Looks Like

Responding to a complaint of a problem bear, I set an old, rusted 55-gallon drum-type bear live trap near a campsite that was used regularly, and proceeded to put up caution signs in all accessible directions, except one side with heavy timber and windfall. Later, a couple of young, inquisitive hikers had left the trail and came down through that area of heavy timber and windfall adjacent to the campground. You guessed it—they came out where the bear trap had been set, and there was a black bear in the trap, unbeknownst to them!

Later, they told me how they saw that odd looking thing made out of oil drums, and wondered what it might be. Of course, they saw the steel trap door and wondered how it worked, so one guy lifted it while standing directly in front, and the other fellow knelt down to look inside the puzzling device.

Anyone can guess what happened next. That bear came out in a rush and went between the one guy's legs holding the trap door up, knocking him off balance, and the other fellow went over backwards from the force of the bear's rush. Neither man had so much as a scratch, but later may have turned white-haired at an early age. I'm still not sure if the droppings that were near the trap when I moved it was from man or beast.

Going forward, I placed warning signs in all directions when I set a bear live trap. I have often thought of how tragic that encounter could have been if the bear had been aggressive, and hadn't been intent only on escape.

Captive Bear Bluff

I have a lot of gratitude for my late wife, Alice. She regularly provided me assistance, and was patient with the demands of a game warden's duties. I remember many times when she had every right to cease being an ex-officio. One such instance was when I brought home a live trapped black bear to release later when time permitted. I asked if Alice would feed and water the bear in the meantime, and to hose down the trap and animal if the day turned warm.

Alice loved animals, and accepted the chore. The next day, she took some food to the bear, which was far back in the trap in a seemingly sulking mood. About the time she was placing the food in a container at the heavily barred end of the trap, the bear made a sudden rush at her, making a frightening woofing sound and blowing snot her way. Naturally, she retreated and the bear received no food. But, he did get a good watering down with the garden hose—from a distance of course!

Lucky Second Time Catch of a Black Bear

On yet another occasion with a live trapped bear being held overnight at my home headquarters, I had used a section of reasonably heavy interwoven gravel screen over the open end of the live trap so the metal body of the trap would not become excessively hot inside before the next day's planned release. At some point during the night, the fairly small bear had separated the sizable screen wires and escaped. I was very surprised at this discovery, and immediately scanned surrounding areas. It wasn't long before I finally saw the bear in a field between my house and town.

I took a gun with me as a precaution and started to get between the bear and town, but the bear ran toward a house at the edge of town and, with me in pursuit, went up a tall tree at the back door of the house. Due to the commotion, the lady tenant's dog was barking and the lady, who knew me, said, "Fitzwater, what is going on?" as she was pointing out the bear up her tree.

Being a local well-known elderly lady and not particularly excitable, I asked her to let the dog keep barking and perhaps she could make some additional noise banging on a couple kitchen pans, while I hurriedly went back and got the bear live trap. Arriving back at the treed bear, and as an enticement to coax the bear down out of the tree and hopefully into the trap, I took a slab of bacon I had in reserve for bear bait and put a piece on a long stick. Fortunately the bear devoured it! Pleased with my progress, I repeated the coaxing as the bear gradually backed down the tree trunk. To my amazement, the bacon pieces extending into the live trap worked perfectly and the somewhat dumb bear was once again caught.

Later in the day, I took the bear to a remote high mountain area for release. The live trap was in the truck bed, and when the trap door was raised and open for the bear to scurry out, it only sulked in the far end of the trap. I pulled my vehicle forward to encourage him to exit, but the bear still stayed inside the trap. I then hastily backed downslope and the bear slid inside the trap to the opening, but quickly went back inside to the trigger end. Once again I repeated the maneuver, and the bear slid down out of the trap to the ground, only to quickly hop back into the trap. I repeated the procedure one more time by quickly pulling upslope, and the puzzled bear was out and finally ran toward a timbered area.

I had taken my terrier dog along, which was a rarity for him. At the release site, I must not have been thinking about my little canine companion because one vehicle window was down about halfway and, to my surprise, the dog squeezed out and ran after the bear for the hundred yards or so to the timber where both bear and dog disappeared.

I thought I'd be in a world of hurt if the dog was lost, so I yelled the dog's name over and over and tooted the vehicle horn, which had been used a couple of times as a call to load up and go. After a frustrating period of waiting, the dog finally reappeared and stood with one front leg held up and looked toward the pickup. After some hesitation and a few bladder-relieving leg lifts on a couple of nearby bushes, the dog came back to the pickup, much to my relief!

Escape from a Trap

When I was transferred to the Dillon district, I brought along the live trap I had built with Rex Smart in the Helena-Townsend district. Not long after my arrival, I received a bear complaint related to a campground where some campers fed a bear, which caused the bear to lose any fear of humans, and the animal become quite dangerous to campground occupants, their children, and dogs.

On a Friday, I set the trap. This meant I had to crawl inside the front to secure bait on a trapdoor release trigger. After getting things set up, I started to back out toward the entry end of the trap and my coverall sleeve caught on the wired-on baited trigger—down went the steel trapdoor! Foolishly, I had not removed the trapdoor from the guide track for the steel door to go up and down.

Being trapped, I was somewhat frantic as to how I might get out. After a couple of unsuccessful tries at lifting the door with my shoes, I spied a finger-sized stick through a saucer-sized hole in the trap bottom and, by picking away around it, finally retrieved it. I scooted back toward the trapdoor, and pushed the stick under the lower edge and tried to lift the door somewhat. I broke the end of the stick twice, then in that doubled-up, cramped position, I finally managed to lift the steel door far enough to get one shoe under it. I then used my

other foot to lift it higher, then high enough to partially get out farther, and finally free.

More cautiously this time, I re-set the trap. As I had worn a soiled, stinky pair of coveralls used for such projects and for beaver live trapping, I removed the coveralls and went to a nearby creek to wash up. I was very relieved to be quite presentable and in uniform when soon afterward a group of campers arrived for their weekend outing. I thought how embarrassing it would have been to be in the live trap when the campers arrived!

Entertaining Encounters:
Hunting Hoopla

A Kill of Last Resort

The late winter extended elk hunt in the Gardiner area brought on several unusual events with local hunters. During one assignment on patrol duty, I drove the Gardiner-Jardine road after the first surge of hunters passed through early in the day. While traveling toward the Jardine settlement, I saw a fresh blood trail coming from the open hunting area to the north, and across the road to the closed steep slope below. After finding a roadside turnout, I went back to the blood trail, and some distance down below the road I saw some movement among the trees. I waded through the deep snow and finally saw a fellow holding a sizable rock high over his head and scurrying around in a semi-circle.

As I came closer to the fellow, I could see the antlers of a bull elk moving around. When I approached the hunter, I asked what was going on, and the fellow replied, "I shot this bull and he kept going and going until I ran out of ammo, and crossed the road into this closed hunting area. Out of desperation, I'm trying to finish him off with a rock to his head before he might go farther down this steep slope."

The blood trail was evidence that the bull was indeed shot in a legal hunting area, so I handed him my .357 service revolver to cinch his kill. Later, I advised a couple of other wardens, Harold Gartside and Al Boston, about the bull elk below the road in the closed area so they wouldn't needlessly pursue any investigative actions.

When the desperate hunter came to the old Eagle Creek patrol cabin, resident warden Red Burke told the fellow that he and I would drag the bull up to the road for him the following day with a couple horses. What a difficult hillside drag it was, finally getting the bull up the steep Bear Creek slope!

Elk Minced Meat

During a late season elk hunt, there were few animals to be found at the lower and more easily accessible areas. Three hardy hunters had heard that some elk were seen in a high, remote, deep snow basin beyond where most hunters would normally hunt. The three hunters struggled through deep snow and very cold temperatures to this relatively small basin, which drained toward the river and the highway, then down over some sheer, rocky ledges and cliffs, making it nearly impassable for animals and humans alike.

Once the three hunters had fought their way up the steep slopes and could look into much of the basin, sure enough, there were some elk. This raised their spirits and seemed to make the tough trek worthwhile. While taking a much needed break from the grueling steep climb, their better judgment surfaced and they agreed that a couple calf elk would be more appropriate rather than a larger adult animal which would be difficult, if not impossible, to drag out of the area.

They proceeded to hunt fairly close together and managed to bag one calf elk. By the time they dressed out the carcass and pondered what might be the best route to get the animal out of that snow bowl, it was decided that the most likely and easiest way would be down slope toward the river. Little did they know what terrain lay ahead of them!

During this time, I had seen the three men earlier that day struggling up the snow covered slope toward the basin. I was familiar with the basin, and when it was evident they were dedicated hunters intent on their mission, I decided to snowshoe there since there was no hunter activity elsewhere nearby. Once up on the basin rim, I could view the hunters' progress and activities through my binoculars—and man-oh-man, was it cold and windy up there!

I witnessed the shooting that downed the calf elk and, even though it was nearing dusk I continued to watch, all the while wondering if they would attempt to drag the elk up out of that basin after nightfall in the moonlight, or leave it for the next day after a night's rest. Seeing that they decided not to wait, and were going to attempt to take the shortest route down the drainage, I was desperately wishing I was within shouting distance and could call out, "NO, NO! Don't try it!"

Once the men and their bounty were out of sight down toward the rock ledges and cliffs, I snowshoed the long jaunt back to the Eagle Creek patrol cabin. After eating a hasty snack, I decided to drive the several miles around to the highway where I might "glass" the rocky slope and learn if the men were successful in getting down that treacherous terrain. I had no success seeing them and finally surmised they gave up that attempt and would struggle back out of the basin the way they had entered.

I went to the checking station further down the highway and stayed there quite a long while visiting with Old Jack, the station operator. About the time I was leaving, a pickup truck pulled in and three men came into the station. They were wet, cold, downright miserable, and very disgruntled. The checker asked, "Does anyone have any game to be checked?"

One of the sad approaching hunters said, "Hell yes, why do you think we are here?"

The checker and I went outside the shelter of the warm station, and what a pitifully sad elk carcass was to be seen! Much of the hair had been dragged off both sides and it was a broken, mangled mess. Also, there was no obvious carcass tag so the checker went back inside the station and inquired about the tag. Loud voices could be heard and one of the hunters exclaimed, "The damn tag was on there, and if it's gone you can have the elk for what it's worth."

Of course the checker maintained the carcass must be tagged before it could be cleared through the station, and the three very miserable and exhausted hunters were very vocal in declaring the carcass had been properly tagged and it wasn't worth haggling, so just take it off their hands. Intervening before things really escalated, I explained that a replacement tag would be provided so the men could keep their well-earned elk.

Once the hunters warmed themselves and drank a couple cups of hot coffee, their attitudes changed for the better and they reviewed the day's hunt, not knowing that I had been up on that frigid, windy rim watching them. I well knew what an ordeal they had experienced plodding through deep snow all day and coming down over that treacherous bluff.

The hunters related that they had gotten down to the steep and treacherous rocky slope, and certainly did not intend to go back up to that basin. They had taken their three lengths of drag rope and tied them together, then onto the calf elk carcass minus legs and head, then around a stout cedar shrub, and proceeded to slowly lower the animal until it seemed to have stopped in a stable position well below them. Then about the time they released their hold on the rope, it literally whirred around the cedar trunk and they could hear the elk thumping and bumping as it fell down, down, down.

The men had a treacherous climb downward through, over, and around rocks, bluffs, and cliffs and retrieved the pathetically mangled elk, but were conscientious enough to claim it and drag it to the highway. The hunters indicated the elk probably would only be good for dog food, but I suggested they soak the bruised and bloodshot meat in cold water to draw the blood out then grind it into elk burger for a try at edibility before giving it to the dogs.

Ranch Boy Does Well

The late season elk hunt in Gardiner brought in hunters of many kinds, ranging from young to old, experienced and inexperienced, legally inclined and some not so legally inclined, and some real "dudes" that by appearances and acts didn't really know which end of a gun was which. On one occasion, two well-dressed "hunters" were noticed around the Eagle Creek hunter vehicle parking area. I had snowshoed back into an area where hunters were likely to bag elk, and then came out prior to noon with the intent of assisting Warden Burke in dragging a confiscated elk carcass out of Bear Creek.

As I arrived at the parking area, I noticed the two dapper looking hunters were standing near a couple calf elk carcasses, which had been dragged out of lower Eagle Creek by horse. The strange part was that neither of the dead elk had been gutted, so I established that the two dudes claimed the elk which were tagged, but I doubted that either of the two had actually shot the elk. I advised them that the elk had better be gutted promptly, and one of the guys said, "I don't think I can do it right. It would be worth ten bucks if someone would help," to which his partner agreed.

There were a couple young ranch hands nearby who were looking at the elk carcasses, and one of them asked the dude if he meant it. When assured, the young man pushed up his sleeves and hastily opened one elk paunch with his knife and rolled out the greater portion of the entrails. The one dude handed the young guy a ten dollar bill, so he proceeded to clean his hands and arms with snow as the second dude asked, "What about my elk?"

The young guy said, "I understood it was ten dollars for each elk." The hunter reluctantly agreed, so the young guy again went to work and asked the hunter to hold the elk's leg so he could make the belly cut easier. When the knife penetrated into the paunch area and a hiss of accumulated bloat gas penetrated the air, the poor dude lost his hold and quickly turned away as his wind-reddened face changed to an off-color pallor.

The young butcher left with his quickly earned cash, and I, realizing that the elk gutting procedure was hasty and not too good, informed the two well-dressed hunters that the lungs, hearts, and windpipes should be removed before too long, but they didn't seem too eager to recruit someone else and perhaps pay again. At a monthly wage of $225 I was thinking if it had been appropriate and permissible that it would have been an easy chore for that amount of money, but refrained from offering to complete the butchering.

Fit to Eat

I put in many, many snowshoeing hours patrolling the often snow-drifted and inaccessible areas away from vehicle travels, parking areas, and horseback trails. On one occasion, as I was heading into snowed-in areas, I was stopped by a hunter inquiring where he might best have a chance to bag what he termed a "dry cow elk" for choice meat. I advised the hunter that without snowshoes it would be an almost impossible hunt, but the several horseback trails would be a fair choice as elk also traveled some of the horse trails. We parted ways and I continued on my snowshoe patrol.

Later in the day while on a high snowy slope, I heard a couple gunshots coming from the Eagle Creek bottom area, so I snowshoed in that direction. I stopped once to scan the area with binoculars, and finally spotted a fellow walking around an elk carcass in the snow. When I arrived at the site, I could see the elk was not yet field dressed. I asked the hunter for his hunting license and inquired why he hadn't gutted the elk. The fellow replied with his own question, "What in the hell is it?"

I then realized it was the same hunter who wanted to kill a dry cow elk, so with reluctance I told the hunter it was a de-antlered bull elk from Yellowstone that had been released from the relocation holding pen near Gardiner earlier that morning. The hunter said, "I don't want it! I specifically told you earlier that I wanted a dry cow elk!"

As the hunter had not yet tagged the de-horned bull, I explained that the elk must be tagged but that I thought a replacement tag might be issued under such unusual circumstances. As consolation, I offered to help field dress the animal. Looking the carcass over, there was minimal show of body fat so, again with reluctance, I told the fellow the elk carcass looked to be in good shape but it appeared to be an old bull, perhaps beyond breeding age and consequently in good shape by just resting and foraging. The hunter's face lit up as he then said, "Do you really think so?" I nodded, and without hesitating, he tagged the bull and soon went down the horse trail to find a horse-backer to drag the carcass to the vehicle parking lot.

I have often wondered if the elk meat was fit to eat. It comes to mind that years ago a couple dedicated old-time poachers and wild game connoisseurs told to me that they had thrived on wild game meat and a vegetable garden through many years of hard living, along with their knack for preserving old sage grouse roosters, old buck deer and elk, and "trash fish" like suckers. They noted that the processes of aging, freezing, smoking, canning, and marinating combined with the know-how of cooking was the answer to good grub.

An Unintentional Hunter Target

While I was patrolling a popular elk hunting area on foot, I had reason to confiscate a recently killed calf elk that had been field dressed and was frozen stiff. Due to the snow on the ground and a forecast calling for even more snowfall, combined with the scant number of landmarks in the widespread timbered area, I propped the stiff elk carcass with the legs down and head quite upright up over a stump. I planned to return later and retrieve the elk and bring it through the standing timber, windfall, and rough terrain.

I then left the area to continue my patrol and had not gone far when I heard two rifle shots back in the direction of the elk carcass, followed by some loud, excited shouting. I hurried back and could soon see where a horse had stirred up quite a lot of the snow, and there was a hunter approaching the calf elk carcass. As I drew nearer to the hunter, who was examining the frozen elk, he said, "I don't know what in the hell is going on here, so maybe you can figure it out!" Then he added, "And what is that red tag dangling there?"

I soon learned that the hunter's horse had spooked at the sight of the calf elk, and was the cause of the man's excited shouts and low-key rodeo. The hunter was still puzzled by the somewhat lifelike position of the elk carcass, so I explained that I had placed it that way to discourage birds and animals from feeding on the elk meat. Frustrated, the hunter made it quite clear that he was upset to have been tricked and made to look foolish.

Against good judgment, rules, and guidelines, considering there had been no citation issued as related to the confiscated elk, and keeping in mind the distance factor to an easy access area, as well as the type of terrain one must cross to get to an access point at all, I asked the fellow if he was interested in buying the elk for a very nominal fee and then be issued a certificate of sale. To sweeten the deal, I told him that he would not have to surrender his valid elk tag. The certificate of sale required a fee, and as the irked hunter said that he had no cash on him, I offered to pay a minimal amount to be submitted to the Fish & Game Department headquarters. Sensing his good fortune, the fellow quickly agreed and inquired as to the best and easiest route out of the area. Later, I felt quite bad to have shifted the labor of getting the elk carcass out of that remote area filled with thick timber, jack pine thickets, and wind-fallen trees.

Misinterpreted Instructions

During the late season Gardiner elk hunt, hunters of various skill levels and categories seemed to be there to participate in that "hunt of last resort." Game Warden Pinky Sears was one of the regulars patrolling the area, and as most of his fellow warden coworkers knew, he was definitely one of the more conscientious working wardens.

One particular day, a couple of young elk hunters had bagged an elk and were soon afterward checked by Warden Sears. In an effort to help them take home a good piece of meat, the warden suggested that they let the dressed elk carcass cool out, and said if they managed to get it to the wardens' patrol station, there was a meat rack where it could cool.

Some time later, reports were received that a couple fellows in a vehicle were seen dragging an elk carcass down the Gardiner-Jardine road, through east Gardiner, and northbound on the paved highway toward the game checking station. Old Jack at the checking station was quite upset by the condition of the elk carcass, which was very well-worn by the long drag over quite a few miles. When the two young hunters were quizzed why they did such a foolish thing, they replied that a game warden had suggested they drag the elk to the station so it could be hung to cool.

Jack, the checker, realized there had been a misunderstanding and that Warden Sears really meant the Gardiner-Eagle Creek patrol cabin, which was only a short distance from where he had first contacted the young hunters and had conscientiously and helpfully given them the good advice that went awry.

Graft in the Hunters' Ranks

Game wardens operating law enforcement checking stations are confronted with a wide range of situations, from humorous to serious. One time, I was assisting with a hunter checking station when an out-of-state vehicle was flagged in to be checked. There were three buck deer lashed down on the vehicle top, and when the three hunters were asked for licenses and advised the deer would be checked for proper tagging, one of the hunters said, "Don't look too close, warden." Of course, the statement was reason for me to look extra close.

The carcass tags were on the hind legs of the deer and were legal and proper, so I looked over the animal carcass and noticed something strange about the deers' heads and antlers. A closer inspection revealed that all three animals were doe deer, and antlers were fitted into the skulls of the does. A V-cut had been made in the skulls, then a matching cut from a buck deer head was made and carefully fit into place, with nails driven in at various angles to hold the antlers in place until the hunters arrived at their out-of-state destination.

I asked the men what the reasoning was for the antler grafts, and they laughingly explained, "We live in a very small community, and when we left for Montana to hunt, most everyone knew about it and recognized us as good hunters. On previous hunts we had always returned with buck deer, which was a mark of pride."

Evidently, on this hunt they had very limited hunting time and did not bag any bucks. So, out of desperation, and not wanting to go back empty-handed, they bagged the legal doe deer instead. At that time, and in the area they claimed to have hunted, either sex deer were legal. In fact, two deer of either sex were allowed, but they settled for one doe deer each and explained, “Once we arrive home, we will drive around and let friends and neighbors see our ‘buck deer’ on the car top.”

The local response would probably be, “The men are back with their bucks!” The men indicated they would then drive to their farms and unload and butcher their game, and go to town later and tell of their great Montana hunt.

As in most instances, the pride of a deer hunter bagging a buck still stands, as it has through the years. I have pondered whether this buck antler grafting incident constituted “destroying evidence of sex” as stipulated under Montana Fish & Game laws, or whether the caper might have fallen into some other category such as “altering sex,” which now seems to be acceptable in the human ranks.

An Unorthodox Style of Public Relations

The late H.L. Sneed was a Montana Fish & Game Department license sales agent and sporting goods dealer for many years. As a state license agent, he established a couple records related to monthly license sales receipts. Due to frequent discrepancies in the total amount of money due to the department, Mr. Sneed would submit the duplicate copies of all sales and a signed, blank check to the department cashier, Margaret Jennings. Some of his monthly sales amounted to about $25,000 or more! During those days, people were much more trusting than in later years.

Sneed sets record

DILLON – Figures indicate that H. L. Sneed, owner of Sneed's Sporting Goods, has set another record for fish and game license sales.

Sneed remitted some $76,500 to the State Fish and Game Department in 1969, an increase of about $21,000 over the previous year when he held the state record for license sales. 1969 was also his largest year for out-of-state licenses with 344 sold. When Sneed opened his business in 1966 he processed 259 out-of-state licenses. In 1967 there were 247; in 1968, 217.

(Source: *Montana Standard*, Butte, MT, February 8, 1970)

Sneed was a shrewd businessman, and a somewhat unorthodox public relations man, as supported by the following story: A couple non-resident hunters came to his store and browsed around for some time, looking at the variety of hunting and fishing merchandise and grumbling about the high prices. They then applied their gripe to the cost of a non-resident hunting license. They added that for the cost, a hunter should be assured of getting an animal, and for that much money, they could just buy a lot of beef instead. In reply, Sneed mentioned the names of a couple local ranchers who would gladly sell them some beef if they wanted to save themselves the trouble.

After listening to continued complaining about the cost of a non-resident license, Sneed shared that there were a couple areas in the state where big game hunting success was nearly a cinch. This quickly quieted the complainers, who now listened with eager ears. Although Sneed exhibited some reluctance to say where, he finally said a few areas outside of Miles City were very good.

The two hunters had not yet purchased their non-resident licenses, so Sneed had a short discussion with his clerk. Soon afterward, the clerk called out loudly, "I received a phone call from the Fish & Game office that non-resident big game licenses were in short supply, so we had better save back the very few we have for those already spoken for." Almost immediately, the two prospective hunters stated they would buy licenses, because with a shortage, Miles City might not have any.

Late the following day, Sneed received a phone call from the two hunters from Miles City. They were told the nearest elk were north in the Missouri Breaks and miles away. Sneed facetiously replied, "Elk? I'm sure you fellows said antelope."

Warden Fitzwater field checking a sizable buck antelope

Caught with Panties Down

At the old Eagle Creek patrol cabin, the wardens would quite often learn of hunter-wounded elk getting across the Gardiner-Jardine road and into the Bear Creek area. This area was closed to hunting activity and, on a few occasions, a hunter would contact a warden and state that he shot and wounded an elk that went into the closed area. In those instances, old-timer warden Red Burke would ask, "Which one of you lazy ass wardens will go with me to check the hunter's claim of shooting and wounding an elk that got into the Bear Creek closure?"

On several occasions, I offered to accompany him, since I had come to Gardiner well equipped for extremely cold conditions. Riding horseback, which can be miserably cold duty, we would be advised by the hunter just where the elk crossed the road and left an obvious blood trail. Then, to follow it on the steep slope down to Bear Creek on horseback wasn't an easy venture.

Quite a number of times we would track down such an elk, and if it was badly wounded, we would kill the animal and roughly field dress it. When we returned from our expedition, we would then notify the hunter that he could go retrieve the carcass but would need hardy help to do so, even if it was quartered.

On one such ride with Warden Burke, we saw a couple off in the distance doing something puzzling, and Red said, "Fitz, take a look with binoculars and see what's going on."

I replied that a man was holding his coat up in a strange fashion, so Red said, "We'll head over there and check it out."

We hastily made our way at a gallop through the snow. Once we were quite close, a woman raised up from her squat to pee and said, "You boys have me at a disadvantage."

Burke replied, "Not yet, lady!" as we rode off laughing.

Gun on the Run

While patrolling an elk hunting area on foot, I heard a couple rifle shots, and later came across two hunters. When I made contact with them, they said, "Have we ever a story to tell you!"

They then related that one of them shot a bull elk, and once at the elk carcass and feeling quite exhausted, he hung his rifle with leather sling on an antler tine. Needing a break, he lit a cigarette and sat on the carcass to rest. He noted that the blood pattern indicated that the rifle's bullet had struck the neck area ahead of the shoulder, and near the animal's spine. As the hunter was recovering from his exertion, the elk suddenly gained its feet and went charging down the steep slope with the rifle swinging around before the gun finally fell and hit the ground. Just then his hunting partner showed up to the scene and saw the running elk, but couldn't get a shot off through the timber. They surmised that the rifle bullet had hit near the elk's spine, and the shock put the animal down for a short period of time, but then it recovered and fled away. The fellow retrieved his gun, with a broken sling strap and slightly cracked wood stock, and undoubtedly had a story to tell for many years!

Mystery Moose

Many years ago when I was assisting with late season patrol of the upper Gallatin Canyon, I shared the old Sage Creek forest cabin with Warden Supervisor Gene Sherman and Wardens Linn Clark, Pinky Sears, and I. L. Todd, and we used it as our patrol headquarters. They had a good laugh when I relayed the happenings of a particularly memorable snowshoe patrol one evening.

I had snowshoed up Sage Creek and then up the slope toward the Little Wapiti Divide and beyond many times before, checking for hunter activity. Early one morning when I was high up on the slope, I heard a single rifle shot but could not be sure of the exact direction because of the noisy, windy conditions and the muffled sound through timber. I continued snowshoeing the tough, steep slope and came to the edge of an open sagebrush park, then skirted around the edge where the wind was less severe because of the standing timber. Once around, I came across horse tracks going single file because of the snow depth, and I noted that one horse had been turned out of the trail, which seemed somewhat unusual. I used binoculars to view the surrounding area, but saw no hunters.

After considerable looking, I did finally notice what appeared to be an elk antler protruding above the snow, so I proceed to the place out in the sagebrush opening and instead found a dead bull moose. The antlers had not palmed much and could possibly have been mistaken for a young bull elk's rack, but no hunter had approached the carcass, which was still quite warm and hadn't began to stiffen at all.

I once again scanned the area and saw no one, so I proceeded to field dress the moose carcass and arrange and position the legs so when the carcass froze it wouldn't be spread-eagled, in an effort to prevent difficulty in dragging it through the deep snow. I then proceeded back to where the horse tracks were and carefully looked for empty brass rifle cases, and did find one, but that's another story!

The next day, I learned that no horse was available to drag the bull moose carcass out, so I again snowshoed to that same general area and went to the frozen body to see if any birds or animals had been feeding on it. I then proceeded to survey the area to determine the easiest route to get a horse to the carcass once one was available. I noticed the downslope was fairly gentle for thirty yards or so, then it pitched off quite steeply down toward the Sage Creek bottom, all the while thinking how tough it would be to get a horse up to the moose carcass.

I snowshoed back and forth, from the carcass to the top of the steep slope, making a trail to try to drag the carcass. After considerable effort, I did inch the carcass over and with just a couple more shoves it would certainly go downhill, and hopefully be easier to get out to the Sage Creek cabin. Right as I gave the carcass the old heave-ho, I saw a lone hunter struggling in the snow down in the Sage Creek bottom, so once the moose carcass was loosed down the steep slope, it literally snowplowed downward, with snow flying aside and striking a couple of small trees and sagebrush.

The lone hunter must have been conscious of movement up on the slope, and may have possibly heard the sounds made by the flying carcass, which had flipped over belly down with head and antlers first. After momentarily viewing that spectacle of flying snow and what may have appeared as an animal charge, he assumed a "fix bayonet and charge" position and backed up, keeping his gun in readiness. It really must have been a puzzling and ominous sight on a remote, cold, quiet, and snowy mountainside where a hunter might expect to see an elk, but not a moose.

The moose stopped sliding just short of the creek bottom, and all was quiet. Then, after considerable hesitation and looking through his rifle scope at the strange beast, the hunter, with gun in readiness, slowly semi-circled the partially snow-covered moose. He stood for some time looking things over and kept glancing upslope, undoubtedly trying to determine where the creature came from and finally, slowly, walked to it and gave it a couple cautious pokes with the gun barrel.

In the meantime, I had sat down alongside a clump of sagebrush so I could steady my binoculars in the gusty winds and was probably not visible from where the hunter and moose carcass were located. After he completed his inspection, the hunter turned and went back down the trail with an occasional stop and glance backward as though that experience was enough for one day. You can bet he has told of this experience numerous times, and may have caused his friends to wonder about the truthfulness of his hunting stories. Nevertheless, the moose carcass was then easily accessible and dragged out with a horse the next day.

Proud to Have Been Checked by the "Big Boys!"

I was out on patrol with Warden Bill Smith one day, and we stopped to check a particular hunter. Through our conversation with him, we learned that he had a game animal in his vehicle which he admitted was improperly tagged. He also had a couple legal ducks he had shot. We advised him that he was to be issued a citation for the minor tagging violation. The man didn't seem to be at all concerned, and made it quite clear with his remarks and actions that the contact with mere state wardens was unimpressive. The hunter seemed compelled to tell to share his lowly opinion of state wardens, and us specifically. "Let me tell you, I have been checked by the big boys, and not just the run-of-the mill Mickey Mouse game wardens," he sneered at us.

This statement wasn't at all bothersome to either of us wardens, because we were calloused to such remarks and others, which were quite often more pointed and could be downright abusive. Out of curiosity, we asked the hunter about his claim to have already been checked. He shared that he had

An Unproductive Stalk

During the yearly waterfowl hunt, I patrolled a reservoir area frequented by Canada geese. As usual, I gained a vantage point where I could observe hunters' activities. There were several good hunter blinds established with goose decoys nearby. Peering through my binoculars, I observed a hunter very cautiously approaching some well-placed decoys. After watching for a time, I finally determined that the hunter was unknowingly stalking some of the other hunters' decoys. Since the distance between me and the stalker was too great, I couldn't intervene. A hunter in one of the goose blinds finally spotted the decoy stalker, and stood up and yelled some nasty remarks. The stalker quickly hurried away toward his vehicle about a half-mile away. Undoubtedly, he may have had some feelings of embarrassment!

hunted waterfowl earlier in the day on the Federal Red Rock Lakes Refuge public hunting area, and it was there that federal game wardens had checked his licenses and the ducks he had bagged. It was very obvious the hunter was quite proud and impressed to have been checked by what he termed "the big boys," meaning the federal game agents.

Over-Excited Hunter

While I was assigned to the Stillwater County district, the mule deer populations were at a high level and several areas of deer depredations and over-used deer ranges prompted extended hunts beyond the regular hunting season. I patrolled those areas as time and scheduling permitted and, being quite close to Billings, there were no shortages of hunters. While patrolling one region on foot, I had field checked several hunters, and was in an open grassy area when I heard gunshots from a timbered area upslope.

I used my binoculars to scan the range above, and soon saw a doe deer running down toward me. As the deer came closer, I could see some of the deer's entrails hanging below its belly, and what a pathetic sight! Soon afterward, a hunter came charging out of the trees. I wasn't in uniform that day, so as soon as he laid eyes on me, he thought I was another hunter trying to claim his deer. Frantically, he started yelling, "That's my deer, that's my deer!"

About that time, the deer leaped over a barbed wire fence, but didn't get enough clearance and literally pulled its entrails out, which hung on the upper barbed wire strand. The hunter kept charging down slope, and continued his yelling, "That's my deer, that's my deer!"

Once we met at the now prostrate deer, still alive but dying, the hunter realized I was a game warden, and he apologized for his actions. Out of mercy, I fired a fatal shot to the deer's head and helped the hunter with field dressing the animal. In looking at the deer carcass, it was evident that the hunter's one shot had creased the deer's belly and opened it enough that a portion of the entrails dropped out, but the deer kept running and finally collapsed beyond the fence.

Surprise Addition to Bird Hunter's Bag Limit

While I was assigned to the Broadwater and Lewis and Clark County districts, the pheasant hunt in the Townsend, Toston, and Radersburg areas was quite popular, so I concentrated on patrolling for hunter activities. Hunter success was usually quite good for several days after the hunt opening, then the wily cock pheasants stayed in heavy cover and adjacent valley draws and were harder to flush or locate.

As I was traveling along the highway one day heading for lunch with the Broadwater sheriff, Jack Thompson, a vehicle was parked alongside the highway. I stopped, as it appeared the lone fellow was a bird hunter. When I approached the hunter, he was laughing about bagging an extra cock pheasant over his legal limit.

The hunter then explained that while traveling the highway, by surprise, a rooster pheasant flew in the vehicle's open passenger-side window and crashed into the steering wheel column and died. The fellow's shotgun-bagged birds were at the limit allowed, so the extra pheasant was improperly given to a young first-time pheasant hunter instead.

Cooperative Man, Mouthy Woman, Unruly Kid, and a Bad Dog

When a game warden makes contact with people in the field, he many times does not know how an individual will respond to inquiries related to Fish & Game matters. I can easily recall one such interaction regarding a game law violation. Standing on the violator's front porch, I was questioning the hunter about his illegal hunting activities. Through the course of our conversation, he was quite cooperative and admitted to his wrong-doing. I was explaining the details and necessary procedures related to the violation when, surprisingly, behind the front porch screen door, a woman loudly cussed me and said, "Tell him to go to hell! He has no proof!"

The woman continued her tirade, and then a young boy came outside holding back a big dog with only a rather tenuous appearing leash. The dog was snarling and barking and lunging toward me when the boy said, "Dad, should I turn him loose?" and the woman yelled, "Turn him loose!"

Thankfully, the fellow told the boy to take the dog back in the house, ignoring the woman as she continued her lengthy stream of expletives. Soon afterward, the young boy came back outside and, from close quarters, aimed a pistol squirt gun at me and doused me with a red liquid as he exclaimed, "You are bleeding where I shot you!"

Embarrassed now, the man took the squirt gun from the kid, and ushered him back through the front door by the arm. Reappearing on the porch, he apologized for his drunken wife and unruly kid's behavior and said, "The kid probably filled the squirt gun with red Kool-Aid." He then added, "If the violation justified jail time, it would probably be a relief for me."

The fellow appeared before a local justice of the peace, pleaded guilty, paid the fine, and then invited me out for a cup of coffee. I'll never forget the man and his unruly family!

Entertaining Encounters:
Funny People

Coffee with Character and Remembrance

I frequently stopped at summer grazing sheep camps to visit with sheep herders who were observing the activities afield in their areas of work. Many of the herders were conscientious men, and nearly always eager to visit with anyone happening to travel to their remote sheep camps. On one occasion, I stopped at a herder's sheep wagon and noticed that there was another, badly damaged wagon nearby. The herder explained that the damaged wagon had been struck by lightning. He went on to say that during a recent severe nighttime thunder and lightning storm, it had made his hobbled horse "spooky" and nervous, so he had left the sheep wagon during the storm to check his horse. During that short time out of the primitive camper, it was struck by bolt of lightning and literally blew apart some of the wagon.

Further filling in the details, he explained that he had erected a radio antenna for his all-band battery radio between two masts at each end of the wagon, and had driven a metal grounding rod into the ground for better radio reception. It seems this may have attracted and received the full energy of the lightning bolt, and the shaken but dedicated herder hastily erected a tepee tent for the remainder of the night and until another sheep wagon was brought to his campsite.

The man was still visibly agitated by the experience and was eager for human company, so I finally accepted his offer of a cup of hot coffee. The herder quickly had a fire going in the stove, with the help of some pine-pitch kindling. Once the few sups of water in the grimy old porcelain coffee pot were boiling, and amid constant talking about the nerve-wracking experience, the fellow grabbed a fistful of coffee from a can and threw it into the small coffee pot. The coffee was brewing fast and really had a good aroma. During the non-stop conversation, the fellow again grabbed a handful of coffee and added it to the water, which by that time must have boiled down considerably. I had drank some pretty strong coffee at various times in the many camps I visited, but I reckoned this might outdo any past java brewed.

The conversation continued without end, when the herder again reached for the coffee can and for the third time threw in another, smaller amount. This had me seriously thinking of going on my way, with an explanation that I had a lot of ground to cover by nightfall. Before I had a chance to make my escape, the herder poured each of us a cup of that powerful brew. Thankfully, he also had some type of sourdough cookies that helped make that strong, strong coffee nearly tolerable.

Experiences such as these seem to come to mind after all these many years, so one cannot deny that, say what you may, that was coffee with character, and could have passed for a strong name brand like today's Starbucks.

An Unexpected River Dunking

Sadly, during my tenure a fisherman drowned when his inflatable boat capsized as it struck an obstacle in the river. The local search and rescue unit was attempting to find the body, and several local boaters were floating different river areas assisting with the search. A fellow in the category of a local legend, H.L. Sneed, was familiar with boating the river and had accumulated certain types of tools that could be used to probe specific river sections where a body would likely be held by the river current. Since I wasn't available at the time, Sneed got the services of a newly assigned game warden for the Southwest Montana area.

As Sneed and the warden were floating a section of the river not yet covered by the search and rescue unit, they were probing areas of debris lodged in clumps by the river current. The new warden was doing much of the probing, when the pole suddenly caught. As he tried to get it loose while standing upright in the boat, he lost his balance and tipped the boat over. Both men went overboard, and luckily the water was only about waist-deep. Since the river was shallow where they capsized, the two men finally managed to pull the boat to shore.

Sneed was quite upset about the dunking, as he had many, many times floated the river without any such incident. Over the succeeding days he openly let it be known, in a joking way, that it took a damn game warden to cause his first river dunking after years of uneventful river floating.

Ballistics Help from an Expert Revolver Sharpshooter

I once had a Fish & Game violation case where the outcome was mostly dependent on a ballistics report concerning a bullet retrieved from a game animal's carcass, and one fired from a rifle belonging to a suspect in the shooting. I had had a couple of previous experiences submitting similar evidence to an FBI lab, but with a tight timeline I went to a Montana man, Ed McGivern. McGivern was generally recognized as a firearms expert, and I asked him to do a comparison of the two bullets and testify as to his findings. His testimony, stating that the two rifle bullets came from the same gun, won the case with no doubt.

This wasn't my first encounter with McGivern, however. I once attended a revolver shooting exhibition with Ed as the star. In the gathering of spectators, a well-liquored fellow was regularly chiding McGivern, which irritated others in the audience. During a break in the exhibition, McGivern went to a couple of the spectators and asked if one of them would consider grabbing the loudmouth's new-looking cowboy hat and send it sailing into the air during the next shooting session.

The intermission ended, and McGivern kept an eye on the heckling fellow while he introduced the next part of the show. It wasn't long before the jabberer called out, "Hey, short-ass show-off, I'm getting to you, ain't I?"

With that, the fellow standing closest to the blowhard grabbed his hat and quickly sent it skyward while McGivern shot holes through it, with one bullet actually splitting the hat brim. The gathering of onlookers whooped and yelled in approval.

Smiling, McGivern went to the startled fellow and said, "To compensate for the damage to your hat, I'll buy you the best Stetson in town!"

A Circumstance When East is West

During those years when I was working the Montana Beaverhead country, I would often cross the state line into Idaho during the summer months to effectively patrol certain Montana areas where hunter and fisherman access was only available from the Idaho side of the Continental Divide. Blair Lake, part of the Hell Roaring Creek drainage system, is the most distant watershed from the Gulf of Mexico and the Mississippi, Missouri, Jefferson, Beaverhead, and Red Rock River drainages. The best route to the lake is through the Red Rock Pass, over the Continental Divide into Idaho, at the extreme east end of the Centennial and Alaska Basins.

On one such patrol at Red Rock Pass, an out-of-state vehicle was parked, so I stopped to inquire if the traveler might be having vehicle trouble or wasn't sure of his travel route. A fairly large and obvious sign is erected there to clarify the divide between the Pacific and Gulf of Mexico drainages, and I soon learned it was this sign that was of interest to the traveler. The man's reply to my inquiry was, "No trouble. But, that sign sure shows that some bureaucrat didn't know his geography."

What was of interest to the traveler were the arrows pointing east indicating west of the divide Pacific drainage, and the other pointing west to clarify east of the divide Gulf of Mexico drainage. I didn't know if this was the only instance along the Continental Divide as it transverses the U.S. from Canada to Mexico that it makes such a loop, which caused this particular traveler to question the accuracy of the sign. Nonetheless, I offered to explain the lay of the land thereabouts, and proceeded to produce a map and point out the geography of the area. After his brief geography lesson, and accepting the sign as correct, the man took some photographs and apologized for being so critical of others more knowledgeable than he.

Eavesdropping

I was stationed at Columbus in the early 1950s, and mule deer populations were at a high point. Accordingly, deer hunting was extended in areas where deer gathered for wintering and in areas of ranch depredations. It was an immense area to be patrolled, so another fellow warden, Pinky Sears, was assigned to assist me. At that time, the Red Lodge warden had been called back for naval duty, so occasionally I would also patrol some of those areas, but I depended mostly on the local Carbon County sheriff to advise me of the need for a game warden when necessary.

One day, the sheriff notified me that a couple of trappers had beaver and pine marten pelts to be tagged. So with Pinky in tow, I went to Red Lodge and had to stay overnight to complete the pelt tagging. Due to our low monthly wages and shortage of cash, we rented a room in a house that had converted a couple of sleeping rooms for added income. The room we took had a locked door to the adjoining room and, as was common then, had a transom window above the locked door. Outside the rooming house we had noticed a car with "Just Married!" scrawled across the back and crepe paper streamers dangling off it.

Once in our quarters, we could hear laughter and a girl's giggling coming from the adjoining room. Later, while we were in our respective beds and trying to sleep, the sounds next door indicated love making. Pinky laughed at the verbal outpouring, and proceeded to get out of bed. Then he gently opened the over-the-door transom and put his ear to the door to hear better. He stayed up for quite a while, eavesdropping on the newlyweds. The next morning he went out to the makeshift front desk area so he could await the departure of the young lovers and satisfy his curiosity. During the next day's travel, every now and then, Pinky would mimic the bride's, "Oh, honey!" and laugh.

Many fellow wardens remember Pinky as entertaining to be around, and would quite regularly demonstrate his seemingly constant flatulence abilities, which to some was amusing and to others not so much.

Centerline Safety

H. L. Sneed, the record-setting Fish & Game license purveyor, frequently fished the Big Hole River back when catches of larger fish were commonplace. On one trip from Dillon to the river, he picked up a hitchhiker alongside the highway. During the short ride before they parted ways, Sneed mentioned to the fellow that he should watch for rattlesnakes alongside the highway's pavement. The obviously concerned fellow then said, "Man, I sure don't like them snakes!"

Later, Sneed came back out to the highway to go to a different spot along the river, and ahead of his vehicle he spotted a person walking the highway's centerline. As he came closer, he saw that it was the same hitchhiker. Sneed again stopped and picked up the foot traveler, who said he wasn't taking any chances for an encounter with a rattlesnake, and so was keeping to the middle of the road.

As it was nearly noon, the two men proceeded to Melrose where Sneed assured the fellow he was out of rattlesnake territory. Being the generous man he was, he bought lunch for the hitchhiker, and undoubtedly slipped him a few dollars to help along the way to Malmstrom Air Force Base in Great Falls.

Manifold Cookin' and an Explosion

As one might expect, I had numerous vehicle breakdowns through the years, but only twice did I summon a wrecker for assistance. While I did not have to call a wrecker for help this particular time, I remember one occasion when my vehicle was about to stall, so I coaxed it back to town and arrived about noon. I assumed that the repair shop mechanics would have their lunch break and postpone any repair needed. The shop foreman met me and said he would have a mechanic diagnose the problem and try to get it repaired right away, saying, "I realize you have a lot of area to cover." He raised the vehicle hood and then said, "Do you smell that good odor of something cooking? And it's lunchtime too!"

Sheepishly, I reached down to the exhaust manifold and removed a hot can of beanie weenies which I had "cooked" for my lunch. The shop foreman laughed and called to the mechanics to come and see where the appetizing aroma was coming from. I then had to tell them that when I first decided to heat a can of food on the manifold, I failed to punch vent holes in it. The can literally exploded and sprayed beans and weenies all over the engine and hood, and the lingering odor of food lasted several days and attracted several ranch dogs.

Spiteful Acts

No doubt many game wardens, because of the scope and results of their game law enforcement duties, have caused ill feeling with certain law violators, who then felt motivated to commit spiteful acts against the warden. On a couple occasions I was the target of such bad tempered operations. Once, roofing nails were broadcast on my house lane, which resulted in flat tires. I attempted to retrieve the nails with a strong magnet suspended on a short rope, with decent success. Other incidents of more serious nature included the loosening of my vehicle's differential bolts, causing leakage of lubricant and ruination of the differential. Sealed beam headlights were broken, and air let out of tires out in remote areas afield. As a precaution, I carried a diverse arsenal of tools and parts—a hand tire pump, extra valve cores, and always two mounted spare tires, a high lift jack, a come-along, shovel, and saw for fallen trees across mountain roads, etc.

Quite a number of wardens experienced theft from their patrol vehicles due to the knowledge that game wardens possessed binoculars, spotting scopes, and other useful equipment. Fortunately, I never had any such thefts. When I parked my patrol vehicle out in remote areas and was away on foot patrol, I made it a policy to print an obvious note that I wasn't far away. Using any warden names on the note, I instructed them that when they came by to toot the vehicle horn and I would come back to the vehicle. Having done this, there were a couple instances where I was in sight of my vehicle and observed individuals walking around it. Their actions, and obviously scanning the surrounding areas, certainly indicated that they undoubtedly had ulterior intentions.

While living in a larger city as the surrounding district game warden, I frequently used a Grumman canoe for water patrol. As a safeguard against theft in a community known for frequent thievery, I chained and padlocked the canoe to some permanent fixture in the pavement. During one night of stormy thunder and lightning and at a late hour, I happened to look out my house window and noticed a vehicle parked nearby with two men lingering there. Soon afterward, the men went to the canoe and picked up each end and hastened toward their truck. The padlocked chain was quite hidden underneath the canoe, and once the fellows got to the end of the chain, it jerked the canoe from their grasp and the aluminum canoe struck the pavement with a loud metal bang. They certainly didn't linger after that, and made a quick getaway. It was a somewhat comical performance!

Amazing but Intolerable

Within game warden districts, there were license agents appointed to sell the various Fish & Game Department licenses, and the district warden was responsible for periodically checking the license agent's sales records. So, I found myself out checking sales records one day. At one of my stops, the license agent's basic business was a small restaurant with sales of other miscellaneous items, which also served a bus stop on the regularly traveled highway. While I was there, a group of travelers who had just arrived by bus were ordering food and beverages. There was a printed notice behind the counter stating that the proprietor was blind, but would serve them well.

As usual, several customers ordered coffee and were being served when one lady yet to be helped repeatedly stated how absolutely amazing it was that the blind proprietor could serve coffee and never spill a drop or run the coffee over in a cup. After several such comments, a local loafing older fellow who was a regular customer spoke out and said, "It is amazing, but if you will take note when he fills a cup from the coffee urn, he has one finger over the lip of the cup, and when the hot coffee is felt on his finger, he knows it is a cupful."

In the meantime, the lady had been served her coffee, but when the bus driver said, "All aboard," her cup remained full on the counter. After the bus passengers had left, the old local said, "Some people are so squeamish!"

Cadillac in the Muck

When working the Stillwater County warden district, I also covered portions of the Sweetgrass areas and went to Big Timber quite regularly. Having received a call from the Sweetgrass sheriff, I headed that way with stops at Grey Cliff and Reedpoint. The earlier light rain was freezing on the highway, making black ice, and travel was very treacherous and slow. At one point I had the right wheels of my vehicle at the pavement's edge, where some exposed gravel added traction to keep from sliding sideways off the crown of the highway. Because of my slower speed, I kept watch in the rearview mirror for oncoming traffic from the rear and a vehicle was seen coming on very fast, so I put on my hazard lights to be more obvious to the fast-moving driver.

Unbelievably, a Cadillac whizzed past me! As it flew by, I noticed that the two female occupants seemed to be in a conversation and unaware of the black ice. When I caught up with them a few miles farther down the road, I discovered the car had skidded off the right side of the highway and skipped a couple times on a swampy swath of black mud studded with cattails, and thankfully came to a stop right-side up. By then, the vehicle had settled down, hub and doorsill deep in the muck.

I very cautiously stopped my vehicle, and called to the driver to determine if anyone was injured. I got no reply, but could see that the driver was clinging to the steering wheel and seemed reluctant to move or respond. Finally, I convinced her to roll down the door window so we could communicate. After she indicated neither of them seemed to be injured, she pleaded with me to walk out and help them out of the car. Patiently, I explained to her that in the seemingly bottomless swampy area, walking out wasn't possible. The two women were getting quite frantic about their predicament, so I attempted to console them and said I would summon help.

I contacted the sheriff's office by radio and explained the situation, and he asked me what it would take to get the vehicle back to the highway. I decided extension ladders or the ladder fire truck could probably rescue the ladies, and a wrecker vehicle could determine how to tow the car out.

Once assistance with ladders arrived, it was quite tricky getting them extended over the oozy, swampy surface to the car. The disabled vehicle had settled down in the muck so far the doors couldn't be opened, so the ladies were told that the only way they could vacate the car was out the doors' windows. Both ladies were reluctant to try that avenue of escape, so it took some encouraging for them to finally agree. One of their chief concerns was that their dresses would expose much of their lower anatomy when they clambered out of the car.

While it was quite an amusing feat to get them stabilized on a stretcher lying on the ladder, it wasn't an easy chore. Needless to say, it took quite a lot of time to accomplish the rescue. The next concern was to get the wrecker cable attached to the Cadillac in a manner that could tow it back out of the swamp. To get the hook on the cable end in underneath the car body meant you had to put your arm down off the ladder through the muck and attach the hook by feel alone. Once towed out, the muddy, messy Cadillac didn't seem to have been damaged until the towing procedure took its toll.

Game Warden Fitzwater's Accomplishments and Acknowledgments

Reviewing Warden Fitzwater's monthly duty diaries, which were compulsory, yielded an interesting and comprehensive retrospective of his career with the Montana Fish & Game Department. His career highlights demonstrate how well-rounded and highly regarded he was in the law enforcement community as a whole, and in the Fish & Game Department specifically.

During the course of duty, Fitzwater requisitioned a canoe for river and lake patrol, and for investigating beaver damage for trapping permit issuance. Having been assigned districts that included Dillon, Whitehall, Townsend, Helena and Wolf Creek, he canoed the continuous stream waters from Hell Roaring Creek in the Alaska Basin, Red Rock, Beaverhead, Jefferson and Missouri Rivers to Holter Dam, as well as many tributary streams and mountain lakes. He assisted big game trapping foreman Jim McLucas in live-trapping and transplanting mountain goat and antelope. He also live-trapped and relocated many, many troublesome beaver. His snowshoe patrols covered approximately 3,800 miles!

In addition to his regular warden duties, he satisfactorily completed the National Rifle Association Police Firearms Instructor Training Course for the benefit of the required game warden pistol qualifications. Numerous times he, along with others, participated in lost hunter rescues and retrieving victims of lake and river drownings, sadly bearing witness to five deaths. As authorized and requested, Warden Fitzwater assisted the

United States Forest Service in wildfire fighting as a fire line leader several times in rugged mountain terrain.

In all the years he worked in the backcountry, often in very rugged terrain, only once did he summon a tow-vehicle for assistance, and that was due to a broken axle. He survived several life threatening occurrences, which he recognized as "close calls."

1951 Basic Game Warden Training; Missoula, MT

1952 Montana Fish & Game Department Orientation; Helena, MT

1954 Game Management & Law Enforcement Basics; Blackfoot Game Range, MT

1955 Continuing Game Management Principles; Bozeman, MT

1958 Principles of Law & Game Law Enforcement; University of Montana Law School, Missoula, MT

1961 Fish & Game Department Policies and Orientation; Fort Missoula, Missoula, MT

1965 Montana Law Enforcement Training Academy and Shooting Competition (Score 96.8 points out of 100); Bozeman State College, Bozeman, MT.

Warden Fitzwater participated in this course and competition annually starting in 1965.

1965 Arrests, Searches & Seizures—Due Process; F.B.I. Course, Helena, MT

1966 Defensive Driving and Hot Pursuit Training; Montana Highway Patrol, Butte, MT

1966 First Aid Course, Firearms Training & Qualification (Score: 98.4); Bozeman, MT

1966 Court Proceedings; F.B.I. Lab Facilities, Bozeman, MT

1967 Court Decisions and National Crime Information Center Facility & Use; F.B.I. Facilities, Bozeman, MT

1968 Arrests, Searches and Seizures—Miranda Warning Use; University of Montana Law School, Missoula, MT

1968 Montana Law Enforcement Training Academy and Shooting Competition; Bozeman State College, Bozeman, MT

The Certificate of Completion of the academy training course, and presentation of the Otto Fossen Trophy for the highest score on the required competitive pistol shoot was an outstanding accomplishment for Warden Fitzwater. His score of 98.8 points (out of a possible 100 points) beat out the scores of the more than 60 other law enforcement officers in attendance.

1971 Awarded *Wildlife Officer of the Year* by the Fish & Game Department; Montana Fish & Game Headquarters, Helena, MT

Warden Fitzwater was selected as Wildlife Officer of the Year *over 55 other Montana Fish & Game Wardens by a five-person committee from the Montana Fish & Game*

Department. According to the Fish & Game Department's director at the time, the award was based on the recommendations of regional law enforcement division personnel, review of his activities for the year, Warden Fitzwater's duty diaries, and several letters commending him from sportsmen contacted in the course of his duties.

1972 Handling of Evidence and Court Trial Proceedings; University of Montana Law School, Missoula, MT

1975 Diversity in Law Enforcement & Cooperation and Arrest Procedures; University of Montana Law School, Missoula, MT

Before I Was a Game Warden

In the midst of the second world war, I enlisted in the US Army and took my basic infantry training at Camp Walters, Texas. After completion, I was assigned to the prestigious First Infantry Division at Fort Devens, Massachusetts. As the European conflict was growing worse, in addition to the attack at Pearl Harbor, the army units' training pursuits were stepped up with riflemen obstacle courses, long weekly hikes, rifle range qualification, and several physically demanding ship-to shore-assault landing maneuvers at several east coast locations.

In June of 1942, the First Infantry Division embarked on the British liner Queen Mary, en route to Scotland and England. My unit traveled from the Scottish port to the Tidworth Barracks in south-central England, near Salisbury. While there, the unit continued Army maneuvers locally, and also in the Lock Fyne, Inveraray Castle area in Scotland, where our squad excelled.

We were granted a pass one weekend, and I took a bus to London with a fellow squad member. Not the partying kind, we took in the downtown London sights and spent some time viewing the boat traffic on the Thames River. While we watched the happenings on the river, an older Englishman invited us to dangle our legs from the scaffolding of the London Bridge. We carefully scratched our names and the date (August, 1942) on a granite block of the bridge. In later years, up to 2010, the names were still visible on the bridge which was transported to and reassembled in Lake Havasu City, Arizona.

The field maneuvers and hikes continued while we were stationed at the Salisbury Military Post. Then, in early November of 1942, we received orders to pack up with all battle gear, were trucked to a seaport, and boarded the English liner Monarch of Bermuda with no destination announced. The ship, accompanied by many other ships, formed a large convoy assembled in the Atlantic Ocean with no land in sight, then traveled through the Strait of Gibraltar into the Mediterranean Sea. It later anchored off the Algerian, North African coast near Oran.

We soldiers were advised to check our battle gear in preparation to go down the ship-side nets into assault landing craft, and ultimately make a shoreline assault landing. Unfortunately, several boats grounded short of the shore, with several soldiers going over sides and into deep water. With their heavy battle gear and rifles, they found themselves in a critical situation with no means of assistance.

Once on shore, the opposition was light, so we cautiously advanced inland. After gaining some forward ground, orders were received to hold the ground gained and dig-in. As squad sergeant, I verbally checked where my men were located and carefully surveyed the frontal terrain before starting to dig my foxhole. After some thought, I called to my nearest man, the squad scout, and advised him that I was going to instead scout and rough-sketch the forward terrain for better forward advancing and security.

I kept my pack, rifle, and ammo with me, although cumbersome and deterrent to evasive movement, since I had not yet chosen a foxhole site. As trained, I cautiously double-timed from one position to another and rough-sketched the forward terrain. After progressing some distance, a combatant incoming small arms round struck the ground in front of me, causing mostly ground debris to strike my left leg just above the knee. This came as a surprise, so I used every precaution possible getting to places of cover and for better observation, and all the while looking for the position of the combatant shooter.

I had made significant progress forward with my terrain sketching, but as I double-timed to a likely position, two small arms bullets ricocheted off the hard ground, with both penetrating my clothing and pack-straps, and striking my chest. One of the rounds caused quite a shock, and had struck on my dog tag.

With that, I decided to abandon my scouting and sketching foray and head back to my infantry squad's position after one last attempt to gain intelligence. During this last effort to sketch additional forward terrain, I received an incoming small arms round that struck my left side just above the hip, with the bullet passing through but not striking my hip bone or left ribs. Not one to give up, I took time to concentrate on areas likely to be the positions of the combatant shooters, and after considerable scanning I located two combatant positions and noted that their movements were quite open and obvious.

Having excelled as a marksman and hunter as a civilian, and also on the Army rifle range, I patiently waited for the opportune moment and fired two rounds at each combatant. After a decent wait, I was sure I had silenced both. This brought on a moment of elation and Army pride, for previously it was quite degrading as an infantry man, with lots of training to seemingly have been outwitted.

My contentment was somewhat short lived, however, as I fully realized my predicament being so far away from my squad. In my rush to a more secure position, a round from a larger caliber weapon struck the ground nearby. To get out of the line of fire, I jumped off a ledge and landed hard, pitched forward head-first, and was knocked temporarily unconscious.

While recovering, I had serious neck and back pain and removed my backpack with great difficulty. I then crawled to where my rifle was, which had landed a ways off. I decided to open my shirt and trouser waist to look at my chest and left hip to determine the extent of my bullet wounds. The chest injury was mostly quite shallow with little bleeding, and one dog tag had a hole nearly through it. The two misshapen bullets from the chest hits were lodged inside my shirt at my waistline. I kept these as souvenirs, but they came up missing along with my dented steel helmet when I was later transferred from the field medical facility. My hip wound had bled quite a lot, but had clotted up and finally stopped. I laid there for quite a while, thinking I would recover somewhat, but I realized I had been away from my squad for too long, and so I very slowly dragged my backpack and rifle and headed toward the squad.

Evidently, the low silhouette long crawl prevented any more shots. After a long ordeal getting within voice range of the squad, I finally made contact and the first voice reply was, "Sergeant, where in the hell have you been?"

I called out that I had been shot, but was okay, and would soon dig in. Once I found a suitable site, and with only a shovel to work with, I soon found that my hurts made the digging very difficult and slow. Having made only slight digging headway while laying in a prone position, I elevated my left leg only slightly to gain better traction. Soon afterward, a sizable combatant round struck my left thigh, barely missing the left side of my head and left shoulder.

The shock was overwhelming. I looked down and saw my thigh bone exposed, and realized the bleeding was severe. As we had received first aid training in boot camp, I knew to apply hand pressure in my left groin, and sometime afterward a large blood clot formed and the bleeding nearly stopped.

After somewhat recovering from the shock, I called to my squad first scout and informed him that I had been seriously shot. I instructed that the squad Corporal take command, and also that all should lay low to prevent giving away their position.

Due to the dangerous conditions, no first aid man was summoned, but after darkness, four men came and carried me on a blanket to safety. As I was being carried out of the danger zone, I advised the men that I had a detailed, but rough sketch of much of the forward terrain, and it should definitely be given to the I-Company commander for reference when the go forward order arrived, and also that a combatant knew the forward squad's position and was firing larger than small arms guns.

Transporting me out of the battlefield caused more bleeding of my leg wound. Once I arrived at a makeshift first aid station, it was quickly determined that I desperately needed blood. For want of the proper blood type, a French nurse gave me a direct person-to-person transfusion and very likely saved my life!

Later, I was moved to a makeshift field hospital. While still in critical condition, Major General Terry Allen personally presented me with a Purple Heart. The General said, "Sergeant, you have other awards forthcoming." Due to my physical condition at that time, I didn't fully appreciate the honor of the presentation.

A couple of my squad members visited me there too, and

told me that my steel helmet had a very significant dent in it and offered to give it to me as a souvenir of my plunge to get out of the combatants' line of fire. Regrettably, when I was taken aboard the Newfoundland, a hospital ship, to be transported to England, the helmet was not included in my possessions.

Meanwhile, in Ohio, my mother received a letter of commendation from the I-Company commander stating that my conduct and accomplishments in battle were outstanding, and more military awards were forthcoming.

At the general hospital in England, I underwent surgery and stayed for a lengthy period of recuperation. I was then taken aboard the Queen Mary en route to a Staten Island, New York hospital, and was later transferred to a hospital at Fort Harrison, Indiana. Due to my injuries, I was then discharged from the Army.

I wore a left knee brace for quite a long period of time. After tiring of the comments and looks from others, and the persistent trouser-knee wear, I worked at strengthening my leg and ultimately gave up the helpful brace. Once out in civilian life and the work force, I sought the services of many orthopedic physicians for pain relief in my neck and back.

Sergeant Merrill W. Fitzwater, R.S.N. 3549382
Company I, Third Battalion,
26th Infantry Regiment, First Infantry Division

Bronze Star Medal
Purple Heart Award
European, African, Middle East Campaign Award
Combat Infantry Badge
WWII Military Campaign Medal
Presidential Unit Citation to the First Infantry Division
U.S. Army Commendation Medal
American Defense Medal
Expert Rifleman Award
Honorably Discharged Lapel Button

Made in United States
Troutdale, OR
04/24/2025